PARTICIPATORY DESIGN FOR LEARNING

Participatory Design is a field of research and design that actively engages stakeholders in the processes of design in order to better conceptualize and create tools, environments, and systems that serve those stakeholders. In *Participatory Design for Learning*, contributors from across the fields of the learning sciences and design articulate an inclusive practice and begin the process of shaping guidelines for such collaborative involvement. Drawing from a wide range of examples and perspectives, this book explores how participatory design can contribute to the development, implementation, and sustainability of learning innovations. Written for scholars and students, *Participatory Design for Learning* develops and draws attention to practices that are relevant to the facilitation of effective educational environments and learning technologies.

Betsy DiSalvo is Assistant Professor in the School of Interactive Computing at the Georgia Institute of Technology, USA.

Jason Yip is Assistant Professor in the Information School at the University of Washington, USA.

Elizabeth Bonsignore is Postdoctoral Researcher in the Human-Computer Interaction Lab and College of Information Studies at the University of Maryland, USA.

Carl DiSalvo is Associate Professor in the School of Literature, Media, and Communication at the Georgia Institute of Technology, USA.

PARTICIPATORY DESIGN FOR LEARNING

Perspectives from Practice and Research

Edited by
Betsy DiSalvo, Jason Yip,
Elizabeth Bonsignore and
Carl DiSalvo

Routledge
Taylor & Francis Group

NEW YORK AND LONDON

First published 2017
by Routledge
711 Third Avenue, New York, NY 10017

and by Routledge
2 Park Square, Milton Park, Abingdon, Oxon, OX14 4RN

Routledge is an imprint of the Taylor & Francis Group, an informa business

© 2017 Taylor & Francis

Library of Congress Cataloging in Publication Data
Names: Bonsignore, Elizabeth, editor.
Title: Participatory design for learning / [edited by] Elizabeth Bonsignore, Betsy DiSalvo, Carl DiSalvo, and Jason Yip.
Description: New York, NY : Routledge, 2017.
Identifiers: LCCN 2016051422| ISBN 9781138640979 (hardback) | ISBN 9781138640986 (pbk.) | ISBN 9781315630830 (e-book)
Subjects: LCSH: Instructional systems—Design.
Classification: LCC LB1028.38 .P38 2017 | DDC 371.3—dc23
LC record available at https://lccn.loc.gov/2016051422

ISBN: 978-1-138-64097-9 (hbk)
ISBN: 978-1-138-64098-6 (pbk)
ISBN: 978-1-315-63083-0 (ebk)

Typeset in Bembo
by diacriTech, Chennai

CONTENTS

SECTION II
PARTICIPATORY LEARNING AND DESIGN FROM
DIVERSE PERSPECTIVES AND CONTEXTS 43

SECTION III
CASE STUDIES OF PARTICIPATORY DESIGN
IN LEARNING RESEARCH 89

SECTION IV
EMERGING PERSPECTIVES ON PARTICIPATORY
DESIGN AND LEARNING   **155**

SECTION V
CONCLUDING THOUGHTS AND MOVING FORWARD   **211**

FOREWORD

Christopher Hoadley said it well in Chapter 3 of this book (I summarize): Learning scientists have been really good at being forward-thinking and pluralistic in their understanding of learning and their use of learning theory, taking into account in their research and design what we know about learning at many different levels of abstraction, from neurophysiological to cognitive and social and through to cultural. We pride ourselves in bringing a variety of theoretical perspectives to each of our projects. However, we've taken a far more "traditionalist" approach to engaging in design itself. When we design curriculum and technology, we hold the power on our design teams. Experience designers help us make it engaging, and teachers and students help us debug our designs and explain what's not working. But, in general, experienced designers, teachers, students, and other stakeholders are not equal members of our teams. How could they be? We're the ones who know learning, and we're aiming to foster learning. So we design *for* our stakeholders and not usually *with* them.

There's good reason for that. Our community of designers has taken more risks than any other community of designers of educational materials; we're designing the future, not merely the next curriculum or curriculum units or technologies that will be used in the educational environments (schools) of today. And we've been engaged in arguing that theory-driven iterative design is a first-class research activity, along with investigative methods. How can we make the case that theory-driven iterative design is a first-class research activity if our teams include as equal members partners who know little or know only narrowly about learning theory? As well, we are usually designing for the far future; we are trying to lay the groundwork for what will be common 10, 15, 20 years from now. Our knowledge of learning can help us imagine that future better than others can; how can others who don't have our kind of imagination help us with that? I am part of that "we";

in fact, the description fits me and my approach really well. And I've been very successful, thank you, at working this way.

But the truth is, it isn't actually working as well as we want it to. First of all, learning scientists are beginning to have some humility about the lack of influence our designs have had on our educational system and are recognizing the need to work more closely with local stakeholders to bring change. Second, one size doesn't fit all, and a really big intellectual challenge we face in designing educational materials is designing them in ways that allow for adaptation. Learners in different communities have had different experiences and therefore bring different prior knowledge to bear. And the places where learners live often offer opportunities for making the educational experience more engaging and connected to their lives. Poor kids in the Midwest, for example, may never have experienced the ocean; using differences in the temperature between sand and water doesn't work for those kids in thinking about heat transfer. And why would kids who live near the Delaware Water Gap in Pennsylvania or New Jersey want to address an ecology challenge that focuses on the Rouge River in the Midwest? And what about those kids in farm communities who have experienced farm ecosystems and the effects of changing weather up close? Or the kids in fishing communities who are experiencing different types of ecosystems and different effects of changing weather up close? Should they learn about ecosystems in the context of an ecosystem they are already familiar with, or some other one? If the one they are in, how can place be taken advantage of? And, if some other one, how should the connections be made to what the kids are already familiar with?

Making the educational materials we design adaptable requires two things, I think: (1) setting up the kinds of infrastructure that support productive adaptation, and (2) learning to design our curriculum materials and technologies so that they are adaptable. I don't think we can do either without learning better how to include our stakeholders as real partners in our deliberations. The first is happening. Design-based implementation and networked-improvement communities are two approaches to adapting mostly designed approaches for local situations, in the process supporting practitioners (teachers) in understanding important theory that underlies those approaches and developing capabilities necessary for their implementation. This is not easy, and the designers of these approaches have taken lessons from participatory design but are not practitioners of the approach; I am hoping that the chapters in this book might introduce some ideas that will ease the load.

Designing so that curriculum units and use of technology are adaptable to place is, I think, much harder, and I'm happy to report that this book provides ideas about how to do that. A lesson that can be learned from work in design-based implementation teams and networked-improvement communities, and from Polman et al.'s work reported in Chapter 6, for example, is that getting to the point where participants can participate as equals doesn't happen quickly. Multi-stakeholder teams, like interdisciplinary ones, develop understanding of what others bring, understanding of the joint endeavor, and ways of interacting productively only over long periods of time—time counted in years.

Interestingly, both the learning scientists' chapters and those of participatory designers shed light on how to manage evolving partnerships. Participatory designers reflect on what that development looks like, and the challenges and opportunities for fostering joint understanding that arise as understanding emerges among members of a team. For example, Light and Boys (Chapter 12) focus on what collaboration requires and involves when it is happening across and between participants from different disciplinary contexts who are designing toward complex ends, while Sanders's (Chapter 16) autobiographical chapter lays out many of things she's learned, from her long career as a participatory design practitioner, about making teams work.

Learning scientists, on the other hand, reflect on the particular challenges of managing design teams that include experts on learning processes (learning scientists) and the stakeholders they are designing for. Uchidiuno et al. (Chapter 5), Wilkerson (Chapter 10), and Louw et al. (Chapter 8), for example, discuss the work of getting to joint understanding and the roles different participants might play. Uchidiuno et al. discuss how to get to empathy so that joint designing can happen; really hard, but they have ideas about how to do it. Wilkerson focuses on the added complexity of introducing new uses of technology that carry with them the need for teachers to learn new skills and buy into new pedagogies and social configurations. She, too, sheds light on how to include teachers in the planning such that they feel they are part of the decision-making. Louw et al. discuss the level of detail that might go into top-down designs so that local practitioners, leaders, and learners can adapt them to local needs and the roles representative stakeholders can play on those design teams. None of these authors buys in to the radical democratic ideal of participatory design, but they do inform, I think, about ways of managing inclusion, especially when progress is a priority. It's hard to imagine how the radically democratic ideal of participatory design can support large scale-up; these authors discuss the resources to make available to local groups so they can participate in enacting small-scale adaptations and ways of interacting that minimize the power dynamic between participants with different goals, experiences, and expertise.

In a delightful Chapter 17, a participatory design practitioner (Frauenberger), a learning scientist who has done extensive design of learning technologies (Quintana), and just-plain designer of learning technologies (Rogers, who describes herself this way) discuss what they've learned about what works when, and where the synergies between these approaches are. Nicest about that chapter, I think, is that it provides a model of how learning scientists and participatory design practitioners might interact in the future to enhance both endeavors.

In the last chapter, the book's editors express some sorrow that rather than gathering together best practices where the two fields meet, the chapters identify many new challenges that arise when bringing learning into participatory design and when using a participatory design approach to designing learning technologies and curriculum. I'm not surprised, and I don't think there is anything to apologize for. The book sets the stage for continuing the discussion, and difficult discussions are something academics like a lot. I gather from the book that participatory design practitioners enjoy such discussions just as much. I look forward to the continued discussion.

Janet L. Kolodner
Chief Learning Scientist at the Concord Consortium
and Regents' Professor Emerita in Computing
and Cognitive Science at the Georgia Institute of Technology

SECTION I

Introduction

1

PARTICIPATORY DESIGN FOR LEARNING

Betsy DiSalvo, Jason Yip, Elizabeth Bonsignore, and Carl DiSalvo

The goal of the learning sciences is to not only understand the phenomena of learning, but also to impact educational practices and enable more effective learning. To meet these goals, learning scientists use iterative and participatory design methods as they design curriculum approaches, learning technologies, and technology-rich learning environments. Participatory design (PD) is a field of research and design that examines how stakeholders are able to participate with designers on the development of tools, artifacts, and activities that are important to the user group. Design-based research methods allow them to, in parallel, iterate toward better designs and add to foundational understanding of learning processes and how to support learning. Taking a learner-centered approach to design focuses them on the diverse and changing needs of learners (as opposed to sophisticated users) who may be working toward learning disciplinary content and practices at the same time they are getting used to using new software tools. Taking a community-based design approach helps them make sure they are addressing the needs of learners in ways that learners can identify with, that teachers or facilitators find useful, and that are consistent with the culture of the community. Using a combination of these methods, learning sciences researchers design curriculum and activities, technologies, policies, teacher professional development experiences, and other artifacts and systems in support of learning. They and their teams conceive new designs, develop them, put them to work in the world, test them, refine them, and iterate. The best products tend to come from teams that include not only researchers but also students, teachers, parents, community members, and other stakeholders.

Until now, however, the learning sciences community has not focused on design of artifacts for supporting learning as a formal practice, discipline, and field of research. Nowhere is this oversight more evident than with regard to engaging stakeholders actively in the design process. While some research teams have included learners, their families and communities, teachers, and administrators in the design of new learning environments and technologies, to date, there has been little discussion about how to include *direct input* from these multiple participant stakeholders while designing.

We aim, in this volume, to articulate a design practice that is inclusive of those who will use the designed artifacts we are creating and, with that, to begin the process of developing guidelines for such practice. The authors of chapters in this book have been informed by the practice that the Human-Centered Computing community calls participatory design, or "PD." In PD, users and other stakeholders in the life of artifacts that are being designed participate directly in design processes. Our goal is to develop and draw attention to design practices that are relevant to participatory design of learning environments and learning technologies and that directly involve learners, teachers, and other community members in all the different steps of designing. Such designing, if done well, with insure that decisions about how to foster learning rely not only on expertise in how people learn, but also on the context in which the designs will be used and the people who will use them. PD at its best offers a way of gathering together and engaging a pluralistic community to collectively imagine and create designs for new technologies, environments, and types of experiences. Practitioners of PD focus, like learning scientists do, on designs for contexts of use. Learner-centered and design-based approaches in the learning sciences are, like PD, founded on the principle that target populations are best served when designs address the needs of community members. PD focuses on giving such stakeholders a high degree of agency throughout the design process, emphasizing the cultivation of knowledge communities in which content and expertise are *co*-created by experts and other participants working in concert. In particular, PD offers methods and practices for discovering, navigating, and *co*-creating goals in direct partnership with participants, while simultaneously revealing the constraints and opportunities that these participants face in complex contexts. But despite what would seem to be a productive fit between the learning sciences and PD, there is little discussion of how to adapt PD into design of learning technologies and environments. Our claim is that PD is a mostly untapped resource that, if used well, can advance the development, implementation, and sustainability of learning innovations.

We claim, conversely, that systematic use of PD practices and outcomes as we design learning technologies and environments will enrich understanding of how people learn in ways that will ultimately contribute to improved PD practices and outcomes. Learning is increasingly important to designers of user experiences and technology that supports learners' interactions and experiences with knowledge, information, and data. Learning is both an implicit and explicit desired outcome of many designed systems and experiences. But within user design practice and research, there is limited engagement with theories of learning. As a result, claims about learning and the role of design are often weak, such as what learning theories can inform how successful PD is and if PD can also inform the development of learning theories. This does not need to be so. We believe it is possible to bring together PD and the learning sciences to create a vibrant and robust space of inquiry. We expect this book to help create that space and provide the intellectual infrastructure for its growth.

As a first step in crafting a foundation to increase the interaction between PD and learning sciences, our book benefits from a diverse group of contributors across the fields of the learning sciences and design. We have divided our chapters into five sections. The first and last sections serve as bookends to our core collection: Section I provides an introduction to PD and its history with the learning sciences, and Section V offers closing reflections and a call to action for moving forward. The sections in between provide a wide range of working examples and perspectives that cover design practices, audiences, and challenges that designers, education practitioners, and researchers alike will be able to apply in their work.

The first section of papers, beyond this introduction, includes the inspiring reflections of Pelle Ehn (Chapter 2), one of the founders of the participatory design movement in Scandinavia, on the history of participatory design and its shared foundations and commitments with the learning sciences. Christopher Hoadley continues this historical reflection in Chapter 3, describing and analyzing the long-standing interplay between the fields of design and learning. Chapter 4 is the transcript of a conversation mediated by Jason Yip, between Christopher Hoadley, an expert in the history of design in the learning sciences, and Carl DiSalvo, an expert in the field of design. This conversation provides a unique opportunity to see the ways that the field of learning sciences and design approach participatory design and where some of the fundamental differences and similarities lie.

The second section of the book brings together diverse perspectives on the types of participants that can be included in participatory design and ways of working with them. This includes Chapter 5, by Judith Uchidiuno et al., that speaks to the unique ways that families can contribute to participatory design as a research method to better understand how learning happens between generations in a family. In contrast, Chapter 6, by Joseph Polman et al., demonstrates how the unique power dynamic between learning researchers and teachers produces a very different type of participatory design that takes place over semesters and even years. In Chapter 7, Helene Gelderblom looks at students as participants in designing their own course and how that relationship can shape the learning experience. These three chapters taken together offer an opportunity to reflect on the diversity of methods and approaches to integrating participation in design and how they are interdependent upon the relationships between designers and participants, and among participants.

The chapters in third section of the book are case studies on specific projects or practices of participatory design. Chapter 8, by Marti Louw, Nina Barbuto, and Kevin Crowley, provides a case study of collaboration between researchers trained in design and the learning sciences and their interdisciplinary approach to designing learning pathways with families. Chapter 9 is a case study by Juan Pablo Hourcade on the unique challenges in designing with children in the autism spectrum. Chapter 10, by Michelle Hoda Wilkerson, is the post analysis that reflects on the participation of after-school professionals in the development of digital tools. In Chapter 11, Lisa Maurer and Elizabeth Bonsignore reflect on the development of Pearson Kids CoLab and how participatory design principles placed the learner as the central player in the education industry's product design process.

The fourth section of the book looks at emerging perspectives on participatory design. Ann Light and Jos Boys (Chapter 12), who are designers and researchers of design practices, present a number of cutting-edge approaches to participatory design and reflect on the learning outcomes and applications for learning that can be gleaned from them. In Chapter 13, Betsy DiSalvo and Kayla DesPortes explore how applying participatory design approaches, in the form of formative and meta-design, can help to shape learning that is driven by the values of the learners. Chapter 14 is a conversation facilitated by Elizabeth Bonsignore between a human–computer interaction researcher, Allison Druin, and a practicing designer and design educator, Jon Kolko. This conversation reflects many of the differences between the goals of academic researchers and those of design professionals in their respective use of participatory design. Brenna McNally and Mona Leigh Guha in Chapter 15 share perspectives on creating and sustaining co-design teams the allow participants to develop expertise.

In the concluding section of the book, Elizabeth B.-N. Sanders (Chapter 16) provides and autobiographical account of participatory design in her work as a design educator and insights into frameworks for radical ways to move forward with participatory design and the efforts to design for conviviality. Chapter 17 is our final conversation. This conversation, facilitated by Elizabeth Bonsignore, highlights three researchers (Christopher Frauenberger, Chris Quintana, and Yvonne Rogers) and provides a personal narrative of how they each came to use PD and its relationship to learning, which highlight conflicts between PD and the learning sciences and what needs to be addressed to move forward. Finally, Chapter 18 is the editors' critical reflection on design for learning and educational environments and their call to action for learning scientists and design researchers alike to seize opportunities for increased cross-pollination and coordinated, interdisciplinary collaboration between their complementary—but currently parallel—research tracks.

For some readers, this will be the first time they have considered their work in learning with a PD lens; for others, PD practices and methods came first, and learning sciences' expertise adds a new dimension to the negotiation of goals and design outcomes among participants. Taken together, our compendium offers a resource that will support researchers who aim to incorporate PD principles into their learning frameworks, as well as PD practitioners who aspire to incorporate learning constructs and theories into their designs.

2

LEARNING IN PARTICIPATORY DESIGN AS I FOUND IT (1970–2015)

Pelle Ehn

I have had the fortune to be a member of the participatory design community for almost half a century and the privilege to participate in what I today would call democratic design experiments in the small. In the 1970s this was with focus on democratization of the workplace. In the 1980s this engagement was extended to trying to design for skilled work. The 1990s centered on being part of establishing an academic design-oriented community linked to the democratic visions of participatory design. From around the turn of the century this turned into engagements with building a "digital Bauhaus," a design school dedicated to the challenges of participatory design. During the last decades this has also meant coaching younger colleagues in their exploration of democratic design experiments in the small. In all these achievements collaborative learning has been a central theme. So what follows is a personal account of how I found learning in participatory design over these years—anecdotes of wayfindings from a collective designer (part of).

Not Quite a Revolutionary Beginning—Democracy at Work (1970s)

"You have to learn to speak better English if the revolution is going to succeed." We are in a hotel room in the south of Sweden. An international conference on "alternative organizations" is going on. The year is 1974, and it is my first research conference ever.

I had in murmured broken English presented a paper entitled "Emancipation and the Design of Information Systems"—a crude theoretical model for defensive trade union participation" to a hostile academic environment (Ehn 1974).

The "we" is a small group of young researchers from the Scandinavian countries gathered by our much senior mentor Kristen Nygaard to discuss performance and strategy in challenging management prerogatives in the workplace. Kristen is, as inventor of object oriented programming, an internationally most respected researcher within the field of programming languages and with a lot of academic credibility. He is also the leader of a new orientation within computing and social change—the emerging tradition of participatory design. Kristen's critical comment on our English language skills and performance had to do with what it would take to achieve our joint goal of contributing to changes in society toward more democratic socialism at the time in history when computers entered the workplace. Which language skills were needed for this change? English, yes, for academic respect for the new ideas. Programming, yes, for controlling the machines. But more importantly, a "language" for designers/researchers to be able to supportively participate in class struggle at work, to support democratization of the workplace.

Paradoxically, I had, in broken English in my talk, addressed this third "language" challenge. The main inspiration came from two learning approaches. The approach by Nygaard and his Norwegian colleagues on "local knowledge production" and the "pedagogy of the oppressed" by Paulo Freire (Freire 1971).

Nygaard and colleagues had since 1970 worked together with the Norwegian Metal Workers Union (NJMF) on introduction of computers at the workplace (Nygaard and Bergo 1973). A report on potential impact and what could be done was written and delivered, but nothing changed as the report just sat there and collected dust in a shelf at the central union office. In search for a new mobilization and knowledge strategy the researchers took inspiration from a successful movement (an NGO against Norwegian economic integration in the European Economic Community). The geography of Norway with its through fjords and mountains and many isolated villages made communication difficult, and a knowledge strategy based on local activist groups in a network was productively engendered. The NJMF project adapted this strategy to the work of local trade unions and their work with the introduction of computers at the workplace. On central union level textbooks and courses on computers from a trade union perspective was developed with the idea of supporting local activity. Local trade union groups at the workplaces were at the core of the "local knowledge production" strategy. It was programmatically stated that as "knowledge" the NJMF project only considered that which supported and lead to actions by the local union and its members (Nygaard and Bergo, 1975). Typically, this took the form of support to local union collective activities in negotiation with management, whether it had to do with the design and use of computer based planning systems, numerically controlled machines, or other issues of "new technology." The democratic potential of this knowledge strategy is linked to the ideal that workers, as "end users" of a technology, should have a direct influence on its implementation and use. This strategy was followed by most of the computes and democracy projects that emerged in the 1970s all over Scandinavia, and in retrospective this "local knowledge production" learning strategy stands out as a cornerstone in participatory design, and Kristen Nygaard as the founding figure.

In contrast to the many encounters with Kristen as mentor and colleague over many years, I met Paulo Freire only once. I think it was in 1972. Anyway, it was in the Labour Congress hall in Stockholm and I was part of a big audience applauding his encouraging Marxist liberation theology approach. Even if my detailed knowledge of the specific interventions was limited, the impact of the ideas were immense.

Whereas the Norwegian trade union "local knowledge production" strategy had its base in the struggle over the means of production in advanced industrial settings, the "pedagogy of the oppressed" by Freire emerged out of class conflicts as manifested in struggles for better living conditions for poor peasants in Brazil (Freire 1971). Freire's learning strategy was one of liberation. Alphabetization had to do not with disciplining the pupils by the "bank method," with copying already preconfigured knowledge objects into their heads, but with "conscientization," with learning to read and write as a critical practice. "Teachers" worked together with the peasants collaboratively assembling "teaching material" that had two specific qualities. One the one hand, it always took its point of departure in challenges in concrete local well known practices; but on the other hand, though being hands-on practical, it was assembled to open up toward connecting to broader societal controversies and ways to approach them.

When we started the first participatory design trade union projects, which we at that time called the collective resource approach, not only the Norwegian language of "local knowledge production" strategy was with us, but certainly also the Brazilian language of "the pedagogy of the oppressed." In retrospective it also seems that the two strategies complemented each other—top down and bottom up. One focused on organizational decentralization to support "local knowledge production" through central support to local action on conflicting issues at the workplace. The other emphasized concrete local learning as a vehicle for liberation opening up toward engagement in broader societal issues and conflicts.

So when a network of trade union–oriented participatory design project were further developed in Sweden (Demos), Denmark (Due), and Norway (Florence) in the mid '70s (see *Computers in Context* for details (Bjerknes et al. 1987)), the "learning legacy" from Norwegian metal workers (Nygaard) as well as Brazilian peasants (Freire) were key to how the practical work was organized. In the Demos project, on democratic planning and control in working life, where I worked as a researcher, the base for learning was "investigating teams" within the local trade union at different workplaces. At a locomotive repair shop in Örebro they were investigating a new computer-based planning and control system. How would wages and working conditions be affected? Would work be deskilled? Could more democratic alternatives be designed? What direction should they take? What is the role of computers in a more democratic working life? The investigation group, workers on shop floor, would scrutinize the proposals from management and elaborate on alternatives. In this work they would be supported by participatory designers/researcher and more importantly by central levels of the trade union through negotiation expertise and courses for local activity. The work by the investigation groups was, through a "negotiation model," to support the local union in concrete negotiations on the planning, implementation and use of "new technology." In the long run these local experiences were also to have a bearing on national negotiations on laws and agreements regulating democracy at work.

From a learning perspective, the practiced participatory design strategy was very much a merger of "local knowledge production" and "pedagogy of the oppressed." But there was also, with inspiration from the emerging field of "actions research," a critique of traditional ivory tower research. There were influences from the grounding work of Kurt Lewin (1946) but also from Paulo Freire and other Marxists.

In our view, local knowledge production was central but not enough. Through the concept of "praxis research" or "directed basic research," our ambition was to unite participatory actions research in the field with systematic theoretical reflections aiming at a productive interplay between academic and local knowledge production—hence, simultaneously participating in local and academic practices toward democratization of the workplace (and society). (See Sandberg 1981 for an overview of actions research in the early trade union associated participatory projects.)

Ambitions of better English and revolution in all honor, a summary of the participatory design learning ambitions and language from this period read something like a merger between actions research and Marxism "If you want to truly understand something, try to change it" (Lewin 1946); "The philosophers have only interpreted the world, in various ways; the point is to change it" (Marx 1845).

Our textbook, *Företagsstyrning och löntagarmakt* (Management Control and Labour Power) (Ehn and Sanberg 1979), which had a wide circulation, is typical for the learning ambitions at that time. Practical experiences from the local workplaces cases merged with a critical theoretical democracy perspective on design, technology, and learning. The book was written with trade union classes and local study circles as audience and to be supportive to local action and change. This also become the main audience, even if the book also was frequently used at universities all over Scandinavia. On a personal note, I considered this textbook for trade unions my "doctoral dissertation" and had no wish to pursue an academic carrier beyond that. A position that, on the contrary, condemned me to a life-long commitment to academia. But more about that later.

Utopian Language Games—Design for Skilled Work (1980s)

We are now in the early '80s. The Silicon Valley Mac revolution is still to come. But there are crises in the printing industry all over the Western world—at least from the perspective of graphic workers who are challenged by management's introduction of "new technology." Wages are cut, jobs laid off, and strikes defeated. Is an alternative production possible—a technology supporting skilled work rather than deskilling automation? The Utopia project, a participatory design research project, was set up to explore this challenge and eventually to design skills-based technology for newspaper production. It was a collaboration between the graphic workers' unions in all the Nordic countries and an interdisciplinary group of researchers and designers (Ehn 1988).

Based on dialogues about the graphic workers' requirements and wishes, the systems designers in our team produced drawings and flowcharts of a computer-based system for text and image processing. These descriptions were highly appreciated by the graphic workers. But still something was wrong. It gradually became clear that we did not communicate. The systems descriptions were appreciated because the were made by us, their own experts, but they made no real sense to them. A new way of collaborating was needed, and it came rather unexpected in the form of a wooden mouse.

The industrial designers in the team had been asked to mock up the system beyond the display, in the form of ergonomic furniture and controls. The "mouse" was a possible such interaction device. But how should it be designed to fit professional graphic work (and keep in mind we are still some three years prior to the Mac)? A handful of mice mock-ups were produced and explored hands-on by graphic workers. This was a breakthrough in the project. All of a sudden a strategy for joint exploration of design alternatives and their consequences had opened up. The mice mock-ups were followed by all kinds of mock-ups and prototypes of different devices and interactions to jointly explore potential design alternatives for an entire graphic production system. But more importantly, the use of mock-ups and prototypes as design devices was not to test the devices, but to support a shared design process of exploring and designing for future use situations through prototyping and different kinds of design games. We later described this as strategy of "cardboard computing: mocking it up or hands-on the future" (Ehn and Kyng 1991) and "a shift from systems descriptions to scripts for action" (Ehn and Sjögren 1991), and in broader retrospective participatory design terms, a design strategy based on the use of games, mock-ups, and prototyping.

This brings us back to design and learning. In the "academic" environment around the project, the Swedish Center for Working Life in Stockholm, there was at that time a renewed interest in the later works by the philosopher Ludwig Wittgenstein, especially his *Philosophical Investigations* (1953). The focus was on understanding the "tacit knowledge" of crafts work (and how it could not be reduced to algorithmic procedures and taken over by a computer). (See Bo Göranson 1993 for an overview.) I found this most essential also for how we dealt with skills in the Utopia project, but when I later reflected upon our "mutual learning" experiences form the Utopia project, it was rather through an unorthodox reading of Wittgenstein's language games as a vehicle for design. In short, this was the Wittgenstein-inspired participatory design learning theory I suggested in my PhD thesis (and yes, in the end and under protest I ended up as an academic) (Ehn 1988).

We are all part of many different practices. We learn language through participation in these practices. In this we become part of language games rather than acquiring a language. The meaning in language is in its use. We participate in language games because they are meaningful to us. There is no requirement that we transparently understand each other, only that the language game is a meaningful activity to all participants. To participate in a language game is to learn how to follow a rule in practice. We show that we know how to play a language game by performing the unwritten rules. When we perform the rules of a language game we may even change them as we go along. We can progressively learn new language games through their family resemblance with language games we already know. So far Wittgenstein. Now we'll move on to the attempt of a participatory design learning theory.

We could think of the design process as the coming together of many actors all with their different practices and language games. (Over)simplistically, this may to begin with be reduced to two practices: that of "designers" and that of "practitioners/users" in the Utopia project—that is, researchers/designers and graphic workers, respectively. They are both expected to know how to participate in their respective professional language games. But how may they be able to speak or play across language games and practices?

In one of his famous aphorisms Wittgenstein says: "If a lion could speak we would not understand him" (Wittgenstein 1953) and by that suggesting that their *form of life* is too different. This is where a third language game under construction is introduced—a shared design language game and practice. This design language game is composed based on the language games of both practitioners/users and professional designers. Via family resemblance between this shared design language game and the respective language games of practitioners and designers, participation in the design language game is potentially rendered meaningful for both practitioners/users and designers. (It does not matter if their understanding of the design language game is different, given that they come from different professional language games, only that the participation is a meaningful activity given their background.) So with this standpoint a participatory design challenge becomes to find ways for composing such specific design language games.

And this is what brings us back from academia to the graphic workers, the wooden mice and the turn from systems descriptions to scripts for action. Whereas systems descriptions are written in the language of design experts and with no family resemblance to the language games of other participants, they are nonsensical to these practices and language games. In contrast to this, design language games, based on performances with mock-ups, prototypes, and games that are designed to have a family resemblance to both the language games of designers and other professionals/users, have the ability to work as vehicles for expanding both. Through collaborative exploration of mock-ups, prototypes, and joint performance of design games, it becomes possible to "show" what you mean without having a shared language. Participation in this shared design language game, through family resemblance, also potentially expands the professional language games of designers and practitioners/users by opening up for novel but still meaningful ways of performing a rule in those practices.

Well, the Mac came in 1984, and desktop publishing was a fact in 1986. The Utopia system, despite all its merits, could not really compete on the market. But that is another story. "UTOPIA where workers craft new technology. Today Scandinavia, tomorrow may be the rest of the world" as the *MIT Technical Review* in 1985 appreciatively wrote did not happen either. To really change the world participatory design cannot be reduced to intertwined language games of design and use, and it is not enough for speaking with the lions of monopoly capital, as we learned from Harry Braverman (1974). I will return to this toward the end of this text.

Scandinavian Mecca for Participatory Design—International and Interdisciplinary Foundations (1990s)

After the Utopia project I joined forces with my colleagues at Århus University in Denmark for further democratic design experiments. Well at least that was our plan. As it turned out the participatory design politics of Utopia and Demos made me a persona non grata at the computer science department were they were working, and a majority of the staff voted against my enrollment, not wanting to risk that their real computer science colleagues from overseas would be offended and not want to come and visit.

Since my "PhD thesis" (written for the trade unions) was not formally a PhD and hence not a "real" scientific knowledge contribution, it was easy to turn the application down. In the long run this was probably just as good. It forced me to be more reflective and to write a second academic PhD, now with focus upon *Work-Oriented Design of Computer Artifacts* (Ehn 1988) and participatory design in theory and practice. So this was how, among other things, the understanding of participatory design as intertwined language games of design and use was developed.

Anyway, over the years Århus University developed into a mecca for participatory design scholars and many came by, not least from overseas and the Silicon Valley. So Århus is where I encountered the work by Terry Winograd at Stanford University, Lucy Suchman at Xerox Parc, Jean Lave at the Institute for Learning, Yrjö Engeström at University of San Diego, and Donald Schön at MIT, to mention a few important influences for the development of participatory design and learning in what gradually turned into a really curious and eclectic academic environment.

Winograd, Lave, and Suchman were all active in Computer Scientists for Social Responsibility in the Bay area and had a genuine interest in democratic design experiments as explored in Scandinavia. The contact with Winograd was established via Nygaard. A manuscript to the forthcoming *Computers and Understanding* (Winograd and Flores 1986) was the basis for a study circle on computers, design, and learning. Ways to understand participatory design and learning was enriched beyond language games by a *phenomenological take on skills* and the "toolness" of computer artifacts, as well as interaction across *consensual domains of autopoetic systems* as inspired by Maturana and Varela. Suchman's work with photocopiers introduced the fundamental distinction between *plans* and *situated knowledge and action* (1987), and Lave's work on crafts as *communities of practice* (Lave and Wenger 1991) inspired reflecting upon conditions for particippation and how mutual learning also is a power struggle. Engström, sharing a Marxist heritage, influenced participatory design and learning in the direction of cultural-historical activity theory and the interplay among human activity, tools, and community *in learning by expanding* in the zone of proximal learning at work (Engeström 1987).

Last, but not least there was the influence from Schön (1983, 1987) and the notion of the designer as a skillful *reflective practitioner* that practiced and learned in deeply uncertain terrains rather than as the at that time worshiped logical scientist of the artificial as declared by Herbert Simon (1969). Classical are Schön's descriptions of how designers learn and conduct professional artistry through processes of *reflection-in*-action in which knowing and doing are inseparable, and how this is carried out as *on the spot experiments* where the materials of the situation (models, sketches, drawings, etc.) at hand *talk back,* often in a surprising way.

To begin with, the influence from Schön was only indirect, via books and other scholars, but in the long run the influence was considerable, not only as an opening into the pragmatism of John Dewey (1934, 1938), which since has continued to profoundly influence participatory design, but also as generous collegial support. An example is when he, despite age and poor health conditions, came across the Atlantic and participated in a PhD summer school on design of computer systems that we organized. The intensity and mastery in the way he performed his theory of the reflective practitioner left no participant unaffected. Later he also became a key advisor for another learning adventure and the making of a school and research center focusing on democratic design experiments and a reflective practicum in the era of the computer, a digital Bauhaus (Ehn 1998). By that time we were already approaching the turn of the century, and for me the eclectic and controversial learning challenges in Århus was since several years over and with the first biannual Participatory Design Conference (PDC) held in Seattle in 1990 participatory design was now an established international research field that grow out of the USA-Scandinavia/Århus connection. Participatory designers of the world were united—we had learned to speak with peers all over the academic world—but did it change the world, and was there also a design revolution?

Building a Digital Bauhaus—A Participatory Design School ('00s)

"Digital Bauhaus designers of all countries, unite!" (Ehn 1998). These were the commanding, serious, but also self-mocking, final words of the manifesto for a new kind of design school and research center in the era of the computer aiming at critically uniting Scandinavian participatory design with the social and aesthetic revolutionary goals of the Bauhaus school and early modern design before it had become reduced to the "international style" of concrete, steel, and glass.

The learning challenge to shape a school of arts and communication focusing on design and information technology as part of building a new university from scratch was certainly very different from that of conducting participatory design research projects. How to build programs and curricula? How to combine design studio work with academic studies? How to make the school a "living lab" that in participatory, critical, democratic, and "designerly" ways could engage with people in their everyday lives at work and in their neighborhoods? This last question had specific significance, since the new university—situated in the once thriving industrial city of Malmö, since many years plagued by plant closures, segregation, and high unemployment—was seen by the local politicians as an important vehicle to transform the city toward a green, sustainable, and creative hub in the 21st-century economy.

The pedagogy for the study programs that emerged was based on experiences with "problem based learning" (Hmelo-Silver 2004) combined with Donald Schön's vision of a "reflective practicum" and of the architectural studio as an educational model for this kind of reflection-in-action, and the observation of such a conversation as characterized by learning-by-doing, coaching rather than teaching, and a dialogue of reciprocal reflection-in-action between teacher and student (Schön 1983, 1987).

The architecture of the digital Bauhaus was centered on an open public space for group work, exhibitions, and café meetings. Research studios, a performance black box, a lecture theater, workshops for wood and electronics, a music studio, and "home rooms" for the students surrounded this space. All facilities were on the same floor, intended to be supportive of creative meetings and mutual learnings among students, teachers, researchers, artists, and the public.

In many ways this school was a success, surfing on the wave of the IT boom and the grand expectations of the creative class at the turn of the century. Now, in retrospective, the picture is a bit more scattered and lusterless. To begin with, ample resources for studio- and problem-based learning were allocated to the study programs, and the research studios attracted major long-term grants. With a focus on media studies and interaction design, study programs from bachelor to PhD level were initiated. The research studios thematically approached digital media in relation to space, narration, and creative environments respectively. So far, so good. But this was not only the time for the breakthrough of the Internet and new media forms, but also for neoliberalism as the main societal ideology also in Scandinavian welfare states. Seen from the outside, participatory design with a strong focus on democratic design experiments (in the small) was problematic. This did not fit neoliberal market economy, neither as expressed through the unlimited beliefs in the dotcom industry and the creative class nor as in the focus on individualistic libertarianism minimizing the public sphere and the collective welfare state. As a consequence, major research grants were withdrawn, and, in the name of new public management, the education programs were standardized, with more focus on employability than on democratic civic participation.

Still we were producing in accordance with the manifesto. A good example from the earlier years and with relation to a learning perspective was the KLIV-project (Knowledge and Learning in Healthcare). Two of our young design researchers from the school were invited to collaborate with nurses and other staff at the main hospital in the city. Their initial approach was as taken out of a participatory design handbook. Building trust over time. Video ethnographic work to collaboratively articulate problematic situations and ending up with informal learning at the ward as a major challenge. Mock-ups and design games for shared exploration of design openings, resulting in a broad repertoire of short films, an "app" (many years before we had apps), and an accreditation system made for and by the staff to informally and *in situ* share experiences of how to handle medical equipment and problematic situations. When the approach and its implementation in 2005 were bestowed the User Award for IT-support for best working conditions in a Swedish workplace, only nurses were on the stage representing the design. The professional designers becomingly stayed in the background. As design researchers they, however, also participated in academic language games. With their PhD thesis (Hillgren 2006; Björgvinsson 2007) in Interaction design, based on the collaboration with the nurses, they became legitimate participants in design research communities of practice, both by adding to the repertoire of good participatory design practices and by further developing the theoretical interdisciplinary understanding of especially design and learning. Participatory design was both challenged and expanded by exploring participatory design as participation in the formation of communities of practice as well as the role of artifacts as socio-material mediations in this practice. In the beginning the experiences travelled well to other sites and practices, but when commercial actors took over the whole approach was reified and the "technological app" fetishized.

Another research learning initiative during the early years of was the attempt, inspired by Dewey and Schön, to in collaboration with the interaction design students redesign their studios as "creative environments" and "reflective practicum" by enhancing the studios with new media and physical computing devices (Telier 2011). In many ways this was a success. The students loved their new studio and spent most of their time there. There was a kind of "cocooning effect" and students spent less and less time learning in the field in collaboration with others. Hence, the achievements led to a major failure, and the learning program had to be revised with a much stronger focus "out of the box" and on ethnographic fieldwork and participatory design "in the wild," far away from the cozy creative studio environment.

Democratic Design Experiments (in the Small)—Participatory Design and Beyond

The last decade have seen many participatory design interventions from this "digital Bauhaus," but they have been less "digital" and more social or rather "collective" (as in socio-material hybrids) inspired by science and technology studies and especially the work by Bruno Latour and colleagues (Latour and Weibel 2005, Latour 2005) as well as Donna Haraway and other feminist techno-science scholars (Haraway 1991, 2007). At the same time, this participatory design work has in most cases been carried out outside the walls of the design studio and the university in "living labs," long-term interventions serendipitously forging collaboration between actors in heterogeneous expanding networks in the city of Malmö and beyond.

The open access book *Making Futures—Marginal Notes on Innovation, Design and Democracy* (Ehn et al. 2014) is a collection of reflected stories from these design interventions. What is suggested is not an innovation highway to the future, but rather many small capricious situated futures in the making. There are contemporary participatory design stories that goes beyond struggling for democracy at the workplace turning toward social innovation in the neighborhoods, about opening production through maker-spaces and commons, about creative class struggles and cultural production, and last but not least about emerging publics and designerly ways to extend democratic participation. These are not success stories and no Utopias or promised lands are reached, but in the struggles there are openings of hope. As for learning theory the interventions more or less follow on from earlier participatory design experiences. With one major exception—the "project" is no longer where learning primarily takes place. As mentioned above, through "living labs" and an overarching "infrastructuring" approach (Karasti and Syrjänen 2004, Björgvinsson et al. 2012), paying special attention to the "marginalized by hegonomic infrastuctures" (Star 1991), heterogeneous networks of actors and communities of practice are connected over time.

The last decade at the School of Arts and Communication has for me personally also meant a changing focus of learning and participation to a different kind of "we" than in the early days—from being PhD student and "project leader" to PhD supervisor and "mentor." So what I have learned about participatory design during these later years I have fundamentally learned from interaction with my PhD students. To mention a few but important examples: from Erling Björgvinsson and Per-Anders Hillgren I have learned about participatory design not only as a democratic work practice but also as mundane artistic practice and design as long-term engagements through "living labs" and "rhizomatic collisions" (Björgvinsson 2007; Hillgren 2006); from Kristina Lindstöm and Åsa Ståhl, about design research as a truly collaborative practice and participatory design as "patchworking publics" (Lindström and Ståhl 2014); from Anna Seravalli, as "making commons" challenging capitalist modes of production (Seravalli 2014); and from Anders Emilson, about participatory design, as not only social innovation but also as actively preparing in the shadow of "societal collapse" (Emilson 2015).

This privilege to, in the spirit of Dewey and Schön, learn through participation in "educating the reflective design researcher" has also included being a supervisor for many years in the national Swedish design doctoral school (Ehn and Ullmark forthcoming).

I am not sure my younger colleagues think they are doing participatory design or co-design, just as much as we did not think we were doing that in the 1970s. We were doing the "collective resource approach" and they are engaged in "making publics" and "cosmopolitical events," and so on. In my view, however, there is a family resemblance between the language games the old "we" of participatory design was playing and the ones performed by the contemporary "we" of participatory design. They all have a family resemblance in the sense of being engagements in some kind of, what we lately have reviewed as, democratic design experiments in the small, enriching the repertoire of democratic engagement and expressions in a designerly way (Binder et al. 2015).

> What we have in mind is a performative fluid and flickering figuration (Law and Mol 2001) we could name design thinging. This "design thinging" is a flickering between processes of collective decision making and collaborative material making, between "parliamentary" and "laboratory" practices, between engagements with objects of worry as "matters of concern" (Latour 1999) and the transformation of objective matter as "circulating references" (Latour 1999), forging strategies and tactics of participation and representation across these practices. This performative figuration also changes over time as a flickering between gathering assemblies and appropriating objects. The challenge concerns the legitimacy and the skills of codesign to draw these things together, the "parliamentary legitimacy of assembling the assemblies (of drawing them together) as well as the "drawing skills" of making collaborative designing take place.
>
> (Binder et al. 2015)

In such language games, politics and power are not external conditions that design can relate to, but at the very core of participatory design and learning. This was the case in the early days of struggles around workplace democracy, just as it is today, when participatory designers engage with those marginalized in society in making publics and commons or in cosmopolitical encounters, including participation by troublesome nonhuman "significant otherness" (Harraway 2007) as well as "idiots" (Stengers 2005) slowing the participatory engagement down.

In other words, participatory design as design experiments (in the small) will always have to be concurrently concerned both with the challenge of how to extend and find forms for democratic participation and decision-making beyond the representative parliament and with the challenge of doing this in a public collaborative composing experimental way beyond the concealed scientific laboratory. Issues of inclusion and exclusion, not least legitimate participation of those marginalized by hegemonic infrastructures, are specific and situated and will always have to be at the core of participatory design as democratic design experiments in the small. If not, there is just yet another creative design method.

What started as challenges of language and revolution and with reference to Paulo Freire as a "pedagogy of the oppressed" and educated hope has over the years travelled through many language games of small democratic design experiments. These language games have concerned democratization of the workplace (and of innovation) as well as engagements with making publics around everyday mundane practices in neighborhoods and with civic organizations (and democratizing social innovation). They have dealt with supporting everyday learning practices at work and in public as well as the building of academic institutions and with supporting PhD students to become participatory reflective design researchers. This has not been a frictionless, ever more progressive accomplishment of democratic design experiments, and what at times looked like real success stories ever so often faded away or were antagonistically crushed. In these struggles there are, however, still openings of hope, even if there is no Utopia and no promised land. Our ever-so-small democratic design experiments and the pedagogy of the oppressed have to be reinvented again and again as we play along. This is how I found learning in participatory design, now as well as almost half a century ago: Neither consensus with the lions of the market economy nor revolution, but improved democratic design language games—a paradoxical Scandinavian tale, full of melancholy and of hope.

References

Binder, Thomas, Eva Brandt, Pelle Ehn, and Joakim Halse. 2015. Democratic Design Experiments—Between Parliament and Laboratory. In *CoDesign* 11 (3–4), 152–165.

Bjerknes, Gro, Pelle Ehn, and Morten Kyng. 1987. *Computers and Democracy*. Aldershot: Gower Publishing Company Limited.

Björgvinsson, Erling. 2007. *Socio-Material Mediations: Learning, Knowing and Self-Produced Media within Healthcare*. Karlskrona: Blekinge Institute of Technology.

Björgvinsson, Erling, Pelle Ehn, and Per-Anders Hillgren. 2012. Agonistic Participatory Design: Working with Marginalised Social Movements. In *CoDesign* 8 (2–3): 127–144.

Braverman, Harry. 1974. *Labor and Monopoly Capital—The Degradation of Work in the Twentieth Century*. New York: Monthly Review Press.

Dewey, John. 1934/1980. *Art as Experience*. New York: Berkeley Publishing Group.

Dewey, John. 1938. *Logic: The Theory of Inquiry*. New York: Henry Holt and Company.

Ehn, Pelle. 1974. *Emancipation and the Design of Information Systems*. Hindås: Altorg.

Ehn, Pelle. 1988. *Work-Oriented Design of Computer Artifacts*. Falköping: Erlbaum.

Ehn, Pelle. 1998. Manifesto for a Digital Bauhaus. In *Digital Creativity* 9 (4): 207–217.

Ehn, Pelle, and Morten Kyng. 1991. Cardboard Computers: Mocking-It-Up or Hands-on the Future. In *Design at Work*, ed. J. Greenbaum and M. Kyng (pp. 169–195). Mahwah: Erlbaum.

Ehn, Pelle, Elisabet Nilsson, and Richard Topgaard (eds.). 2014. *Making Futures—Marginal Notes on Innovation, Design and Democracy*. Cambridge, MA: MIT Press.

Ehn, Pelle, and Åke Sandberg. 1979. *Företagsstyrning och Löntagarmakt*. Falköping: Prisma.

Ehn, Pelle, and Dan Sjögren. 1991. From Systems Descriptions to Scripts for Action. In *Design at Work*, ed. J. Greenbaum and M. Kyng (pp. 241–268). Mahwah: Erlbaum.

Ehn, Pelle, and Peter Ullmark. Forthcoming. *Educating the Reflective Design Researcher*.

Emilson, Anders. 2015. *Design in the Space between Stories: Design for Social Innovation and Sustainability—From Responding to Societal Challenges to Preparing for Societal Collapse*. Doctoral dissertation. Malmö University.

Engeтröm, Yrjö. 1987. *Learning by Expanding*. Helsinki: Orienta-Konsultit.

Freire, Paulo. 1971. *Pedagogy of the Oppressed*. New York: Herder and Herder.

Göranzon, Bo. 1993. *The Practical Intellect—Computers and Skills*. London: Springer-Vorlag.

Haraway, Donna J. 1991. Situated Knowledges: The Science Question in Feminism and the Privilege of Partial Perspective. In *Simians, Cyborgs, and Women*, ed. D. Haraway (pp. 183–202). Abingdon: Routledge.

Haraway, Donna J. 2007. *When Species Meet*. Minneapolis: University of Minnesota Press.

Hillgren, Per-Anders. 2006. *Ready-made-media-actions: Lokal produktion och användning av audiovisuella medier inom hälso-och sjukvården*. Blekinge Institute of Technology.

Hmelo-Silver, Cindy E. 2004. Problem-Based Learning: What and How Do Students Learn? In *Educational Psychology Review* 16 (3): 235–266.

Howard, Robert. 1985. Utopia—Where Workers Craft New Technology. In *Technological Review* 88 (3): 43–49.

Karasti, Helena, and Anna-Liina Syrjänen. 2004. Artful Infrastructuring in "Two Cases of Community PD." In *Proceedings of the Eighth Conference on Participatory Design 2004* (pp. 20–30). Canada.

Latour, Bruno. 1999. *Pandora's Hope: Essays on the Reality of Science Studies*. Cambridge, MA: Harvard University Press.

Latour, Bruno. 2005. *Reassembling the Social: An Introduction to Actor-Network-Theory*, Clarendon Lectures in Management Studies. Oxford: Oxford University Press.

Latour, Bruno, and Peter Weibel (eds.). 2005. *Making Things Public: Atmospheres of Democracy*. Cambridge, MA: MIT Press.

Lave, Jean, and Etienne Wenger. 1991. *Situated Learning: Legitimate Peripheral Participation*. Cambridge: Cambridge University Press.

Law, John, and Annemarie Mol. 2001. Situating Technoscience: An Inquiry into Spatialities. In *Environment and Planning D: Society and Space* 19 (5): 609–621.

Lewin, Kurt. 1946. Action Research and Minority Problems. *Journal of Social Issues* 2 (4): 34–46.

Lindström, Kristina, and Åsa Ståhl. 2014. *Patchworking Publics-in-the-Making—Design, Media and Public Engagement*. Doctoral dissertation. Malmö University.

Marx, Karl. 1845/1888. *Thesis on Feuerbach*.

Nyggard, Kristen, and Olav Bergo. 1973. *Planlegging, Styring og Databehandling*. Oslo: Tiden Norsk Forlag.

Nyggard, Kristen, and Olav Bergo. 1975. The Trade Unions—New Users of Research. In *Personal Review*, no. 2.

Sandberg, Åke. 1981. Om arbetslivsforskningens metoder och förutsättningar. In *Forskning för förändring. Om metoder och förutsättningar för handlingsinriktad forskning i arbetslivet*, ed. Å. Sandberg. Stockholm: Arbetslivscentrum.

Schön, Donald A. 1983. *The Reflective Practitioner—How Professionals Think in Action*. New York: Basic Books.

Schön, Donald A. 1987. *Educating the Reflective Practitioner*. San Francisco: Jossey-Bass.

Seravalli, Anna. 2014. *Making Commons—Attempts at Composing Prospects in the Opening of Production*. Doctoral dissertation, Malmö University.

Simon, Herbert A. 1969. *The Sciences of the Artificial*. Cambridge, MA: MIT Press.

Star, Susan L. 1991. Power, Technology and the Phenomenology of Conventions: On Being Allergic to Onions. In *A Sociology of Monsters: Essays on Power, Technology and Domination*, ed. J. Law. London: Routledge.

Stengers, Isabelle. 2005. The Cosmopolitical Proposal. In *Making Things Public*, ed. B. Latour and P. Weibel. Cambridge, MA: MIT Press.

Suchman, Lucy. 1987. *Plans and Situated Actions: The Problem of Human–Machine Communication*. New York: Cambridge University Press.

Telier, A. (Thomas Binder, Giorgio De Michelis, Pelle Ehn, Giulio Jacucci, Per Linde and Ina Wagner). 2011. *Design Things*. Cambridge, MA: MIT Press.

Winograd, Terry, and Fernando Flores. 1986. *Understanding Computers and Cognition: A New Foundation for Design*. Norwood: Ablex.

Wittgenstein, Ludwig. 1953. *Philosophical Investigations*. Oxford: Basil Blackwell.

3

HOW PARTICIPATORY DESIGN HAS INFLUENCED THE LEARNING SCIENCES

Christopher Hoadley

This book demonstrates in an important way the linkages between two different perspectives, held by two different communities. In many ways, the dual perspective of these two communities helps contrast two major stances toward learning—the perspective of science, and the perspective of design. Education, more than many other arenas of intellectual inquiry, has spent the 20th century in a dance between these two perspectives. This has been both a core challenge and, increasingly, a core strength. I don't think it's a coincidence that Herbert Simon, author of *The Sciences of the Artificial* (Simon, 1969) and who explored what it means to have a "design science," is still the only person one might identify as a member of the learning sciences to have won a Nobel prize. Simon, John Dewey, Jerome Bruner, Seymour Papert: many of the people who have significantly influenced the learning sciences share this quality of attempting to foster a deep and empirically based understanding of how people learn, and yet have maintained a deeply interventionist stance toward what it means to create an environment that fosters learning, whether in a lab school or a computer lab. And perhaps not coincidentally, as much as each of these scholars is identifiably part of the heritage that led to the learning sciences, each also had a wide-ranging background that makes their discipline hard to pin down—was Dewey an educational scientist, or a philosopher? Bruner is lauded as a psychologist, but spent most of his life as a law professor. Simon's Nobel in economics belies his role as one of the cofounders of artificial intelligence. And Papert's history in AI and computer science (itself a new field) doesn't capture his role in education or media.

As John Dewey stated, every design can be an act of scientific inquiry: "The conjunction of problematic and determinate characters in nature renders every existence, as well as every idea and human act, an experiment in fact, even though not in design. To be intelligently experimental is but to be conscious of this intersection of natural conditions so as to profit by it instead of being at its mercy" (Dewey, 1925, p. lw.1.63). While I wholeheartedly agree with this stance, it contrasts mightily with those who see changing the world as informed by, but not concomitant, with scientific research on how the world works. We might think back to the types of natural science that were conducted in Ben Franklin's time, when scientific research didn't necessarily imply collecting your data in a laboratory, and when data was not as distinct from observation, and when science was seen as "natural philosophy" implying strongly that data without a probing, rational mind was not actually scientific.

On the flip side, science, especially science related to the human sphere, suffers when it is cleaved from its roots of mastering the world. "The contingency of artificial phenomena has always created doubts as to whether they fall properly within the compass of science. Sometimes these doubts are directed at the . . . difficulty of disentangling prescription from description. This seems to me not to be the real difficulty. The genuine problem is to show how empirical propositions can be made at all about systems that, given different circumstances, might be quite other than they are" (Simon, 1969, p. x). And in learning research, this dilemma: how to change the world, based on an empirically derived knowledge of how people learn, when all of the scientific findings on education, "given different circumstance, might be quite other than they are" (ibid.). This dilemma in the 20th century has led to several interesting outcomes. One is the fetishization of "objective" science in learning research. The emergence of research on learning in the 20th century can be seen as a struggle between the faction exemplified by Dewey, aiming for a holistic, grounded, interventionist discipline made rigorous through a balance of empiricism and groundedness, in particular contexts tied together by clear philosophical inquiry, and the faction exemplified by Thorndike and Skinner, aiming for objectivity through a brutal extermination of agendas, irreproducible results, and introspection, with a clear firewall between interpretation and uncontrovertible data. This perspective is not limited to the early 20th century, and in many ways aligns with the US National Academy of Science report titled "Scientific Research in Education" (National Research Council, 2002). Still, in the United States at least, most academic education departments remain a valuable, if eclectic, bazaar of approaches ranging from social theory, interpretivism and activism, and humanistic study to the more standoffish approaches of experimental psychology, sophisticated statistical analysis, and psychometrics. Tucked away on a side street in this bazaar are often designers: instructional designers, curriculum designers, designers of educational communications and technology.

The learning sciences community has been a cluster of scholars who, like some of the boundary-crossers described above, tend less toward questions of policy, or the pragmatics of training the education workforce, and more toward the dual attempt to understand and to change learning in context, or in other words, toward science and design (e.g., Collins, 1992). My own history with this community is as an American scholar, trained in cognitive science and computer science, and studying in northern California just as the technological revolution was spawning the learning sciences, but also as an advocate for deepening the international nature of the learning sciences community through organizations such as the International Society for the Learning Sciences. I've written about this community and its history elsewhere (Hoadley, 2004, 2005; Hoadley & Van Haneghan, 2011; Kirby, Hoadley, & Carr-Chellman, 2005), but I would reiterate that several characteristics help define it as a place that was perhaps uniquely well suited, among all the learning research communities, to think about design. First, there was a strong tradition of straddling this boundary between science and action in practice. Second, the learning sciences has, like cognitive science before it, struggled with the role of social context, including all the challenges it poses to reproducibility, but also with all the opportunities provided by treating learning research as informing a profession, in the sense of Argyris and Schön (1991). Argyris and Schön argued that professional knowledge, unlike other forms of knowledge, is contingent on context, and on judgment. They argue this is why an architect is not merely a technician applying known solutions to problems, and they echo some of Simon's way of treating design as a way of thinking that can't be reduced to closed-form problem solving. Learning scientists tend to take this "your mileage may vary" stance, treating learning research as often a "local science" in diSessa's terminology (diSessa, 1991). And thirdly, perhaps most importantly, the learning sciences as a field is inextricably linked to the emergence of research in and on and with technology. In the 1980s and 1990s, computers were the purview of either computer scientists (an emerging discipline even then) or of science and math experts who had access to the resources for computing. But there was also this incredible moment of opportunity in which cognitive science was providing opportunities for collaborations across psychology, anthropology, linguistics, and neuroscience, with computer scientists at the table (Gardner, 1985; Molnar, 1997). One can argue that the mind-as-computer or mind-as-symbol-system metaphor drove cognitive science for years, and this community included lots of computer folks who were, by inclination or necessity, builders, makers, and designers. They were improvisers and implementers. And in some places, especially Silicon Valley and the Boston area, there was a deep confluence of people who were studying and building our shared future with technology as they went.

As described in Ehn's chapter (this volume), there were important confluences forged in the crucible of technology invention. Xerox PARC hosted not only numerous early human–computer interaction designers and researchers, but also the Institute for Research on Learning. Many of the early groups of learning scientists had strong educational technology emphasis, including those at UC Berkeley's Education in Math, Science and Technology; Northwestern University's Institute for the Learning Sciences; the Cognition and Technology Group at Vanderbilt (CGTV); and MIT's Media Lab. The first learning sciences conference and journal emerged at Northwestern University as an outgrowth of the Artificial Intelligence in Education community. Participatory design and its long tradition, especially in Northern Europe, had some intersection with these groups, which at the time were as likely to send papers to the Computer Human Interaction conferences as to the mainstream education conferences. And researchers like Michael Cole, Jean Lave, Etienne Wenger, and Jim Greeno helped link the learning sciences community to those studying and fostering technology using a sociocultural framing—this supported ties to the cultural historical activity theory being used in Scandinavia. Those ties persisted, especially in the area of computer-supported collaborative learning, such that scholars from the United States and from Scandinavian centers like INTERMEDIA in Norway again provided critical human capital for ideas from participatory design to be visible to those in the learning sciences.

When I first encountered participatory design in the 1990s, it was through the technology design community: one of the participatory design conferences had several education colleagues in attendance, and participatory design methods and its sibling, informant design methods, were being talked about and cited in the human–computer interaction literature (Muller & Kuhn, 1993; Scaife, Rogers, Aldrich, & Davies, 1997). The metaphor of "user centered design," at that time still a newish contribution in human–computer interaction (HCI) (Norman & Draper, 1986), was complemented by the concept of "learner centered design" by Elliot Soloway in the *Communications of the ACM*, perhaps the most widely read journal in computer science (Soloway, Guzdial, & Hay, 1994). These connections between learning research and HCI left a door open for ideas from participatory design to come into the learning sciences. Interestingly, the learning sciences was reinventing some wheels here, in that instructional design also had models for learning design that were participatory: for example, "user-design" (Carr, 1997), which closely resembled participatory design, was proposed in the instructional design community but not widely noticed in the learning sciences. In the late 1990s into the early 2000s, the notion of design-based research was evolving and incorporated some of the ideas of participatory design in the notion of design and research as a partnership-based activity involving stakeholders (although often the stakeholders were teachers, but not necessarily learners) (Cobb, Confrey, diSessa, Lehrer, & Schauble, 2003; Design-Based Research Collective, 2003). Later points of connection included what learning scientists would call "co-design" (Penuel, Roschelle, & Shechtman, 2007) and the idea of "research-practice partnerships," which forms part of the basis for what is now called design-based implementation research (e.g., Penuel, Allen, Farrell, & Coburn, 2015). All of these are framings of design that place a value on empowering (whether in an explicitly political way or not) some of the people whom educational designs would influence, and thereby (one hopes) making the findings of the work more useful, usable, disseminable, and valid.

When I reflect on the ways in which the learning sciences have become more connected to the traditions behind participatory design, I think now is a critical moment in the history of both communities. On the one hand, the prominence of framings such as design-based implementation research takes some of the core questions of educational research, like "How do we understand how people learn in a way that helps us influence it at scale?" and places them squarely under a design framing where valuing participation and mutual respect are key assumptions. On the other hand, the learning sciences community has a bit of a blind spot when it comes to the inherently political nature of this framing, and has historically done less well at empowering learners (as opposed to educators) in the process. Other educational research traditions, such as participatory action research, are much more explicit about and embracing toward the political nature of research that draws on design that is participatory. At the International Conference of the Learning Sciences in 2014, the theme of "learning and becoming in practice" heralded not only a theoretical stance toward culture and identity as core aspects of learning, but also had an unprecedented number of sessions in which the political aspects of learning design were considered, including one symposium on participatory design in the learning sciences (from which this book draws.) For the learning sciences to advance, and to truly draw on the natural affinities between it and the participatory design community, there needs to be an increasing consideration of how design is inherently (if not deliberately) a political act, and that, rather than being a weakness in an objectivist model of rigor, is a strength in a framing where both the science and the design of learning are aimed at producing usable knowledge (Lagemann, 2002; Lindblom & Cohen, 1979). Committing to the production of usable knowledge means committing to the contingency of context, to "local sciences," to knowledge that fits the Argyris and Schön sense of knowledge-needing-judgment, and to a version of cumulativity very different from that held in today's natural sciences. By doing so, it may be that we can create a reciprocal benefit to participatory design—one in which, as Dewey says, we can profit from the contingencies and intersectionalities of designing and implementing learning environments, rather than being at their mercy, by generating insights that endure about how people learn, and what to do about it.

References

Argyris, C., & Schön, D. A. (1991). *Theory in Practice: Increasing Professional Effectiveness* (1st Classic Paperback ed.). San Francisco: Jossey-Bass Publishers.

Carr, A. A. (1997). User-design in the creation of human learning systems. *Educational Technology Research and Development, 45*(3), 5–22.

Cobb, P., Confrey, J., diSessa, A., Lehrer, R., & Schauble, L. (2003). Design experiments in educational research. *Educational Researcher, 32*(1), 9–13, 35–37.

Collins, A. (1992). Toward a design science of education. In E. Scanlon & T. O'Shea (Eds.), *New Directions in Educational Technology* (pp. 15–22). New York: Springer-Verlag.

Design-Based Research Collective. (2003). Design-based research: An emerging paradigm for educational inquiry. *Educational Researcher, 32*(1), 5–8, 35–37.

Dewey, J. (1925). Volume I: 1925. In J. A. Boydston (Ed.), *John Dewey: The Later Works* (electronic ed.). Carbondale, IL: Southern Illinois University Press.

diSessa, A. (1991). Local sciences: Viewing the design of human-computer systems as cognitive science. In J. M. Carroll (Ed.), *Designing Interaction: Psychology at the Human-Computer Interface* (pp. 162–202). Cambridge, England: Cambridge University Press.

Gardner, H. (1985). *The Mind's New Science: A History of the Cognitive Revolution*. New York: Basic Books.

Hoadley, C. (2004). Learning and design: Why the learning sciences and instructional systems need each other. *Educational Technology, 44*(3), 6–12.

Hoadley, C. (2005). The shape of the elephant: Scope and membership of the CSCL community. In T. Koschmann, D. D. Suthers, & T.-W. Chan (Eds.), *Computer-Supported Collaborative Learning (CSCL) 2005* (pp. 205–210). Taipei, Taiwan: International Society of the Learning Sciences.

Hoadley, C., & Van Haneghan, J. P. (2011). The learning sciences: Where they came from and what it means for instructional designers. In R. A. Reiser & J. V. Dempsey (Eds.), *Trends and Issues in Instructional Design and Technology* (Third ed., pp. 53–63). New York: Pearson.

Kirby, J., Hoadley, C., & Carr-Chellman, A. A. (2005). Instructional systems design and the learning sciences: A citation analysis. *Educational Technology Research and Development, 53*(1), 37–48.

Lagemann, E. C. (2002). Usable knowledge in education: A memorandum for the Spencer Foundation Board of Directors. Chicago, IL: Spencer Foundation.

Lindblom, C. E., & Cohen, D. K. (1979). *Usable Knowledge: Social Science and Social Problem Solving*. New Haven, CT: Yale University Press.

Molnar, A. R. (1997). Computers in education: A brief history. *T.H.E. Journal, 24*, 63–68.

Muller, M. J., & Kuhn, S. (1993). Participatory design. *Communications of the ACM, 36*(1), 24–28.

National Research Council. (2002). *Scientific Research in Education*. Washington, DC: National Academy Press.

Norman, D. A., & Draper, S. W. (1986). *User-Centered Systems Design: New Perspectives on Human-Computer Interaction*. Hillsdale, NJ: Lawrence Erlbaum Associates.

Penuel, W. R., Allen, A.-R., Farrell, C., & Coburn, C. E. (2015). Conceptualizing research-practice partnerships as joint work at boundaries. *Journal for Education of Students at Risk (JESPAR), 20*(1–2), 182–197. doi: 10.1080/10824669.2014.988334

Penuel, W. R., Roschelle, J., & Shechtman, N. (2007). Designing formative assessment software with teachers: An analysis of the co-design process. *Research and Practice in Technology Enhanced Learning, 2*(1), 51–74.

Scaife, M., Rogers, Y., Aldrich, F., & Davies, M. (1997, March 22–27). *Designing for or designing with? Informant design for interactive learning environments*. Paper presented at the CHI '97, Atlanta.

Simon, H. A. (1969). *The Sciences of the Artificial*. Cambridge, MA: MIT Press.

Soloway, E., Guzdial, M., & Hay, K. E. (1994). Learner-centered design: the challenge for HCI in the 21st century. *Interactions, 1*(2), 36–41.

4

CONVERSATION

Viewing Participatory Design from the Learning Sciences and the Field of Design

Conversation between Christopher Hoadley and Carl DiSalvo

The following conversation took place on April 2, 2016, for approximately 60 minutes. Jason Yip moderated the conversation between professors Christopher Hoadley (New York University) and Carl DiSalvo (Georgia Institute of Technology). The main points of this discussion about participatory design and the learning sciences focused on several themes:

- How each of the discussants came to become involved in participatory design (from learning to design and from design to learning)
- The challenges of learning and participatory design, particularly as the boundaries between user/design and teacher/learner are blurring
- How participatory design can be disruptive to learning design
- The future challenges of involving stakeholders in the design of their learning environments, including how public funding shapes design and learning

From Learning to Design and from Design to Learning

Jason Yip: So what does participatory design mean to both of you, considering how it relates to (1) design and (2) learning?

Carl DiSalvo: Let me take those questions individually first and then try to combine them together. I did not start off doing participatory design work, I came to it later on in my graduate degree and then really full on in my post-doc.

For me, participatory design was a way to broaden the discussion about who or might be involved in the activities of design and it was appealing to me because it was a practice of design that was explicitly engaged with political issues.

That was and is something that's important to me. And participatory design is one of the few areas of design where there is an up-front discussion about the politics of doing design, as well as the political situations that design operates in.

Participatory design grapples with the political with both a big "P" and a small "p." It's political in terms of thinking about the relationship to government, but also political in terms of thinking about issues like worker's rights, and working conditions, identity, politics, and the political aspects of the everyday. Participatory design [PD] is a way of doing design that broadens a conversation about who gets to take part in design and designing.

The reason why that's important to me is that I think that the key thing about what sets practicing designers apart is first a recognition that the world is constructed, and then, second, a recognition that therefore it can be constructed differently. I think understanding a design perspective is really that simple: the world is not taken as a given. When it comes to learning, then, this perspective opens up the conversation about who gets to create learning environments and what are these learning environments? I think actually almost any endeavor of PD also includes some aspect of learning. Successful PD is when we are learning from each other in the process of reconfiguring the world.

Christopher Hoadley: I guess I come at the area of participatory design in a different way. It was learning first, participation second, and design third. So, as a young technologist, I was very excited by exactly as Carl says, this idea that the world can be different than it is, and that certain people have the agency to change what exists. That's one of the things that's really enchanting about technology. As a kid, I used computers at a time when it was under the purview of experts, hobbyists, and specialists. I had a lot of access to that world through just dumb luck at a time when kids generally weren't counted in those three categories of people who had that same level of access. But I had some familiarity with the technology at a time when I was beginning to get interested in how we could use all the tools at our disposal to improve learning and education.

Over time, I grew to understand that learning was a much bigger phenomenon than education on purpose in schools. So, my perspective as somebody who saw learning as a goal and saw technology as a possible means, led naturally to me not only trying to make technologies to serve my own learning and education needs, but also being incredibly frustrated by the lack of access that other learners might have to these kinds of technologies. As sort of a privileged insider in the temple of technology, I was able to do things like programming in concert with my increasing use of technology. But as personal computing became more and more prevalent, we saw that there were a lot of people using technologies who had no means with which to tailor, understand, or remake those technologies for their own purposes. It was in that vein that I realized that some kind of bridging was needed between the creator and the user when it comes to learning. It was around that time that I was first exposed to some of the literature on design. I was lucky enough to meet some of the early folks doing HCI [human–computer interaction] work, and also some mechanical engineering faculty who were doing work on product design, and the early participatory design conferences were just starting to happen. So, for me, that was a language that I could use to explain something that I was already seeing as a disconnect between users and makers in the learning space. I was really happy to discover that there was a long illustrious tradition.

Your comments, Carl, about politics are really interesting to me, because I think at the time, I would have characterized myself as not only apolitical, but anti-political. It was really only by doing this kind of design that you start to realize that anything that's important has power, and anything that has power has politics. That includes the power to design a better word processor. So, starting to see both education and design as inherently political fields I think is one of those awakenings that people can come to at various points in their lives, or various points in their careers. It certainly doesn't mean that we have to treat everything as a contentious or zero sum situation. I think when people hear politics, that's what they assume: You mean somebody's running for election, or somebody wants to be in charge of an organization or some kind of resources. Especially when you're thinking in terms of learning, which is often seen as a generous, collaborative, selfless kind of endeavor, I think that the way that politics plays out is maybe quite different than the way it plays out in a competitive or corporate space. As such, I think learning design in the technology field especially is one of those areas where the politics could be embraced and understood perhaps earlier and less contentiously than in some other domains where the technology might have been really more entwined in a direct conflict between winners and losers. As I think back on the history of Scandinavian participatory design and its relationship to labor and social justice, I realize that these kinds of interactions or contentions are just ever-present. It's up to us whether we treat them as something to worry about.

Why Learning Can Be Difficult for Participatory Design

Jason Yip: What's interesting with this conversation is that you both are coming from different places. So, Carl talked about starting in design being motivated by politics, and then going into learning. In contrast, Chris went from learning into design, and then recognition of politics. It's pretty fascinating to think about it, because we have these challenges with learning.

I wanted to ask both of you what are the challenges of learning when it comes to participatory design. What makes participatory design challenging, in that its goal is to design learning environments through methods that involve politics, and involves power, and involves users?

Carl DiSalvo: One of the challenging things is that, frankly, as designers and design researchers, no matter what area you're coming from, understanding learning often isn't part of our training. That's a real problem. A lot of times I find when someone is doing PD work and they haven't come from a learning background, the conversation about learning is absent. So, there's immediately a challenge of getting designers to recognize that learning is happening, or learning needs to happen. Then there is the challenge of getting designers to realize that people other than designers actually know some things: some people know things about how learning happens. So, designers don't need to approach learning by accident. We can approach it in a really planful way that's informed by learning sciences research, and that this awareness can benefit whatever it is that we're trying to do as designers, whether we're working in a community setting, or other kinds of collaborative settings, and it can benefit whatever it is that others are trying to do through design. Really approaching PD as a challenge of learning and as an opportunity for learning, changes the way—or should change the way—we do design. But the first challenge is getting designers to realize that they are involved in activities of learning.

My introduction to learning was through informal learning, not through classroom-based activities. We were trying to figure out how to scaffold learning about sensor-based technologies. The challenge for us was not so much the complexity of the technology, but rather understanding how scaffolding occurs so that we could design for it. Then we had to ask how to extend that scaffolding of understanding a technology to developing technological fluency—how do we scaffold experiences where, for example, adults are able to learn how given technology might be used to achieve some goals in their community? Through that process, we began to understand the ways in which access to technology is or isn't granted within that community, the ways in which certain voices are or are not present. All of that is a learning process. I think if we approach community-based participatory design through learning methods, we can achieve a kind of PD with a goal of enabling others, and we can get to that goal much more effectively and in a much more robust way if we take the learning aspect of it seriously.

But learning often isn't front and center in design discourse. Instead, we use other terms about discovery and innovation, which I think too often make it seem like the designer or someone should just be immediately inventive on their own, and not actually look towards research or other kinds of informed practice.

Christopher Hoadley: I would wholeheartedly endorse that idea that learning is pervasive and that designers may ignore it at their peril. Again, drawing on the historical perspectives in HCI, there was a time when learning and HCI were seen as intersecting in exactly two places. One was the learning curve that people needed to traverse to get to be able to use the technologies, and the other was the application of computer technology interfaces in educational settings where there's an explicit goal of school learning. I think when we look at the phenomena of learning, the most general definition is human change and development over time. I think we can see that it's one of the central processes that describes the human experience. So, supporting that process as people are learning, whether it's learning facts for a school exam, or perhaps more poignantly, things like learning how to deal with a difficult illness, or learning how to achieve one's career goals, or learning how to become a better parent. These are the kinds of things that aren't your traditional school book subjects, but are definitely areas in which technology and other designed artifacts have been used to try to empower people. The successful designs are ones that change what people do. One can reasonably expect that the individuals who change what they do are themselves changed. That is learning. Given that we do have this rich and robust literature from decades of research on how people learn, it's a powerful set of perspectives in research-based techniques that we have for supporting people that designers can have in mind as they think about their users or their clients.

But in the world of participatory design, there's this special attention given to role differentiation and whether there is this designer on high and this user down below receiving benefactions from above. There is a parallel idea in education that learning is a struggle between a goal to respect democratic ideals of how knowledge comes into being, to respect constructivist ideas about how people are the masters of their own learning, versus the literally paternalistic models in which we do schooling. Back in one of the first courses I took on education, there was a somewhat heartfelt consideration of this issue, an excerpt we read from A. S. Neill, who's most famous for creating a form of democratically enabled schooling in which children had just as much of a say in how the school was run as the adults did. Learning is this interesting paradox, because on the one hand, you can see that there might be something where somebody knows better and wants to transmit that knowing to someone else. On the other hand, there's an inherent reduction in autonomy if someone else gets to decide what you're supposed to learn. So, the political was always there in learning from day one—maybe not from the first learner, but certainly from the first teacher—there were some kind of politics around expertise and differences of expertise, and how that creates barriers between people. Sometimes those are productive barriers. Sometimes they're not. Regardless, they need to be sort of buffered and managed. The kind of contested role, the relationship between teacher and student in that sense is mirrored in a relationship between designer and user. So, in the learning space, it's been sometimes said that this is an area where participatory design wouldn't work, that we should use words like informant design instead, because people aren't able to fully participate in the design process. But I would say that all individuals bring to bear a different set of abilities and predispositions with which they can participate in an effective design process. One of the things that I think sets apart participatory design, which resonates well with the culture of education, is this idea of deep respect for the individual and for their dignity and autonomy. Again, of course, a lot of the best educational systems also respect the autonomy and dignity of individuals. It's not always easy. It is tempting to sort of expediently jettison that idea when it seems inconvenient. But on the other hand, it's a core value, I think, for a lot of people in both the fields of designing and education.

The Blurring Boundaries between User and Designer

Jason Yip: Carl, do you have a response to that, to anything that Chris has mentioned?

Carl DiSalvo: No. I agree with what he's saying. I think that one of the challenges that we're seeing in PD now is an expansion of the field that actually speaks to some of the things that Chris mentions where the role between the designer and the user has always been questioned. In fact, there were times when it was easier to question that because those roles were clearer, because designers were creating products or systems. Users were the people who were literally using them. Increasingly, what you see in PD projects, particularly PD research, is engaging with communities in much more informal ways in which there isn't a clear product or service. It may be a question of looking at a particular issue and beginning to work with that community and say, "How do we develop capacity around that issue? How do we develop literacy?" And I think increasingly, that word literacy is becoming important. How do we develop literacy so that we can make decisions about the things that are being designed?

One of the challenges here is that those individual roles of designer and user are changing, where the designer is less and less of the person who's actually making the system. Instead, she may be making something that rests on top of the system or interfaces with the system. Because of the way that technology is developing, and because of the ways that our systems are becoming more responsive, designers are beginning to talk differently about when design happens. This has actually long been a discussion within PD and it's coming up again to say as users use this system, as people make use of these systems, to what extent are they themselves actually redesigning them by the ways in which they're interacting with them? I think what you end up with is a situation that's very complex, because in some ways, PD has succeeded in blurring those boundaries between the designer and the user. The condition of technology has blurred them even further. So, you end up with a situation that's a bit of a mess, but kind of a productive mess, particularly when you see that what the goals that we're shifting towards now are.

I think, at least in PD, the goal is less and less "How do we enable someone to use something?" and more and more about "How do we work together to understand what the capacities and issues of something might be?" What's interesting is to tie this in a loop back to learning, I think this is one of the reasons why again and again in PD, we have been fascinated with the American pragmatists, particularly John Dewey, but others as well. It started off with discussions of experience and how do we understand the experience, and then discussion of learning and how do we understand learning and education. Now, there's a number of us who are really fascinated with these questions about publics and how do we bring groups of people together around issues.

Christopher Hoadley: It makes me think of the emergence of critical pedagogies and emancipatory learning philosophies in education. I think this messiness of who's the learner, who's the teacher, and what's the curriculum: in the olden days, those were a little tidier. Explicitly blowing up those roles is part of the advancement in trying to increase people's engagement with, and agency within, systems of education and learning. When it comes to design, we've gone full circle. There was a time when everything was sort of hand-crafted, and everybody was making their own stuff. Ideas were transmitted, but there was not a sharp distinction between the makers and the users. Then through the industrial age, we've seen incredible role differentiation in division of labor where the designer became separated from the craftsperson or the user.

We're at a point now where we're beginning to see tools being made that, again, put choices about how to change the way the world is, and how to remake the world in a different image, into everybody's hands and not just the hands of those with enormous amounts of capital with which to manufacture goods. Especially in the digital space, this kind of radical decentralization of creative power has arguably spawned the "dot com boom" and the technology economic revolution. But I think we're only just beginning to see the ways in which participatory digital culture is upon us and how things are going to be, again, very much more democratized in the 21st century, much as the enlightenment in Europe helped decentralize the institutions of knowledge to popularize the creation and sharing of knowledge, and take it out of the hands of literally a priesthood. We may be on the cusp of a similar kind of phenomenon in the 21st century when not just the means of creation, but the inclination and skills of creation being held by many instead of by the few.

Disruption of Learning through Participatory Design

Carl DiSalvo: I agree. I'm going to throw a "but" in there. I want to begin by saying I agree and I'm excited by these things.

But I think it's important to remember is PD is really a very small part of the field of design. At the institution I'm at now, I actually don't think we have a participatory design class. When I was a graduate student, we didn't have a participatory design class. PD was not covered in my Design Methods course in HCI. So it's important to remember that PD is still not the prevailing perspective in design. In a way, I would say that the majority of design education, at least in the States, seems to be a fairly top-down structure. Participatory design education is still sort of niche encounters within both design and with learning. I think one of our challenges is to grow PD education, and to grow it in authentic ways so that design education continues to be both participatory, and frankly has the capacity to also continue to be critical, so that as people are participating and people are learning, they're still participating in learning in ways that are authentic and meaningful to them, and it's not sort of a shallow participation in learning that's just happening for the sake of, let's say, Facebook.

Christopher Hoadley: I would add that, I think, there's an inevitable pushback as well. It's not just that these kinds of more democratized, emancipatory, critical tactics in both education and in design are fringe and therefore not noticed. It's also that they inherently threaten certain power structures. So, if you look at the history of writing and literacy, there's certainly many societies over time where this technology was sort of kept under wraps, and learning to read was criminalized for dispossessed people whom the powers that be intended to keep that way.

You know, we can certainly already see that. I think of the example of the teenager (Ahmed Mohamed, a child of Muslim faith) who cobbled together a maker-style projects of an alarm clock and then was jailed at his school for something that seemed to be threatening the dominant order of things. In much the same way, I think although inquiry teaching and inquiry learning are the kinds of things that have gained traction and explicit support of people in certain quarters (whether in the Next Generation Science Standards, or through explicit endorsement of educational bodies), it's still pretty rare in practice in schools. So, there are an awful lot of folks that, despite these progressive curricular standards, think people should "take what they're given" and that could apply to a third grader studying in a stultifying classroom, or it could apply to a call center employee using an Orwellian computer system, or it could apply to a consumer going to Best Buy and purchasing a shiny new device. I think the more we have conversations about what is our own determinacy in this, the more principled that those decisions will be.

Carl DiSalvo: I'm increasingly interested in that last example that you gave. Right now, so many designers are interested in the so-called Internet of Things, and how do we have all these devices that are going to talk to one another. One of the questions that keeps coming up when thinking about this space is how do we use learning strategies to let someone understand what it means when they buy this device that's going to come into their house. Maybe it's going to connect to another device, or maybe it's going to send information back someplace else, and not that that's necessarily a bad thing. There are times when we may want that. There are times when we may be willing to make that choice.

To me that is a great example of where design, and learning, and participatory design and learning can come together to say, "How do we develop capacities to understand this increasingly complicated world so that when we make our choices, they're *informed* choices?" So, if we're choosing to install a network device that's going to send data about our homes back someplace else, we have an awareness of that choice. We understand what that's about. Then, similarly, that we develop in people the capacity to say, "How can you think about *not* doing that?" What if I want to have an automated thermostat, but I don't want it to send the data back someplace else? I think this is where you get into this interesting mix of hacker culture, and maker culture, participatory design, and learning. How do I come to have the literacies and the capacities to make those choices and act on those choices in an informed way?

Christopher Hoadley: Yeah. It makes me wonder. At one point in time, the British government had sort of been repurposing, as I understand it, what sort of used to be Shop and Home Economics curriculum through what they call the Technology and Design curriculum. There were some researchers there who were beginning to use the phrase "capability" as a term of art to mean essentially the agency with things in your environment, this agency for making use of things. You know, it's an interesting thought experiment to think about what does it mean to teach even the youngest kids to see the world as something that can be remade, to see themselves as being able to use lots of techniques to do that. Think about how our society either fosters or defeats that. In the technology space, there are countries like the United States where intellectual property reigns supreme. The laws around, for instance, digital rights management and copyright are used to sort of lock things up in a way that people don't have the right to mess around with them. In a place like China, intellectual property rights are not really a barrier to messing around with stuff. But what is a barrier is the politics of the government and its old censorship of what people can and cannot do. There are a lot of different potential ecosystems we can imagine which people do or don't have a lot of design capability at their fingertips. And we can also think about cases in which that ability really is too dangerous to unleash. One thing that springs to mind is lethal self-defense designs that people came up with in post-apartheid in South Africa, from flame-throwers to tire spikes, sort of spy-novel stuff that was intended to harm. What happens when everybody has lots of design capability? It could go badly.

Carl DiSalvo: It's a great question. I struggle with this now. I think the obvious one is the person who 3D-printed the parts for a pistol, if I remember correctly. There are a series of these YouTube videos in which people have done drone hacks. One was able to fire a handgun, and another one was able to fire a sort of homemade flame-thrower. You look at this and you say on the one hand, "Yeah, this is ingenious." Someone has figured out some fairly complicated engineering things here. They're abstracting a model of technology that exists and is a sort of top-down model. Then they're appropriating it within their own context. There are lots of ways we could look at this and celebrate it. At the same time, we think, "My God! They made a flying robot that shoots bullets," and that's terrifying!

So, it gets to the question about how do we begin to have limits on some of these discussions? For me, this is a question where I think it becomes really important to ask, "What are the roles of institutions coming back in a highly participatory culture?" Because at the end of the day, I do think I don't want us to evolve sort of into this neoliberal nightmare where everyone is on their own and everything has been privatized, and there's no accountability. With both design and learning, it does come back to a question about rethinking what these institutions are, what are the regulatory bodies, what are ways of talking about ethics in a massively participatory culture in which I can go online and learn to do just about anything I want to do this afternoon, a lot of which may be very stupid.

Involving People in the Design of Their Learning Environments

Jason Yip: One of the things that I was really interested in, while listening to both of you talk, was also: how do these philosophies help each other, particularly where does participatory come in? Where does the learning sciences need help, and consequently how does participatory design also learn from learning sciences? So, we're in a conversation that I think is really fascinating with regard to the intersections right now. So, how do these actual intersections begin to start supporting each other?

Christopher Hoadley: So, one example I can think of is there's been tremendous progress in the learning sciences understanding at multiple layers of abstraction, what are the conditions that support learning? So, ranging from cognitive, all the way down to neurological, up through sociological and cultural. There's a lot of good research out there about the kinds of mechanisms that exist. When it comes to design though, I think the field of learning sciences has historically had a little bit more of a traditionalist, non-participatory model of design. Design has a long history within the learning sciences as a first-class citizen of inquiry, as a conscience to hold up against social science research findings, to try to make things both true in a psychological sense, but also applicable in a design-oriented sense. That yet has not been applied well to scaling up. So, a lot of the learning sciences' best findings still have had relatively small impact on the world, because the learning sciences hasn't done as much of a good job of understanding how these things grow and scale. A big part of that is understanding how to involve people in the design and redesign of learning environments.

One area where I think it's very exciting to see this happening now in the learning sciences is the design-based implementation research community, which is beginning to look at ways in which research can be conceived of as a form of mutual capacity building at scale, where scale becomes something that you bake into your research questions from day one. It's an area in which there are a lot of heterogeneous participants, different kinds of stakeholders with different backgrounds. And the sort of impedance mismatch between those participants being able to get everybody on the same page, having everybody have a seat at the table and be able to participate fully in what essentially becomes a co-design process is one of those things that I think certain subfields within learning have tackled. The instructional systems design folks, for instance, have looked at this to some extent. But I think participatory design is a field that has a little more maturity in some of the techniques and processes that can be used to help ensure a productive meeting of the minds across very disparate kinds of backgrounds or agendas. I do hope that those learnings, the wisdom that exists around how to engage heterogeneous stakeholders towards common goals, that may be ill-defined or under rapid evolution. I think that's an area where PD is ahead of the curve of learning sciences.

Carl DiSalvo: At the same time, I would say what PD has done well is to take really large concepts from the learning sciences and try to work with them in small ways. Early and ongoing discussions of situatedness and thinking about situated learning are an example of where the two fields have drawn from each other in productive ways and informed each other. There's an opportunity to more directly try to stage collaborative research efforts that can bring together people who really have a commitment to the learning sciences and really have a commitment to participatory design and the rich tradition in both of those.

So, I'll give you an example. One of the things that many people are interested in with participatory design right now is how people develop attachments to issues. This ends up being discussion about trying to understand the ways people come to have sort of affective engagement with design things, and then crafting design things so that people have those kinds of attachments. It becomes a way to get at issues, whether those issues are environmental issues, or social issues. A lot of that comes down to discussions of craft and aesthetics that I think designers are particularly attuned to, but not particularly good at communicating about.

Rather than putting the question of aesthetics aside because it seems difficult, particularly with regard to "science," let's take these questions of aesthetic seriously and say, "How do these notions of aesthetics in a participatory environment end up affecting the kind of learning that happens or doesn't happen?" I think we need those sorts of directed questions that are asking, "What is the expert knowledge of the PD researcher? What do they really know when they're out doing their observations, or they're out doing their workshop? What is it that they know so well that is hard for them to convey that?" The same is true with the learning sciences. That process of hard interdisciplinary discussion then becomes a fundamental part of the project, as well as with the communities we're working on, to figure out how these things about design participation and learning mesh in really rich ways.

Influence of Public Interest and Funding on Participatory Design and Learning

Christopher Hoadley: I applaud that goal, and I think that it would be exceptionally fruitful. One thing that I see as a barrier is that in the United States, design is often not taken as seriously as it is in other places. When I think about, for instance, in Europe, the degree to which there's government support for design research in the traditional sense, not in the learning sciences design-based research sense.

There's a sense in which designing in education has always been present, but it's always been to some extent a second-class citizen compared to social science research. So, "I'll sneak design in on the back of social science research through learning sciences research techniques like design-based research methods." But there is knowledge to be contributed on the design side as well. On your comment about "What is the expert knowledge of an expert participatory designer?" it has two parts, one of which is what do they know about how you convene a workshop, or bring people together, or facilitate a particular kind of knowledge exchange.

But there's also the question of what does that participatory designer know about just design in their discipline? That knowledge squares with the ways in which design as an activity is a byproduct of being a learning scientist and your learning research. I think the phrase "curriculum designer" may be falling out of favor. But I've recently been seeing a phrase "learning experience designer" analogous to the user experience designer starting to gain some traction. I think that's a word that's come to the educational publishing industry from the dot-com world. Nonetheless, it shows that bubbling under the surface, there is this interest in understanding what it means to really be able to make good stuff even if you're not into the social science research endeavor. I do think that in terms of production of knowledge, if the learning sciences and the PD communities got together truly, it would be nice if the knowledge contributions could be in all three of those areas. How do people learn? How do we design things in collaboration with people? And how do we design better things?

Carl DiSalvo: Some of the most exciting work right now that's happening is work that's actually happening in the UK around the role of design, the public understanding of science, and public engagement of science and technology. That work happens in part because the funding there, my understanding is that there's a requirement for scientists to engage in public understanding and engagement programs, and designers are able to engage in research from a design perspective. So, design researchers are able to write grants as designers, not having to pretend to be social scientists or something else, and actually say, "Yes. I have a particular way of doing research, and I will be able to conduct research on this topic." Design research is, seemingly more so, considered legitimate research. To have research taken on the grounds of being design is something that is missing in the States. I think we're going to need to figure out other ways to do that work. I don't think that organizations like the National Endowment for the Arts are going to step in and provide that kind of support. So, as design researchers in the States, we have to continue to be creative in how we get work funded. We see exciting work in other places, in part because the infrastructure and material resources are provided to support it in ways that it's not here.

Christopher Hoadley: I mean, I'm also reminded of India's National Institute of Design, which is a combination of between sort of a school and a government agency with a role that is inherently participatory, not necessarily because there was a such a liberal philosophy of design at its founding, but because the problems that their design gaze is pointed at tend to be problems of great scale, and pressing problems of development in India are intractable without mass participation. So, a lot of the design questions that they consider, inherently become participatory design at some level just because their implementation hinges so much on whether you can get, for instance, an illiterate craftsperson from the village to learn a new technique for using bamboo as a building material, or whether you can get everyone from multimillionaires to the disabled, impoverished, or elderly to use the same kind of National ID card. These problems of design often bump up against issues that are best tackled through a participatory approach. I believe that learning as a design problem is inherently one of those problems where the participation comes along for the ride. If you don't put it there in the beginning, you'll discover it in the end, because the problems themselves are so non-self-contained.

Jason Yip: So, we have nine months left (as of the date of this interview, April 2, 2016) in the Obama administration. I think there's time for you to walk down the streets and lobby for a funding agency.

Christopher Hoadley: Well, I'll tell you, as a reflection of the times, and I should state unequivocally I'm not speaking in my role as a temporary worker in the US government, but this is the first administration that held a Maker Faire at the White House. I mean, I think that some of that may be around ideals connected to democratization of technologies. But I think at some level, it's similar to what I was saying about India's development problems. America has a challenging, drastically shifting economic landscape in which jobs like unskilled manufacturing labor are endangered. So, this question of what replaces it is a pressing question of the moment in 2016 and beyond.

No matter who's in the administration of the US government, I do believe that these problems will favor PD and hopefully society, public/private sector, nonprofit sector, everybody will be focusing on those problems in a way that will allow us to take advantage of everybody's contributions or wisdom. It's likely that the shape of that commitment from government to make things better is going to look different from administration to administration just because everybody has to put their mark on things. So, I don't expect a Maker thing, whatever the next administration is. But I do think this idea of participatory culture will be underneath the surface of lots of things that happen in the next decade or two.

Carl DiSalvo: One of the things I find very hopeful is that the person who's leading the making effort for Intel, and Intel was very wrapped into the White House Maker Faire, has a PhD in design. There's very few of us in the States who have PhDs in Design. Jay Melican has a PhD in design from Illinois Institute of Technology. He's now Intel's Maker Czar. Jay has been able to lead that maker movement from within a corporate environment that has real-world public impact. I think that there's something hopeful in that.

Christopher Hoadley: And, you know, we saw in the press. I remember it felt like it had gone mainstream when *Wired* had an article, that design became a trendy corporate idea as a way to understand, for instance, the success of Apple Computer as a corporation. There is a need for, if not participation or literacy in design, there's a need for at least awareness of, or appreciation for design. What does it bring you? What is it good for? That's one of those areas where, whether you're talking about engineering literacy, maker literacy, design literacy, there's an area in which the public would probably benefit from a greater awareness. Again, things come into being not fully formed like Venus on the Half Shell, but there are processes by which people decide that which should exist and bring it into existence that have foibles just like any other human endeavor.

Carl DiSalvo: To go back to one of the things I said to start and to play off of what you just said, learning is not something that ends when you leave class, we should be constantly learning; learning how the world works (or doesn't work) and then learning to change it: "Look, the world is constructed. It's made and it can be made differently. Then you can add to that and you can learn how to do that."

You can develop those capacities for change, and you can do that whether you're age 6 or 60. Obviously, you're going to be able to affect the world differently at age 6 or 46 or 60, but in any case, you can learn to affect the world.

Christopher Hoadley: Aha. I agree.

Jason Yip: Both of you have arrived at a key question, which is, how can the learning sciences and participatory design together affect social change?

One idea could be that as people design learning environments, they begin to understand that those learning environments are socially constructive and that people can participate together.

Maybe that's part of that social change?

Overall, it's fascinating to think that it's not the whole participatory design in learning as the outcome. The actual outcome is not just about the designed curriculum or better learning activities.

Rather, it is a meta-outcome of people understanding that those things that we built—learning activities, learning experiences—came from somewhere. They came from either power, politics, and the things that we allow in the designing together.

Carl DiSalvo: One thing that I hope people get from this conversation and the book is that participatory design and the learning sciences have many methods, techniques, theories, and practices to share with each other. There have been a lot of people and groups that have moved between these fields, filling the in-between spaces, since the 1970s. We are not the first to bring these fields together, but there is more work to be done.

SECTION II

Participatory Learning and Design from Diverse Perspectives and Contexts

5

LEARNING ABOUT LEARNING THROUGH PARTICIPATORY DESIGN WITH FAMILIES

Judith Uchidiuno, Tamara Clegg, June Ahn, Jason Yip, Elizabeth Bonsignore, Daniel Pauw, Austin Beck, and Kelly Mills

Family Learning

The value of family in the physical, emotional, and intellectual growth of children is indispensable. Family life is a primary context for children to learn, and the importance of the family unit is widely accepted as a driver for academic achievement (Goldman & Booker, 2009). Families also influence a child's personal, social, and cultural development, and events that happen at home have the ability to affect a child's progress in school (Bronfenbrenner, 1986). The vital role that families play in children's development and achievement underscores the need to understand how learning occurs within family contexts. Similarly, we must also understand family interactions that directly or indirectly affect how technological systems used by families are designed.

A significant amount of research has been conducted that offers insights on family learning contexts across a wide variety of sub-domains. Some studies have focused on how family members engage school-age children with subjects such as mathematics. For example, Goldman and Booker (2009) conducted a series of studies to understand how parents engage and utilize mathematics in their homes. By interviewing and observing families in their natural environments such as at home, work, and school, they found that families engage in complex mathematical processes such as setting goals, using "approximation, estimation, and they make decisions based on priorities, multiple conditions, and variables" (p. 383). They also found that families routinely use skills taught in formal mathematics curricula as tools to navigate their daily lives, although they did not recognize that they were engaging in those skills. In a follow-up study, Goldman et al. (2010) interviewed 20 families for two hours each to "identify the social, cultural, and material contexts that are relevant to and create opportunities for mathematics learning" (p. 381). Overall, the researchers found that the mathematical problems that received the most attention were those for which the end goals matched their family needs, such as cooking and budgeting, and that families used different socially distributed situations as opportunities to engage in mathematical thinking.

In addition to understanding how family interactions affect students' formal learning, various researchers have investigated how family interactions affect the design of communication- and learning-based interfaces. This body of research covers a wide range of topics, including understanding how families manage their competing schedules (Beech et al., 2004; Davidoff, Zimmerman, & Dey, 2010; Neustaedter, Brush, & Greenberg, 2009; Park & Zimmerman, 2010), how families use technology to coordinate their routines (Davidoff, 2010; Davidoff, Zimmerman, & Dey, 2010), and how families manage communication in co-parenting and distant parenting situations (Odom, Zimmerman, & Forlizzi, 2010; Yarosh, Chieh, & Abowd, 2009). For example, Dalsgaard and colleagues developed a mobile application, eKISS, to mediate intimacy and communication with parents and children who are physically separated (Dalsgaard, Skov, & Thomassen, 2007). eKISS supports asynchronous sharing of experiences from children to their parents and relies on pictures and text messages sent through their mobile phones, while simultaneously sharing the experiences on a website available to the entire family. They found that eKISS enabled opportunities for parents to see things they otherwise would not have, like school projects and places the kids go. It also made it easier for parents to initiate conversations, since they now had more to talk about. The pictures gave the parents a feeling of being present, and made them more aware of the family's mood. It also made children more aware of their parents; children started to think about how sending a picture would make their parents feel better at different times in the day. Davidoff et al. also studied family interactions to understand how their routines influence how they go about their daily lives and, most importantly, how scheduling platforms can better support their routines. They conducted six months of nightly interviews with six families and found that only about 40% of the families' daily activities center on their routines, and that families do not rely on calendars, reminders, and scheduling tools to support their regular routines but rather the deviations from their routines.

These example studies not only highlight the diversity of research available on the subject of family learning, but also emphasize the focus on understanding current family practices through interviews and observations as a methodology for understanding family learning dynamics. Employing natural observation methodologies as a means of understanding family interactions is intuitive. In order to effectively design for families, it is important to have a firsthand understanding of how families naturally interact (Gardner, 2000). However, the dependence on natural observations and research on current practices is not without its drawbacks, especially when the goal is for parents to *improve* their communication with their children, or when parents and their children are meant to contribute *equally*, such as in collaborative design research studies. In natural interaction situations involving multiple parties with different levels of authority, there is a tendency for the more authoritative or "informed" party to take the lead and become the primary contributor in the interaction (McQueen, Rayner, & Kock, 1999). This one-sided contribution phenomenon can be found even in parent–child interactions, especially with parents with authoritative or authoritarian parenting styles.

In addition to observing families in naturalistic settings, we argue for participatory co-design methods as another strategy to facilitate family interactions and observe family learning. Participatory design (PD) methodologies, in particular, show great potential for fostering balanced parent child interactions by creating a rich context that can illuminate and enhance the ways in which families learn together (Muller, 2003). In this chapter, we discuss how PD can be used to gather rich contextual information that can improve family dynamics and guide the design of systems and artifacts aimed at supporting family learning. Specifically, *we are leveraging parent–child interactions around design thinking as a rich context for family learning.*

Background on Design Thinking

Design thinking is a movement that elevates the philosophy and approaches of design into a disposition, whereby design is a lens through which one engages in thinking and doing with the goal of innovating for a better world. As designers make this leap from design *doing* to design *thinking*, they move from bringing an already existing idea into fruition to actually creating the *idea* (Brown, 2008; 2009). The movement emphasizes making abstract ideas and concepts tangible through real-world innovations that are developed using an iterative, collaborative, multidisciplinary process and then communicated simply and concretely (Brown, 2009; Faste, Roth, & Wilde, 1993). Although there are various types of design processes, common elements include *empathizing* with end users, or deeply understanding the context and constraints in which users are operating (e.g., via *in situ* interviews, observation, or participatory practices) (Liedtka & Ogilvie, 2011). The design process emphasizes *ideation* and a dynamic, free-flowing process of developing new ideas (Faste, Roth, & Wilde, 1993). Ideation processes often initially require blue-sky optimism, or the imagination of a perfect world in which anything is possible. *Iteratively*, ideas are then elaborated, narrowed down, prototyped with increasing fidelity, tested, and refined (Liedtka & Ogilvie, 2011). As ideas are iteratively refined, they are communicated simply and concretely, with visual prototypes and oral storytelling (Brown, 2008; 2009). Throughout the design process, design teams share, integrate, and critique ideas to develop collaborative innovations.

This process of empathizing, brainstorming, and iterative testing could be promising for informal family learning interactions. With an emphasis on collaboration, creativity, storytelling, and free-form dynamic experiences where learning is driven by real-world everyday problem-solving, the practices espoused by designers might naturally facilitate collaborative learning within families. Drawing on this approach, we document and present ways to engage families in co-design, and articulate how these methodologies not only help in the design of new ideas and learning tools, but also give us insight into family learning dynamics. In our research, we have engaged a group of families in a local community in a series of design sessions in our efforts to create new social media, ubiquitous technology for science inquiry and investigation (Yip et al., 2016). These technologies are aimed at increasing scientific inquiry among youth and their families alike. Our process of designing with families also led to insights about ways to understand and promote family learning dynamics, which we expand upon in this chapter.

Overview of Our Family Co-Design Initiative

We recruited 16 culturally diverse families from a local neighborhood in a metropolitan area in the United States to participate in weekly co-design sessions with both parents and children as participants over a period of 10 months (October 2014 to July 2015). The research team and participants met at a community church that hosted the project. In addition to being design partners, the children were also involved in an informal science-learning program, so we alternated between co-design sessions with families to build the new social media application, and informal science learning activities with the children. This process of both co-designing and engaging in science learning served the purpose of helping children develop expertise as both designers and subject experts—a key need that was found in prior co-design studies with children (Yip et al., 2013).

We utilized a method of PD called Cooperative Inquiry (Druin, 1999; Guha, Druin, & Fails, 2013), which emphasizes close design partnerships with children (Druin, 2002). Each co-design session lasted approximately 90 minutes and emphasized two goals. The first goal was to use contextual inquiry methods (Holtzblatt & Jones, 1993) to understand the values of the community, which has been established as a critical aspect of the technology design process in human–computer interaction (HCI) (Friedman, Kahn, & Borning, 2002). Our project, called Science Everywhere, included techniques to understand families' knowledge and perceptions about their neighborhoods, science learning, rules around technology, and learning at home. This process revealed their community values, and provided insights on how to design technologies for their unique needs.

The second goal of the sessions focused on design of a mobile application. The Science Everywhere application is based on prior work done in social media technologies for science learning (Ahn et al., 2014; Clegg et al., 2014; Yip et al., 2014) and was redesigned to better facilitate adult–child interactions around science learning within a neighborhood ecosystem. In the sessions, both children and parents created low-tech prototypes that revealed the types of user interactions and experiences required to connect parents and children together for science learning. We photographed and video and audio recorded all design activities, including artifacts. For each session, there were two to four researchers who conducted and documented extensive details of the participant observations. At the end of all of the sessions, we conducted semi-structured interviews with eight children and five parents to get their perspective of the design sessions. The interviews were video recorded for analysis and the questions focused on feedback from the design sessions and understanding how family values of learning and community could inform the design of technology-mediated, social learning experiences.

Each month in the design sessions, the families engaged in different activities around several goals as outlined below:

- *September 2014*: To learn about their family and community values, we had children and youth interview each other, and then interview their parents about their existing values and perceptions of science.
- *October 2014*: Continuing with the goal of learning about the family values, we had families bring in photos and describe their neighborhood, places at which that they felt learning occurred, and the technologies used in their neighborhoods. The children created and presented posters on how science was relevant to their everyday lives. We also conducted focus groups with parents and activity sessions with children to understand how technology was used in their families.
- *December 2014*: The activities, focus groups, and interviews for this month centered on understanding the rules that parents set surrounding technology use in their homes, as well as how they help their children use technology for learning. Between the months of January and May 2015, we shifted focus to collaboratively designing, prototyping, and testing the Science Everywhere application.
- *May 2015*: Insights from the testing phase of the prototype application revealed that the older youth used the Science Everywhere application much less frequently than the younger children. Sessions in May focused on gathering design ideas to better support the youths' diverse needs.
- *July 2015*: July sessions focused on improving the user interface of the Science Everywhere application, as well as designing the user interface for the parents. We also conducted a design session focused on developing large-screen community displays that provide information and gather feedback from the community.

This work has led to key insights with respect to technology design for STEM learning, but it also suggests important implications that inform our understanding of how families learn together and the type of help they might need.

Empathizing Reveals Engrained Norms and Routines

The products of our PD process reveal important insights for family learning regarding the effects of existing rules and routines. After the children interviewed each other and their parents about how they learn with their parents, we created a video montage from the interviews that we showed parents and children. The parents then stayed behind and discussed their reaction to the videos as the children moved on to another activity. During these *empathizing* activities, it became increasingly evident that children's routines, norms, and rules are often engrained in and largely driven by what happens at school. During parent–child interviews, parents emphasized schoolwork in how they help their children learn. In fact, they often framed out-of-school learning activities (e.g., reading, solving word problems) in terms of school-related practices (e.g., referring to such activities as summer "homework"). However, as parents watched the video montage of interviews, they were surprised by their children's accounts of how their parents frequently struggle helping them with schoolwork and often do not have time to help them. In the parents' subsequent discussion of the video, they focused on their own perspectives of helping their children with schoolwork. Parents reported they were often not familiar with the specific methods being taught in their child's class and therefore did not always know how to help them in a manner consistent with how they were learning in class. They discussed the challenges that they had communicating with teachers to get more information about what their children were doing in class so that they could better help them. During these empathizing sessions, parents also emphasized time limitations for themselves as they manage their responsibilities at home, work, and in the community.

Additionally, parents expressed concern about their children's time limitations. In another focus group with parents, we solicited parents' feedback about the logistics of our program (e.g., time, frequency, content). Parents wanted to make sure that the time we held the program did not conflict with time the children needed to do their schoolwork and that the program was not held too often, so that it would not conflict with their school commitments. While our program is designed to enrich children's learning, and parents deeply appreciate this, if it interfered with school norms and routines, the parents perceived it as being in conflict with their children's learning.

Implications for Family Learning

Parents are constantly balancing a myriad of work and home responsibilities as they help their children grow and learn. The constant tension that parents face between making time for their children's learning and making time for other work-life tasks highlights the importance of finding ways to integrate opportunities to learn into the activities and routines that families already engage in as well as problems and issues they face on a daily basis (e.g., cooking meals, eating and playing together). By leveraging such everyday opportunities, new learning activities are less likely to overlap or conflict with time already allotted for other important activities.

As children conducted interviews with one another and their parents around this topic, some of these contexts became evident. Families shared their everyday experiences of learning about their cultural heritage, language learning (particularly for parents who were English language learners), outdoor experiences (e.g., farming, traveling), and cooking. In these contexts, participants described how they benefitted from the expertise of both children and parents. For example, some children help their parents with learning English and technology use. Consistent with prior work on parent–child interaction in museums and parent roles (Barron, Martin, Takeuchi, & Fithian, 2009; Swartz & Crowley, 2004), these findings suggest that such everyday contexts can shift the dynamic of parent–child learning from a one-way interaction where parents are expected to help their children, to a two-way interaction where both parents and children serve as helpers and learners.

While the empathizing process incorporates an interview approach, the ensuing discussions shifted our perspective on family learning and influenced the design of the program. The logistics discussion, for example, revealed specific tensions families face as they balance their goals to provide enhanced learning experiences for their children with the complex demands of work, school, and family life. We initiated this conversation about program logistics for two reasons: we wanted parents' feedback about when to hold our weekly meetings, but we also wanted to encourage parents to become more engaged in the design process. Initially, we noted that many parents were reserved and hesitant to share their ideas in design sessions. However, we observed that parents often asked us prior to and after meetings about program logistics. We therefore thought that asking for their feedback and ideas on this topic might prompt a more open and direct dialogue. Indeed, this prompt led to a lively discussion about families' busy routines and norms and helped us realize the importance of integrating the Science Everywhere meetings and activities within the constraints of their current practices and provided specific insights for doing that. Prior to this meeting, we had planned to hold the after-school program during the afternoon, immediately after school. Through this discussion, however, we learned that holding the program later in the evening would enable parents to get home from work and drive their children to sessions, which was preferable to them in light of their routines and norms.

Ideating Reveals Parents and Children Need Help Negotiating Roles for Learning Interactions

Our design work with families also revealed patterns of engagement among parents and children that have implications for family learning. This was particularly evident during ideation phases of the design process. During ideation activities, our research group presented families with a design prompt (e.g., design a community technology that would enable parents and kids and others in the community to be able to share and extend their learning). The families then worked in groups, either with their own families or in intergenerational groups with other families, to create a low-tech prototype using markers, paper, and/or crafting materials. At the end of the session, groups made short presentations of their designs as a researcher/facilitator took notes on the big ideas or themes that arose from the designs. The facilitator then presented these themes back to the whole group. During these ideation activities, we observed roles and challenges that parents and children took on that have implications for family dynamics that influence family learning experiences.

During design sessions we observed that parents initially tended to assume roles as quiet observers. With encouragement, some parents began to take on more active roles, facilitating their children's design process, yet not contributing their own ideas. As parents began to take on more active roles in the PD process, they initially exhibited an authoritative tone as they focused on managing children's behavior and prompting them for ideas and participation. Parents themselves needed prompting to assume more collaborative roles, contributing and elaborating upon the group's ideas. Additionally, parents expressed that they felt more challenges than children with developing "blue sky" or open-ended, futuristic, creative ideas and then iterating those ideas into prototypes.

Children on the other hand, were quite engaged in the creative and collaborative processes of design. The children had more experiences engaging in design than their parents as a result of the informal science learning activities the children had participated in during sessions without their parents, so this may have eased their transition into the design sessions. However, we observed that children were often uncomfortable talking in front of the whole group. For example, some learners shied away from group presentations, did not face the audience, or presented their ideas quickly in front of the group. Over time, many have grown increasingly comfortable expressing their ideas in the large group. For example, the following research field notes describe one learners' reflection on his ability to speak in large groups:

> Jorge also said that participating in Science Everywhere helped him to get better at presentations. He said that in Science Everywhere you have to make a lot of presentations in front of a "hard audience" because there are older kids, adults, and really young kids. So he said that has helped him in school when he has to make presentations there. (Researcher Field Notes July 15, 2015)

Likewise, as children work in groups with parents, they often become shy or reluctant to express their ideas. This could be exacerbated when parents take especially authoritative roles, as they may lean toward over-instructing and dominating their children, given their high performance expectations (Spera, 2005). Thus it was important for facilitators to emphasize that all ideas must be valued and encouraged and adults should be careful to solicit and value the children's ideas.

Implications for Family Learning

Our findings suggest that parents may find it challenging to negotiate their more authoritative parenting roles and the collaborative learning roles needed to facilitate informal learning activities and investigations. First, as parents participated in the design process with their children, the parents began to observe their children's strengths, particularly in areas of their own difficulties (e.g., technology expertise, creative brainstorming). Observing their children's strengths, parents began to leverage these talents in the design process. For instance, in earlier weeks, children were more open to sharing their creative ideas. As comfort set in for the parents and they saw children engage in such creative practices, in the later weeks we observed parents engaging more in presenting their creative ideas (Yip et al., 2016).

Similarly, parents and other adults may need to be careful to solicit, encourage, and draw upon their children's ideas when learning. Even when parents do not agree with their children or see the potential of the children's ideas, parents need to make sure children feel comfortable taking part in the collaborative learning process. While these roles and challenges became evident during the ideation phases of design, the collaboration that emerged during these activities suggests that *design projects serve as an authentic space for diverse knowledge and expertise to come together to address real-world challenges.* Our PD process revealed that parents and children had different, complementary knowledge and expertise to contribute, and as they observed this, they begin to leverage these differences to take on more collaborative roles.

Iteration Reveals Importance of Developing Mutual Understanding between Parents and Children

The iteration process of our design with families revealed that parents and children have different perspectives about values, learning, and engagement that shape family learning experiences. Our initial process of iterative design with families involved first designing separately with parents and children. Families then iterated upon the ideas generated in new sessions where both parents and children came together either to give feedback on one another's ideas or to integrate ideas from both perspectives into new designs. In some sessions, we conducted focus groups with parents to gather their ideas and feedback on practical aspects of our program (e.g., time, frequency, and location of meetings) and their perspectives on science learning and their children's technology use. Simultaneously, we engaged children in ideation sessions where they created design ideas for the Science Everywhere mobile application and community displays. We then gathered families back together to present their ideas and high-level overviews of their discussions. Because we met more often with the children in our study, several design sessions were conducted only with children who then received feedback from their parents in short presentation and feedback sessions.

This iterative process of separate then integrated design sessions revealed differences between parents and children with respect to morals and dispositions for success in life. While parents placed a high value on discipline, morals, and structure, unsurprisingly, children wanted more opportunities to use technology, view media, chat, and play video games. For example, in a focus group with parents, the adults expressed great concern about children's technology use. One parent noted how uncomfortable she was with the bloody nature of a video game that her son played, with police chasing "the bad guys." She used her son's experience with the video game as an opportunity to illustrate what happens when people decide to break the law.

In a design session with children alone, we asked participants to choose a rule about technology they did not like and then consider their parents' rationale for that rule (from their parents' perspective). Children then designed a modification of this rule that took both theirs and their parents' perspective into account. Most children had trouble reflecting on their parents' perspectives in the context of an issue they were so personally attached to (i.e., using their devices, interacting with their friends) and did not take their perspectives into account in their new solutions. For example, one learner wanted to stay up later to watch basketball games. His resolution of this rule was for his mom to extend his bedtime. When we asked him to describe his compromise for his mom, he simply replied, "There is none." When children presented these resolutions to their parents, the parents were naturally not in agreement with their children's suggested rules.

However, in one set of iterative sessions, we had parents and children work collaboratively to build upon ideas generated initially by children. Based on a method called mixing ideas (Guha et al., 2004), children shared ideas they had developed in a previous session for large, interactive, ubiquitous community displays to promote science learning. Building from these initial ideas, participants (working in intergenerational, across-family groups) designed new large interactive displays, keeping the perspectives of both parents and children in mind. During this session, we found that parents and children were able to leverage their diverse perspectives to create novel designs. Specifically, most children emphasized social media and creative new technologies. Adults on the other hand focused on finding information about practical logistics. In intermixed groups of children and adults (not grouped by family), participants intertwined these ideas and perspectives in their prototypes. For example, one group created a large screen blimp that would display Science Everywhere event information as it flew over their neighborhood.

Implications for Family Learning

Our iterative design sessions revealed the challenges parents and children face with understanding one another's perspectives and values, which have implications for dynamics at play in family learning. First, without a more mature understanding of the disciplinary boundaries that should be in place for children's success, we must consider the ramifications of complete equal partnership in learning and design between parents and children. While it is important to facilitate children's agency and voice in design and learning, we must also maintain some boundaries between parent and child roles to ensure learners' safety and success in the long run. Our experiences engaging parents and children in iterative design and ideation suggest that iteratively working together on open-ended design processes may begin to help parents and children see and value one another's perspectives. However, this mutual understanding among parents, children, and researchers is a slow-developing process that may need scaffolding over time. It then becomes important to talk about boundaries and rules as parents and children learn together, so that children can begin to understand why they need certain boundaries. At the same time, care should be taken by parents to listen and value their children's perspectives. As families learn together and design activities, these design contexts can become a safe space for discussing such considerations because of the emphasis on collaboration, brainstorming new ideas, and iterative testing.

Conclusion

The insights we have garnered through PD with families inform our understanding of the diverse contexts and challenges that comprise family learning and guide us to considerations for supporting family learning. Our findings suggest that empathizing activities can spark conversations that reveal parent–child roles (e.g., collaborator, help seeker, helper) and context-specific dynamics that influence family learning. These activities promote open conversation and reflection about ways parent–child roles and learning contexts can become more collaborative and conducive to everyday learning opportunities. Similarly, we found that open-ended ideation design experiences can be a space for family members to reflect upon existing, more traditional roles and to develop more collaborative, two-way partnerships. Finally, our findings suggest that iteration can be useful for scaffolding mutual understanding between parents and children as well as sparking a deeper appreciation between them for their diverse perspectives.

Another key to the family learning insights we gathered is how participatory design sessions can engender collaboration across families. In our study, families worked together with other families to engage in design. Alternating between within-family and interfamily groups may have been helpful for families to step outside their day-to-day relationships and work with other parents and/or children to gain a broader perspective of the roles they could play and the collaboration approaches they could take. Participants could then apply their shifting perspectives within their own families. Similarly, alternating between parent-only and child-only design groups and intergenerational groups may have facilitated similar shifts and reflection.

Likewise, parents have expressed their appreciation of the opportunity to learn and design together with other families. One mother told us that she loves the program, not only because of the learning activities we have for the children, but also because she really values having a context to meet and talk with others about parenting struggles, and how to adjust better to their children's needs. Within and between families, we believe PD is important for informing the design of learning innovations in family learning contexts, and also for promoting everyday learning practices and opportunities. By engaging in PD, parents and children may gain more explicit awareness and understandings of their individual, everyday life perspectives and challenges, which in itself is an important element of lifelong learning and echoes the original philosophical underpinnings of PD (Leong & Iverson, 2015). These findings also have implications for PD, as fostering such communication and learning interactions helps parents and children engage fluidly together in the design process. Additionally, understanding such learning benefits may help motivate more families to engage collaboratively in PD.

References

Ahn, J., Clegg, T., Yip, J., Bonsignore, E., Pauw, D., Gubbels, M., . . . Rhodes, E. (2014). Seeing the unseen learner: Designing and using social media to recognize children's science dispositions in action. *Learning Media and Technology*, *41*(2), 252–282.

Barron, B., Martin, C. K., Takeuchi, L., & Fithian, R. (2009). Parents as learning partners in the development of technological fluency. *International Journal of Learning and Media*, *1*, 55–77.

Beech, S., Geelhoed, E., Murphy, R., Parker, J., Sellen, A., & Shaw, K. (2004). *The Lifestyles of Working Parents: Implications and Opportunities for New Technologies*. HP Tech report HPL-2003-88 (R. 1). Retrieved from www.researchgate.net/profile/Abigail_Sellen/publication/228827452_The_Lifestyles_of_Working_Parents_Implications_and_Opportunities_for_New_Technologies/links/0912f511a2ced9eb3e000000.pdf

Bronfenbrenner, U. (1986). Ecology of the family as a context for human development: Research perspectives. *Developmental Psychology*, *22*(6), 723.

Brown, T. (2009). *Change by Design: How Design Thinking Transforms Organizations and Inspires Innovation*. New York: Harper Collins.

Brown, T. (2008). Design thinking. *Harvard Business Review*, *86*(6), 84–92.

Clegg, T., Bonsignore, E., Ahn, J., Yip, J., Pauw, D., Gubbels, M., . . . Rhodes, E. (2014). Capturing personal and social science: Technology for integrating the building blocks of disposition. In J. Polman, E. Kyza, K. O'Neill, I. Tabak, W. Penuel, S. Jurow, . . . L. D'Amico (Eds.), *Learning and Becoming in Practice: The International Conference of the*

Learning Sciences (ICLS) 2014, Volume 1 (pp. 455–462). Boulder, CO: International Society of the Learning Sciences.

Dalsgaard, T., Skov, M. B., & Thomassen, B. R. (2007). eKISS: Sharing experiences in families through a picture blog. In *Proceedings of the 21st British HCI Group Annual Conference on People and Computers: HCI . . . But Not as We Know I. Volume 1* (pp. 67–75). British Computer Society.

Davidoff, S. (2010). Routine as resource for the design of learning systems. In *Proceedings of the 12th ACM International Conference Adjunct Papers on Ubiquitous Computing—Adjunct* (pp. 457–460). New York: ACM.

Davidoff, S., Zimmerman, J., & Dey, A. K. (2010). How routine learners can support family coordination. In *Proceedings of the SIGCHI Conference on Human Factors in Computing Systems* (pp. 2461–2470). New York: ACM.

Druin, A. (1999). Cooperative inquiry: Developing new technologies for children with children. In *Proceedings of the SIGCHI Conference on Human Factors in Computing Systems* (pp. 592–599). New York: ACM.

Druin, A. (2002). The role of children in the design of new technology. *Behaviour & Information Technology, 21*(1), 1–25.

Faste, R. A., Roth, B., & Wilde, D. J. (1993). Integrating creativity into the mechanical engineering curriculum. In C. A. Fisher (Ed.), *ASME Resource Guide to Innovation in Engineering Design* (pp. 93–98). New York: American Society of Mechanical Engineers.

Friedman, B., Kahn, P., & Borning, A. (2002). Value sensitive design: Theory and methods. *University of Washington Technical Report*, 02–12.

Gardner, F. (2000). Methodological issues in the direct observation of parent–child interaction: Do observational findings reflect the natural behavior of participants? *Clinical Child and Family Psychology Review, 3*(3), 185–198.

Goldman, S., & Booker, A. (2009). Making math a definition of the situation: Families as sites for mathematical practices. *Anthropology & Education Quarterly, 40*(4), 369–387.

Goldman, S., Pea, R., Blair, K. P., Jimenez, O., Booker, A., Martin, L., & Esmonde, I. (2010). Math engaged problem solving in families. In *Proceedings of the 9th International Conference of the Learning Sciences, Volume 1* (pp. 380–387). Chicago: International Society of the Learning Sciences.

Guha, M. L., Druin, A., Chipman, G., Fails, J. A., Simms, S., & Farber, A. (2004). Mixing ideas: A new technique for working with young children as design partners. In *Proceedings of the 2004 Conference on Interaction Design and Children: Building a Community* (pp. 35–42). New York: ACM.

Guha, M. L., Druin, A., & Fails, J. A. (2013). Cooperative Inquiry revisited: Reflections of the past and guidelines for the future of intergenerational co-design. *International Journal of Child-Computer Interaction, 1*(1), 14–23.

Holtzblatt, K., & Jones, S. (1993). Contextual inquiry: A participatory technique for system design. In A. Namiokoa & D. Schuler (Eds.), *Participatory Design: Principles and Practices* (pp. 177–210). Hillsdale, NJ: Lawrence Erlbaum Publishers.

Leong, T. W., & Iversen, O. S. (2015). Values-led participatory design as a pursuit of meaningful alternatives. In *Proceedings of the Annual Meeting of the Australian Special Interest Group for Computer Human Interaction* (pp. 314–323). New York: ACM.

Liedtka, J., & Ogilvie, T. (2011). *Designing for Growth*. New York: Columbia Business Press.

McQueen, R. J., Rayner, K., & Kock, N. (1999). Contribution by participants in face-to-face business meetings: Implications for collaborative technology. *Journal of Systems and Information Technology, 3*(1), 15–34.

Muller, M. J. (2003). Participatory design: The third space in HCI. *Human-Computer Interaction: Development Process, 4235*, 165–185.

Neustaedter, C., Brush, A. J., & Greenberg, S. (2009). The calendar is crucial: Coordination and awareness through the family calendar. *ACM Transactions on Computer-Human Interaction (TOCHI), 16*(1), 1–48.

Odom, W., Zimmerman, J., & Forlizzi, J. (2010). Designing for dynamic family structures: Divorced families and interactive systems. In *Proceedings of the 8th ACM Conference on Designing Interactive Systems* (pp. 151–160). New York: ACM.

Park, S. Y., & Zimmerman, J. (2010). Investigating the opportunity for a smart activity bag. In *Proceedings of the SIGCHI Conference on Human Factors in Computing Systems* (pp. 2543–2552). New York: ACM.

Spera, C. (2005). A review of the relationship among parenting practices, parenting styles, and adolescent school achievement. *Educational Psychology Review, 17*(2), 125–146.

Swartz, M. I., & Crowley, K. (2004). Parent beliefs about teaching and learning in a children's museum. *Visitor Studies Today, 7*(2), 1–16.

Yarosh, S., Chieh, Y., & Abowd, G. D. (2009). Supporting parent–child communication in divorced families. *International Journal of Human-Computer Studies, 67*(2), 192–203.

Yip, J., Ahn, J., Clegg, T., Bonsignore, E., Pauw, D., & Gubbels, M. (2014). "It helped me do my science": A case of designing social media technologies for children in science learning. In *Proceedings of the 13th International Conference of Interaction Design and Children* (pp. 155–164). New York: ACM.

Yip, J. C., Clegg, T., Ahn, J., Uchidiuno, J. O., Bonsignore, E., Beck, A., ... Mills, K. (2016). The evolution of engagements and social bonds during child-parent co-design. In *Proceedings of the 2016 CHI Conference on Human Factors in Computing Systems* (pp. 3607–3619). New York: ACM.

Yip, J., Clegg, T., Bonsignore, E., Gelderblom, H., Rhodes, E., & Druin, A. (2013). Brownies or bags-of-stuff?: Domain expertise in cooperative inquiry with children. In *Proceedings of the 12th International Conference of Interaction Design and Children* (pp. 201–210). New York: ACM.

6

EVOLVING CURRICULAR DESIGNS THROUGH TEACHER ADAPTATION AND IMPLEMENTATION WITH STUDENTS OVER TIME

Joseph L. Polman, Angela M. Kohnen, Michelle P. Whitacre, Rosemary McBryan Davidson, and Engida H. Gebre

In this chapter, we describe five years of an ongoing curricular design and enactment effort involving multiple stakeholders with diverse roles. We aspired to the participatory design tenet that multiple stakeholders should contribute meaningfully to designs for learning. In what follows, we focus primarily on particular individuals with roles of high school classroom teachers, and their interactions with university-based faculty and doctoral students involved in research and development. Other stakeholders, including high school administrators and students of the high school teachers, participated in the ongoing design, enactment, and refinement.

We will describe how particular teachers in diverse learning environments adapted a curricular model for involving adolescents in the authoring of science news stories and infographics for authentic publication. We focus on this work of adaptation that teachers made to the curricular model as a key aspect of participatory design that involved the teachers interacting with the university-based researchers and educators who had originated the model, curricular resources made by the university-based researchers and other teachers, and incorporating the teachers' ideas about making the model work in interaction with their particular students and local curriculum. Thus teachers made adaptations to fit their particular purposes, contexts, and students, in a distributed reform effort with varying degrees and qualities of interaction between university-based researchers and school-based educators who collaboratively developed the model and related curricular materials. The overall effort began with a project referred to as Science Literacy through Science Journalism, which came to be referred to by participants as "SciJourn" (see Polman, Newman, Farrar, & Saul, 2012; Polman, Newman, Saul, & Farrar, 2014). Many of the teachers and researchers (including the authors) continue to be involved in some version of or outgrowth of SciJourn, but this chapter will focus on the adaptations between 2009 and 2014 as instances of participatory design.

We take a sociocultural perspective on human action and learning, using the notions of mediated action (Wertsch, 1998) and ideas from practice theory (Lave & Wenger, 1991; Wenger, 1998). We consider the set of school, out-of-school, and university sites which implemented some version of the youth journalism curricular model to be a distributed "sociotechnical system" (Fischer, 2013) with persons using cultural tools to carry out and mediate educational activities. This sociotechnical system had loose couplings across sites, and richer interactions at the local site level. Tools of particular importance for this distributed system were the publication venue with a rigorous editorial process (a youth-targeted, online science newsmagazine called *SciJourner.org*), and curricular materials encapsulated in the book *Front-Page Science: Engaging Teens in Science Literacy* (Saul, Kohnen, Newman, & Pearce, 2012) and a teacher website (teach4scijourn.org). Within this system, teachers acted as designers (Brown & Edelson, 2003; Kali & McKenney, 2012; Recker et al., 2007) *with* university faculty and students and the nascent, developing, curricular materials.

Research Methods and Context

Our method is case study based on reanalysis of data from several design-based and descriptive studies. The primary data sources are interviews, supplemented by observational notes from professional development meetings and teacher artifacts (lesson plans, handouts), taken from multiple studies from 2009 through 2014. We examine the process of design adaptation by focal educators at eight school sites in the Midwestern United States: four chemistry teachers, one biology/ chemistry teacher and one physical science teacher at the high school level; and two middle school science teachers. The teachers were deliberately selected to vary on several dimensions. As a set, the sites included ethnic, socioeconomic, and geographic diversity (described below). The teachers ranged in when they began in the project, from 2009 to 2012. They also varied in the curricular resources and professional development interactions available to them. And finally, the teachers differed in the implementation strategies they employed.

We synthesize eight cases from three dissertation projects focusing on teacher work within the larger SciJourn project.

- Four of the cases are from Kohnen's (2012, 2013a, 2013b, 2013c, 2013d) study of genre and authenticity, based on interviews, artifacts, and observations.
- One case is from Davidson's (2014a, 2014b) teacher action research study of her own practice of integrating journalism and infographics.
- Three of the cases are from Whitacre's (2014; Whitacre & Saul, 2015) study of teachers' changing professional identities, knowledge, and classroom practices, based on surveys and interviews.

We have some additional follow-up data on particular cases. From 2009 to 2012, 40 SciJourn teachers of various subject matters across 25 schools participated in a series of professional development experiences and implemented some version of the science journalism model in their classes. There were three "cadres" of teachers. Wendy Saul, an experienced and talented teacher educator, led the large and growing professional development team, which initially included university researchers and educators and subsequently included a growing number of the teachers themselves in the professional development leadership positions (similar to the National Writing Project model, e.g., Lieberman & Wood, 2002). Among the authors of this chapter, Polman was part of the initial university-based team, Kohnen and Whitacre were initially participating teachers and subsequently R&D staff members, and Davidson was initially a participating teacher and subsequently a teacher leader and researcher. Kohnen, Davidson, and Whitacre all completed dissertations related to the project.

Figure 6.1 shows the timeline of participants and cases described in the chapter. The Pilot Cadre, Cadre 1, and Cadre 2 all had several professional development experiences. These included a one-week summer institute beginning with teachers writing science news stories themselves, then planning for adaptation and integration of journalism in their classrooms, four follow-up meetings per year with check-ins, and targeted work on emergent and standing issues and themes. Each year had increasing structure, a larger existing community of practitioners, and a greater number of curricular resources. As noted above, a National Science Teachers Association (NSTA) press book on the approach, with an accompanying teacher website, was published in 2012.

The SciJourn project intentionally recruited participating teachers from socioeconomically, culturally, and geographically diverse locations across two central midwestern states, as shown in Table 6.1 (all teacher names, other than Davidson,

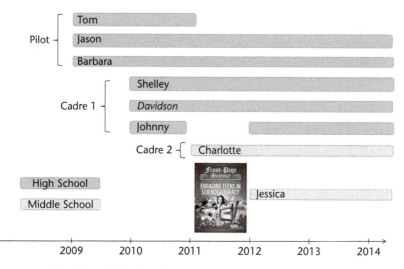

FIGURE 6.1 Timeline and Teacher Cases

TABLE 6.1 Teachers and School Demographics

Teacher	Level	School Performance	Demographics	Socioeconomic
Tom	High School (HS)	Very High	85% White, 12% African American	Suburban; 19% free/reduced lunch (FRL)
Jason	HS	Mid-High	63% White, 29% African American	Suburban; 33% FRL
Barbara	HS	High	90% White, 7% African American	Suburban; 16% FRL
Shelley	HS	Low-Mid	97% African American	Urban; 69% FRL
Rose	HS	High	93% White, All Female	Suburban private; mid-high SES
Johnny	HS	Mid-Low	50% White, 45% African American	Suburban; 46% FRL
Charlotte	Middle School (MS)	Mid-Low	60% White, 30% African American	Urban; 65% FRL
Jessica	MS	High	93% White	Suburban; 22% FRL

are pseudonyms). By this, we mean the schools they were in ranged from relatively advantaged to relatively disadvantaged, included various mixes of primarily White and African American students, and were situated in urban, suburban, and rural locations. The data in Table 6.1 on school performance, demographics, and socio-economic status are based on state sources for the public schools, and published school data from the one private school. The cases in our set were purposefully selected for different reasons based on the originating study, but represent most of the diversity in our overall participant pool. One exception is that there are no rural teacher cases here.

Results

We present the main themes of our case analysis in the following subsections, with aspects of particular cases embedded.

Comprehensiveness of Curricular Materials

In the first summer institute, the emphasis was on helping participants under-stand science journalism. A veteran science journalist (Alan Newman, the editor of *SciJourner* and a part of the R&D team) led many of the workshop sessions, including a session where he modeled the reading of a science news article using a common elementary literacy strategy, the "read aloud-think aloud." Participants were given a handbook that included a variety of kinds of science news articles—the "explainer," an interview, an "evergreen" (i.e., a topic that could be covered every year), and more—as well as a diagram of the inverted triangle and a list of websites to find science news ideas. Participants were required to write two science news articles themselves. Materials for use with students in the classroom were co-created throughout the first summer institute, but teachers returned to the classroom with limited materials in common.

Tom enrolled in the Pilot SciJourn workshop at the urging of a colleague who knew he had an interest in science literacy. Initially, Tom found the summer institute disappointing, describing the experience as "the blind leading the blind." He was frustrated with the lack of curriculum and thought writing a science news article would be too difficult for his students. He also was near retirement and did not wish to invest in major changes. As a result, Tom took up the most developed activities from the summer institute: the "read aloud-think aloud" and a worksheet on the structure of a science news article. Neither of these activities were intended to be adopted wholesale in the classroom, but project research and ongoing interactions between teachers, university faculty, and doctoral students informed the next design. Tom's classroom implementation convinced both the university researchers and other Cadre 1 teachers like Jason and Barbara that the "read aloud-think aloud" could both be easily integrated because it took limited time, and helped shift the relationship between teachers and students in positive ways (students got a sense of what made their teachers find science interesting and relevant). On the other hand, the use of handouts on the structure of science news articles in Tom's and several other teachers' classrooms proved to be far less productive, so in our Cadre 1 teacher institute in 2010 we discouraged focus on that.

Jessica began implementing the model in 2012 after the NSTA book came out (Saul et al., 2012) and based her instruction on the recommendations found there. Despite the book and the accompanying website, she found it overwhelming at first to assist her students in choosing their own newsworthy topics. But eventually she adapted the process by using a website referred to in the book, Eurekalert.org, a source of science-related press releases from research institutions provided by AAAS. The project did not publish rubrics for assessing science news articles, in part because of the plethora of research on how rubrics get abused in writing instruction. But Jessica adapted one of the classroom tools that came with the book, a "Science Article Filtering Instrument." This was a kind of checklist of positive features that an article could have, and problems that it should avoid, which she modified into a rubric that helped her middle school students understand the task and dimensions of quality. Her students did not have to write an article, but instead, had to submit a final "product," which could be anything as long as it met the rubric expectations.

Multimodal Communication of Science

Processes of participatory design resulted in the project moving toward more multimodal communication. Although our originating model involved student production of traditional text science news stories, communicating about science is more than just text-based; it's an opportunity for multimodal expression and representation, such as infographics.

Like many science teachers, Jason (Cadre 1) did not have a strong "writer" identity. He also was very interested in integrating data graphing and visualization in his class. These two factors influenced his adaptation of using science new infographics, rather than just text-based news stories. Building on the adaptations of others, he did "read-alouds" of infographics in 2009, where he revealed his sensemaking to the students. He also gave students the opportunity to author their own infographics. Given the project's focus on text article authoring, Jason at first gave students the choice of either writing a traditional text article or a news infographic; all but a few chose infographics the first year, and they turned out to be quite compelling. The second year, he continued to give students choice between infographics and text news articles, but given how successful the prior year's students were with infographics, all in the second year chose to author infographics. Jason enjoyed being seen as an innovator by project personnel, and he worked closely with project staff to develop infographics curriculum; seven years later, he continues to be involved in our subsequent infographics grants.

Johnny (Cadre 2) was at first surprised by the project's view of science literacy, but saw it as appealing because he realized few of his students were pursuing science careers per se. Despite his affinity for the project, implementing it in his classroom was a struggle. Between navigating a new curriculum and teaching new elective courses, it took him three years to make SciJourn work. Like Jason, he was influenced by the importance of visual representation in chemistry and thus chose to focus on infographics, which he felt were more time-efficient than writing articles. He also found value in having his students focus more on graphical representations because they had difficulties analyzing and interpreting visual data. Infographics, therefore, provided a way for students to research and also work with "making data meaningful." Johnny built his infographic project around the periodic table. His students worked in pairs and were randomly assigned an element. Students were asked to find relevant and interesting information about their elements and then create an infographic showing what they had learned.

Barbara, Jessica, and several other teachers tried out variations of the student news projects as presentations supported by PowerPoint slides on their topic. In order to avoid becoming a typical school research presentation, these adaptations depended on students referring to the SciJourn guidelines and other supporting curricular materials to assist their research and self-assessment.

Increasing the Relevance of Science to Students

The project's most engaged teachers were motivated by personal goals to find new instructional approaches that could increase the personal relevance of science topics and scientific inquiry for their students.

At the time she joined the project, Barbara (Pilot Cadre) had been teaching for 28 years and was a doctoral student. She saw the project as a way to make science relevant for students and embraced the freedom to adapt the project for her own needs. Classroom community was important to Barbara, and she insisted her students write about topics they found "personal" and work in small groups to edit each other's writing. During the summer institute, the "read aloud-think aloud" resonated with Jason (Pilot Cadre), and he realized that science news could allow him to share his passion for science in everyday life with students. Jason joined the SciJourn project at a point when he was considering leaving the teaching profession, and it reignited his engagement with the profession. Jessica (Cadre 2) was also interested in the SciJourn approach as a means to make science relevant and engaging, and resonated with our perspective on science literacy.

Teens Communicating with Stakeholders on Science Issues

Shelley (Cadre 1) and two other teachers from her school joined the project together, motivated in part by a school-wide emphasis on writing across the curriculum. Shelley encouraged her students to interview experts and stakeholders for their articles, a key practice in professional journalism that we had not emphasized due to concerns about time and communication constraints of schools. Jessica also taught her students how to identify experts and stakeholders and how to communicate with them. She required that her students either conduct an interview with an expert or use a survey. At that stage, many of her students contacted press officers at EurekaAlert! or scientists who specialized in their field and "freaked out" when they got responses back. Jessica also described how her students "loved" to do surveys using Google Forms and particularly enjoyed surveying their peers.

Local Curricular Fit

Like Shelley, Rose Davidson (a co-author of this chapter) came into the project partly because the project's overall aims meshed well with her own and her school's: she wanted to cultivate lifelong learners who used contemporary science in their lives. She had a strong desire to tightly integrate SciJourn activities into her existing curriculum and activities. Thus, it's not surprising that she worked on incorporating journalistic research and writing into the science fair and eCYBERMISSION projects her students had been doing in previous years.

As Davidson worked with SciJourn in her classroom, the work gradually changed from that of the typical student research process to one with a science journalism perspective. The student participants underwent training in journalistic methods, which included choosing a research topic, carrying out online research, interviewing experts and stakeholders, attributing information to sources, and crafting a science news article on their topic. They then carried out controlled experiments to develop answers to problems which arose in their research on the topic. They then wrote press releases on the findings of their own experimental results in the context of their previous research on the work of others.

Davidson found that integrating science journalism with the research projects of her students brought about significant changes to the process. Topic selection became more relevant for students through the practices of brainstorming, modeling through read-alouds, reading the news, and connecting it to science. Teacher-and-student dialogues about topics and the development of topic ideas through fishbowl activities provided for the selection of more robust topics that were connected to students' interests and to the events unfolding in the scientific community. Background research for projects was improved by the online research and interviews needed to successfully craft a science news article on their topic. The students' ability to communicate their findings to others were given another facet with the addition of a news release about the findings of their research. These changes in Davidson's teaching practices brought the science research project into the classroom, where it is a community event, rather than one which is carried out in isolation by the student.

Charlotte was the first middle school teacher involved in the project, and because of her previous experience with the National Writing Project, she came in with a strong interest in cultivating writing in science. Her students worked in pairs, choosing their partners. According to Charlotte, "I just feel with seventh graders, they're so social that when you tell them they can pick their partner, they immediately become more comfortable with the project." Charlotte also required that all her students write a finished, revised article, and, like Shelley, she set up very strong systems of peer support and teacher edits and revision.

Discussion

Our results show that the project's aim of preparing students for using science in life after graduation from school provided a key orientation for teachers' adaptations (Polman et al., 2014). The principle-based aspect of the project's "guidelines" left room for significant adaptation for different contextual circumstances and local purposes by all teachers (Kirshner & Polman, 2013; Kohnen, Saul, & Singer, 2016).

We were hoping that the opportunity for publication would be motivating to students and teachers, and it does have a great deal of appeal. Writing was a positive pull for many teachers, but intimidating to other teachers on their own and their students' behalf. Those teachers who found the writing aspect challenging did find other adaptations possible in other genres. The genre of infographics was particularly appealing to chemistry teachers, who had a strong affinity for the power of visualization. The researchers and the growing body of curriculum were resources that made entry into this ambitious work easier.

We saw a number of adaptations to the curriculum over time. One was marrying article writings to existing projects and activities, such as Davidson's science fair projects. Each cadre of teachers had more curricular resources to work with, and this had its pluses and minuses. The early waves of teachers had a great deal of ownership and agency in helping to build a new venture. The later waves had lower barriers to entry, which helped them get started, but less ownership of contributing new resources. We started out focusing on students writing text-based science news stories, but the genre of targeted products was heavily adapted in different sites. The varying genres are not all necessarily created equal, however. All the genres were good vehicles for students seeking out and interpreting multiple sources, and thinking about their credibility. But only infographics strongly push toward visualizing data. And some of the genres do not connect to public audiences (e.g., PowerPoints made only for the classroom).

An important aspect of the work over time is that the project adapted based on findings from teachers' implementations, summarized in Figure 6.2. Some boundary objects from journalism went awry in the classroom; we introduced teachers in the first year to the notion of the Inverted triangle structure of science news stories, and the 5 Ws (who, what, when, where, and why). Almost all teachers latched onto them, and "taught" them to students in a transmission fashion, with little positive result. We found this did not help science literacy for everyday life, and no longer stress it.

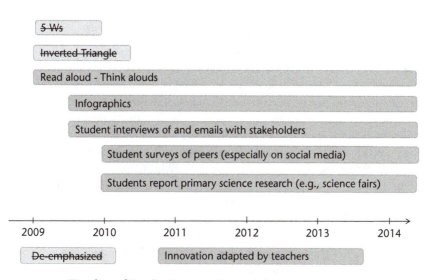

FIGURE 6.2 Timeline of Key Participatory Design Changes

Our project staff at the university engaged in dialogue not only with the teachers but also with their situations, which enabled us to better appreciate unexpected curricular possibilities as they emerged. For instance, *SciJourner* editor Newman, who came from a professional science news background, did not expect students to be able to collect relevant data from surveys they conducted over social media. But when some did that successfully, he encouraged it. As mentioned, we at first did not appreciate how valuable and exciting stakeholder interviews could be in school settings, despite adding some complexity of orchestration.

Early on, instructional activities and resources that the project provided varied in their usefulness to teachers and students. Some of these were counterproductive, so we had to adjust. Our SciJourner.org website proved to be a valuable resource, especially because it included student-generated models of completed work, and inspiration that newcomers could do this kind of reporting.

There are some assets we need to try to maintain over time. These include maintaining high degrees of teacher agency, and having a community with genuine teacher-researcher dialogue. To do this, we need to maintain both a sense and a reality that we're not stagnating, but instead continuing to make progress on significant challenges together.

Conclusion

We close this chapter by discussing future directions for organizing distributed socio-technical systems for participatory design involving teachers and their students. Throughout our project's evolution, our project's primary goals have been—and continue to be—to maintain teacher agency by ensuring that they have authentic opportunities for adaptation and sustained dialogue with university-based staff. As in the field of human–computer interaction, participatory design in education can be carried out with a merely technical orientation of understanding the "user's" experience (Carroll, 1996), but the spirit of participatory design as it emerged in the Scandinavian model (e.g., Bødker, 1996) requires richer interactional possibilities as well as a recognition of power dynamics. Accordingly, we see promise in the idea of reframing our ongoing work with teachers as "co-design" with expectations of continuing adaptation, and building in expectations of ongoing, mutually beneficial research-practice partnerships involving university and school staff (Penuel, Bell, Bevan, Buffington, & Falk, 2016).

In addition, we see promise in engaging students more actively in the participatory design process through "practical measures" that capture their perspectives on their experiences (Bryk, Gomez, Grunow, & LeMahieu, 2015; Krumm et al., 2015). When combined with educational activities that have authenticity from the standpoint of the learners as well as the real-world communities conducting literacy practices (Kohnen, 2013a; Polman, 2012); practical measures for capturing students' experiences, such as short end-of-week surveys, could be valuable tools for time-pressured teachers and researchers to quickly gain more appreciation of student perspectives on their learning experiences, so that adjustments to instruction could be made. In addition, student panels to advise teachers and university staff would allow students to participate more fully in curricular design.

We look forward to working, together with each other and with students, to improve the educational opportunities available to all. The ongoing design journeys are themselves key learning experiences.

References

Bødker, S. (1996). Creating conditions for participation: Conflicts and resources in systems development. *Human-Computer Interaction, 11*(3), 215–236.

Brown, M., & Edelson, D. (2003). Teaching as design: Can we better understand the ways in which teachers use materials so we can better design materials to support their change in practice? (Design Brief). Evanston, IL: Center for Learning Technologies in Urban Schools.

Bryk, A. S., Gomez, L. M., Grunow, A., & LeMahieu, P. (2015). *Learning to Improve: How America's Schools Can Get Better at Getting Better*. Cambridge, MA: Harvard University Press.

Carroll, J. M. (1996). Encountering others: Reciprocal openings in participatory design and user-centered design. *Human-Computer Interaction, 11*(3), 285–290.

Davidson, R. M. (2014a). Researching the real: Transforming the science fair through relevant and authentic research. Doctoral dissertation, University of Missouri-St. Louis.

Davidson, R. M. (2014b). Using infographics in the science classroom: Three investigations in which students present their results in infographics. *The Science Teacher, 81*(3), 34–39.

Fischer, G. (2013). Meta-design: Empowering all stakeholders as co-designers. In R. Luckin, P. Goodyear, B. Grabowski, S. Puntambeker, J. Underwood, & N. Winters (Eds.), *Handbook on Design in Educational Computing* (pp. 133–145). London: Routledge.

Kali, Y., & McKenney, S. (2012). Teachers as designers of technology-enhanced learning materials. In J. van Aalst, K. Thompson, M. J. Jacobson, & P. Reimann (Eds.), *The Future of Learning: Proceedings of the 10th International Conference of the Learning Sciences* (Vol. 2, pp. 582–583). International Society of the Learning Sciences.

Kirshner, B., & Polman, J. L. (2013). Adaptation by design: A context-sensitive, dialogic approach to interventions. In B. Fishman, W. R. Penuel, A. Allen, & B. H. Cheng (Eds.), *Design-Based Implementation Research: Theories, Methods, and Exemplars. National Society for the Study of Education Yearbook,* Volume 112, Issue 2 (pp. 215–236). New York: Teachers College Press.

Kohnen, A. M. (2012). Teachers as editors, editors as teachers. In C. Bazerman, C. Dean, J. Early, K. Lunsford, S. Null, P. Rogers, & A. Stansell (Eds.), *International Advances in Writing Research: Cultures, Places, Measures* (pp. 303-317). Fort Collins, CO: The WAC Clearinghouse.

Kohnen, A. M. (2013a). The authenticity spectrum: The case of a science journalism writing project. *English Journal, 102*(5), 28–34.

Kohnen, A. M. (2013b). Content-area teachers as teachers of writing. *Teaching/Writing: The Journal of Writing Teacher Education, 2*(1), 29–33.

Kohnen, A. M. (2013c). "I wouldn't have said it that way": Mediating professional editorial comments in a secondary science classroom. *Linguistics and Education, 24*(2), 75–85. doi: 10.1016/j.linged.2012.12.007

Kohnen, A. M. (2013d). Informational writing in high school science: The importance of genre, apprenticeship, and publication. *Journal of Adolescent and Adult Literacy, 57*(3), 233–242. doi: 10.1002/JAAL.220

Kohnen, A. M., Saul, E. W., & Singer, N. (2016). Developing support for teachers and students in secondary science classrooms through writing criteria. In S. Plane, C. Bazerman, F. Rondelli, C. Donahue, A. N. Applebee, C. Bore, P. Carlino, M. Marquillo Larruy, P. Rogers, & D. Russell (Eds.), *Recherches en écritures: Regards pluriels* (Writing research from multiple perspectives) (pp. 211–232). Lorraine, France: Centre de Recherche sure les Médiations.

Krumm, A. E., et al. (2015). Practical measures of learning behaviors. In *Proceedings of the Second (2015) ACM Conference on Learning@ Scale* (pp. 327–330). Vancouver: ACM.

Lave, J., & Wenger, E. (1991). *Situated Learning: Legitimate Peripheral Participation.* Cambridge: Cambridge University Press.

Lieberman, A., & Wood, D. R. (2002). *Inside the National Writing Project: Connecting Network Learning and Classroom Teaching.* New York: Teachers College Press.

Penuel, W. R., Bell, P., Bevan, B., Buffington, P., & Falk, J. (2016). Enhancing use of learning sciences research in planning for and supporting educational change: Leveraging and building social networks. *Journal of Educational Change, 17*(2), 251–278.

Polman, J. L. (2012). Trajectories of participation and identification in learning communities involving disciplinary practices. In D. Yun Dai (Ed.), *Design research on learning and thinking in educational settings: Enhancing intellectual growth and functioning* (pp. 225–242). New York: Routledge.

Polman, J. L., Newman, A., Farrar, C., & Saul, E. W. (2012). Science journalism: Students learn lifelong science literacy skills by reporting the news. *The Science Teacher, 79*(1), 44–47.

Polman, J. L., Newman, A., Saul, E. W., & Farrar, C. (2014). Adapting practices of science journalism to foster science literacy. *Science Education, 98*(5), 766–791.

Recker, M., Walker, A., Giersch, S., Mao, X., Halioris, S., Palmer, B., . . . Robertshaw, M. B. (2007). A study of teachers' use of online learning resources to design classroom activities. *New Review of Hypermedia and Multimedia, 13*(2), 117–134. http://doi.org/10.1080/13614560701709846

Saul, E. W., Kohnen, A., Newman, A., & Pearce, L. (2012). *Front-Page Science: Engaging Teens in Science Literacy.* Arlington, VA: NSTA Press.

Wenger, E. (1998). *Communities of Practice: Learning, Meaning, and Identity.* New York: Cambridge University Press.

Wertsch, J. V. (1998). *Mind as Action.* New York: Oxford University Press.

Whitacre, M. P. (2014). Teacher transformation: An exploration of science teachers' changing professional identities, knowledge, and classroom practices. Doctoral dissertation, University of Missouri–St. Louis.

Whitacre, M. P., & Saul, E. W. (2015). High school girls' interpretations of science graphs: Exploring complex visual and natural language hybrid text. *International Journal of Science and Mathematics Education*, 1-20.

7

CO-DESIGNING AN HCI CURRICULUM WITH COLLEGE STUDENTS AND TEACHING THEM ABOUT PARTICIPATORY DESIGN IN THE PROCESS

Helene Gelderblom

Introduction

When participatory design is applied in educational contexts for the purpose of course or curriculum design, it is typically a long-term project with groups of students and educators who collaborate to improve general practices and curricula (Bovill, Cook, Sather & Felten, 2011). For instance, Bovill et al. (2011) discuss three examples where students co-designed courses or curricula. However, those students were not the ones who would directly be taught the newly co-designed curriculum or experience the co-designed teaching methods.

In my search, no documented cases could be found in which a class co-designed the content of a specific course that they were subsequently taught. The reasons are obvious:

- If a course spans a semester and there is a syllabus to cover, it could be challenging to fit a participatory design goal into the time allocated for course content—especially if the outcomes need to be applied in the same course.
- Getting the actual students of the course to participate in its design before the course commences will be difficult to arrange, since students have different class and extra mural schedules. How can they be motivated to participate?
- Assuming the design process could be fit into the beginning of the course, the resultant design would have to be implemented immediately. What if the outcomes of the design process suggest a need for content or methods in which the teacher lacks experience?

Despite these challenges, my reasoning was that we cannot engage in teaching participatory design techniques without fully embracing a participatory design process with the very students who have come to learn it from us. In this chapter, I explain how I overcame these obstacles in the design and delivery of a fourth-level university course in human–computer interaction (HCI). I also demonstrate how the students' participation in the design of their own course improved their learning experience, engagement, and overall performance, as well as the teacher's pedagogical experience.

Rationale

Referring to the development of HCI curricula, Fincher, Cairns, and Blackwell (2012) explain how HCI educators with experience in methods such as participatory design and user-centred design refrain from using these techniques when designing their courses. Their course design tends to be based on how they were taught or how other subjects are taught rather than being focused on the particular characteristics of HCI as a subject. Fincher and colleagues also claim that there is a lack of "appreciation of what might be innovative or unusual approaches that best fit HCI pedagogy" (p. 2708).

Bovill et al. (2011) promote the participatory design of university courses, saying that students should not only be consulted, but teachers must find ways to make them full participants in the design of courses, curricula, and teaching approaches. Treating students as peers who can provide valuable input will support the development of a collegial relationship between lecturers and students. Bovill et al. believe that such a relationship will also improve classroom practice. Involving students in this way does not mean that the teacher's experience and knowledge are less important. Rather, the emphasis should be on enabling students to realise that participation in design is as authentic in the class they are taking as it is in any other design and learning process. False claims of participation will alienate students and be detrimental to the success of the teaching and learning experience (Bovill et al., 2011).

Grounded by these philosophical and theoretical foundations, I embarked on a process of applying participatory design in a new HCI course through co-design with the same students enrolled in that course.

Context

I was newly appointed in the Informatics department at the University of Pretoria (UP), South Africa, in 2013 and hence taught this HCI course for the first time in 2014. It is an elective module in the Honours BCom (Informatics) degree. In South Africa, students complete a bachelor's degree after three years of study and can then acquire a more specialised Honours degree, which is a coursework degree with a 25% research component.

The academic year at UP is divided into two semesters, and in 2014 and 2015 the HCI course was offered in the second semester (August to October). The class spans eight two-hour lectures supplemented by compulsory group and individual assignments, and ends with a written examination in November.

Most of the students who enrol for the module have completed a bachelor of commerce (BCom) degree that does not include any HCI component. A few students have completed a BSc Computer Science or a Bachelor of Information Technology degree, the latter of whom may have completed a third-level Interaction Design course. Around one-third of the class consists of part-time students who have full time employment in the information technology industry. In 2014, only two students in the class had previously encountered HCI in their studies.

Since this was a new course, I was responsible for designing the curriculum and the delivery mechanisms. The task of designing an Honours-level course that should also serve as an introduction to HCI poses one challenge: the students are in their fourth year of study and academically mature. The HCI basics cannot be conveyed to them in the same way as would be done for entry-level students. These students have extensive theoretical and practical knowledge of systems design, databases, project management, and so on, on which one could build in the HCI class. So, although they need to learn the fundamentals, this course had to be designed with their level of knowledge in mind.

As a participatory design practitioner, my immediate response to a design issue of this kind is to ask those who will be affected by the design for their opinion. In this case it was the students enrolled for the course. By kicking off the course with a participatory design exercise that involved co-designing the course curriculum with the students in class, we would kill two birds with one stone—the students would help to design the course and in the process learn through experience how participatory design is carried out. The problem of using up course time diminished. The time spent on the co-design of the course would also be time spent on teaching students a core HCI design technique.

Overview of the Participatory Design Process

The process that I followed was guided by Spinuzzi's (2005) three stages of participatory design: (1) initial exploration, (2) discovery, and (3) prototyping. Each of these is discussed in detail below.

Initial Exploration of Whatever Is Being Designed or Redesigned

In this phase, designers become familiar with the users' world and how they function within a specific context. At the time of this study, I was a new member of this Informatics department. My previous experience had been in Computer Science departments, where I taught introductory HCI courses to undergraduate students and more specialised HCI topics to postgraduate students. Consequently,

I had never taught HCI to BCom students, nor had I faced the challenge of teaching mature students the basics. This unfamiliarity meant that I needed to do some research to understand the students' context, their knowledge, and their expectations. To achieve this, I consulted with various lecturers in the department and engaged in informal discussions with assistant lecturers who were also Honours students. I studied the undergraduate curriculum and the content of other Honours courses taught alongside the HCI course. Because the Honours degree serves as entry into a Masters degree programme, I also considered the research interests of academics in the department who would act as Masters supervisors to students who advanced to a research degree.

With regard to HCI content, I studied the Association for Computing Machinery (ACM) and Institute of Electrical and Electronics Engineers (IEEE) (2013) recommended HCI curriculum and collected information on what was taught in HCI courses at leading international universities. I also consulted the results of Churchill, Bowser, and Preece's (2013) investigation on HCI curricula. Analysing all this information gave me a sense of how I could equip our students with knowledge and skills that would compare well with international standards.

The outcome of my analysis of all the information gathered in the exploration phase was a list of ten core HCI topics to use as a starting point for the discovery phase. These core topics are listed and briefly explained in Table 7.1.

Discovery

During this phase, the participants (designers and users) understand and prioritise the current situation and envision future solutions. Users' goals and values are clarified, and they come to an agreement on the desired outcome. The course began with a two-hour lecture, which I kicked off with an explanation of how we would proceed through the participatory design process toward a goal of co-designing the rest of the course together. Figure 7.1 provides a visual timeline that shows the various parts of the first lecture.

Successful participatory design requires that participants have tools that will enhance dialogue within the design team (DiSalvo & DiSalvo, 2014). The ten core HCI topics that emerged during the exploration phase served as a starting point for discussion during this first lecture and participatory design exercise. Since almost none of the students had any HCI experience, they were not sufficiently informed to make decisions about course content without receiving some introduction. To provide them with the tools to have an effective participatory design dialogue together, I followed my introduction to our design exercise with five-minute presentations on each of the ten topics. I put in a lot of effort to make each of the ten topics seem equally interesting and beneficial, focussing on exciting examples and innovative aspects of the topic. We then engaged in an open discussion about these topics and about HCI in general, during which students had the opportunity to ask questions and express their opinions.

TABLE 7.1 Ten HCI Topics That Were Discussed during the Discovery Phase

Topic	Brief description/motivation for inclusion
Interaction design	Core ACM/IEEE topic
UX/usability evaluation	Part of two core ACM/IEEE core topics
Cognitive psychology	Core ACM/IEEE sub-topic
Eye tracking in interface design and evaluation	Conducting a quantitative evaluation and discussing and reporting the results are part of a core ACM/IEEE topic (Designing Interaction). Since eye tracking is one of the lecturer's fields of expertise it was included as implementation mechanism of this topic.
Social impact of technology	ICT for development (ICT4D) is one of the research focus areas of the department. The social impact of technology is an integral theme of ICT4D and including it would provide future Master's students in this field with some grounding.
HCI and education	IT in Education is another research focus area in the department and including this topic could lead to IT in Education research that focuses on HCI aspects.
Designing for special user groups	This includes designing for users in developing environments and since we are situated in such an environment it makes sense to deliver Informatics graduates that are sensitive to the design issues relating to special user groups. This topic would also cover universal accessibility—an HCI topic included in most programmes at leading international universities.
Data visualisation	An increasingly important, multidisciplinary topic that is also featured in international curricula.
Designing online communities	It appears in some international curricula and seemed like a good opportunity to introduce practical design work that is relevant.
HCI for IT managers and Business Analysts (HCI4BAs).	This topic appeared in the curriculum of one prominent international university. I decided to include it because these students have had no previous exposure to HCI, and many of them end up in Business Analysis (BA) positions. This would provide them with knowledge of how HCI relates to BA activities.

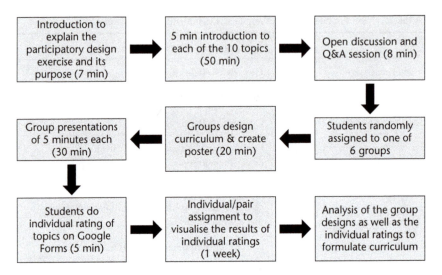

FIGURE 7.1 Timeline of the Parts of the Participatory Design Exercise in Lecture 1

Prototyping

Iterative prototyping is a staple technique in several design disciplines (Jacobson et al., 1999; Vredenburg et al., 2002; Wasserman, 1996). For participatory design in particular, prototyping enables designers and participants to collaboratively and iteratively create a design outcome that builds upon ideas that emerged during their exploration and discovery design phases (Spinuzzi, 2005).

Thirty-nine students attended the first lecture. In the second half of the lecture—after the ten topics listed in Table 7.1 were introduced and discussed— students were randomly assigned to small groups by drawing candy from a bowl. Those with the same brand formed a group. The six groups consisting of four to ten students each were given 20 minutes to come up with a curriculum based on what they had learnt about HCI thus far. The instructions were simple—they could include any selection or combination of the ten topics in their course design that would span the remaining seven lectures. This could range from suggesting one of the ten topics to be covered over seven remaining lectures, to including all ten topics to be covered during the seven lectures. During the design session they had access to the Internet to do further research, and they could revisit my PowerPoint presentation on the ten topics.

After 20 minutes of group work, each group was given the opportunity to present their proposed curriculum, along with a rationale for their proposal. They had to create a poster that communicated their design and explained how the chosen topics should be spread across the remaining lectures. These presentations prompted further discussion of the topics.

At the end of the lecture, I asked students to complete a survey on Google Forms, where they had to individually rate the ten topics from 1 (least favourite) to 10 (favourite). In group work not all voices are heard, and this survey allowed each individual to provide input into the design. I also gave students an after-class assignment to (1) create three different visualisations of the individual rating results, (2) have the visualisations evaluated by at least three people, and (3) write a short report on the three designs and their evaluation. Students had the choice to do this assignment individually or in pairs, and they had one week to complete it. This was their final contribution to the participatory design exercise. The main purpose of the assignment was to engage students with the set of individual preferences as a means for developing an accurate impression of what students in the class prefer. Knowing what their fellow students prefer would help them acknowledge and accommodate decisions about the curriculum that might not align with their own choices.

Outcomes of the Participatory Design Exercise

From the group presentations it was clear that the students were intrigued by eye tracking and the possibility of doing practical work using the eye trackers in our UX lab. Similarly, most groups expressed excitement about data visualisation, with two groups linking it to data science, which they regard as an important aspect of informatics. Students' motivation to include interaction design mostly related to understanding the important fundamental concepts of HCI. Since they had only five minutes, their explanations were generally superficial, and I relied primarily on the content of their posters when analysing their feedback.

Figure 7.2 summarises the HCI topics that each group included in their proposed curriculum. Five groups wanted interaction design, all the groups included eye tracking, and four groups chose data visualisation. The rest of the topics received one or two votes, with the exception of HCI and education, which received none. Three groups wanted only three topics to be covered, one group included six topics, and the remaining two groups requested four and five topics respectively.

Thirty-six students completed the individual survey, and each of them had to give a topic a unique rating from 1 to 10 (i.e., no two topics could have the same rating). Figure 7.3 shows the sum of all the individual scores per topic. Eye tracking and interaction design were the most popular topics, with data visualisation and HCI for business analysts not far behind. I also analysed the individual ratings per group to determine to what extent the group results reflected the preferences of the individuals in the group. In Table 7.2 I present this alongside the group preferences. In line with the group results, HCI in education, designing online communities, and the social impact of technology received the lowest individual ratings.

The combined individual ratings, as depicted in Figure 7.3, corresponded well with the group preferences, but there were some notable differences when

		Group						
Topics		1	2	3	4	5	6	**Count**
1.	Interaction design							5
2.	Social impact of technology							1
3.	HCI and education							0
4.	Eye tracking in design and evaluation							6
5.	Designing for special user groups							2
6.	UX/usability evaluation							2
7.	Cognitive psychology in HCI							2
8.	Designing online communities							1
9.	Data visualisation							4
10.	HCI for IT managers and BAs							1
No of topics per group		3	3	3	6	4	5	

FIGURE 7.2   Topic Choices per Group

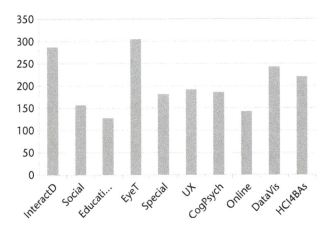

FIGURE 7.3   Sum of Scores Given to Each Topic by Individual Students

comparing the group preferences with the individual ratings within the respective groups (Table 7.2). Consider the following observations:

- Most groups included interaction design, eye tracking, and data visualisation and the aggregated individual student ratings also positioned them as topics of highest interest.

TABLE 7.2 Comparison of Group Choices with Choices of Individuals in the Group

Group number	Topics selected by the group	The four topics that received the highest average individual score from individuals in the group (ordered from high to low score)
1	Interaction design; Eye tracking; Data visualisation	Eye tracking; Data visualisation; Interaction design; Cognitive psychology
2	Social impact; Eye tracking; Online communities	HCI4BAs; Interaction design; Special user groups; Eye tracking
3	Interaction design; Eye tracking; Cognitive psychology	Eye tracking; Interaction design; Data visualisation; UX/usability evaluation
4	Interaction design; Eye tracking; Special user groups; UX/usability evaluation; Cognitive psychology; Data visualisation	Eye tracking; Interaction design; Data visualisation; UX/usability evaluation
5	Interaction design; Eye tracking; Data visualisation; HCI4BAs	Eye tracking; Interaction design; HCI4BAs; Data visualisation
6	Interaction design; Eye tracking; Special user groups; Cognitive psychology; Data visualisation	Eye tracking; Interaction design; HCI4BAs; Data visualisation

- Although the individual rating of HCI for IT managers and BAs (HCI4BAs) was almost as high as that of data visualisation, four groups selected data visualisation, while only one group selected HCI4BAs.
- Group 2's selection differs from the individual preferences in the group. Although the social impact of technology and designing online communities were included in the group's curriculum, interaction design, designing for special users, and HCI4BAs received higher individual ratings from group members. The group's overall and individual preferences also differ notably from those of the rest of the class (I speculate about the reasons in the discussion below).
- Group 3 selected interaction design, eye tracking, and cognitive psychology, although the latter topic was placed only sixth in the group members' individual ratings. The individual scores of both data visualisation and HCI4BAs were higher than that of cognitive psychology.
- Group 5 selected data visualisation and not HCI4BAs, although the individuals in the group preferred HCI4BAs.

- Group 6 included UX/usability evaluation that was placed seventh individually, and they left out HCI4BAs, which received the third highest individual score.

These results indicate that in some groups the individual preferences of group members were overridden by in the group discussions. Overall however, the most preferred topics (eye tracking and interaction design) and the least preferred topics (HCI in education and designing social communities) were similar, whether they were considered in groups or as aggregate individual ratings.

Group 2 can be regarded as an outlier. Since the way I wanted to design the curriculum for this course challenged the standard procedures in the Informatics department, I discussed my plans with the head of the department beforehand. She was intrigued by my plan and asked if she could observe the first lecture. During the group sessions, Group 2 incidentally sat close to her, and she became involved in their discussion. I believe the power relations played an important role here. I felt I could not ask her not to contribute to the discussion, and the students' choices were probably influenced by her input. This was confirmed by the fact that Group 2 is the group where the group's collective and individual preferences diverged the most.

What we learn from the results is that group decisions were probably influenced by the stronger voices in the groups and that it is crucial to supplement the group feedback with the individual ratings of the topics. If I had based the curriculum only on the group results, I would not have included HCI4BAs as a separate topic and there would also have been less emphasis on UX/usability evaluation and cognitive psychology. One should also be aware of power relations between group members and should preferably not allow academic staff to participate in the group activities.

The final co-designed curriculum used for the remainder of the course is given in Table 7.3. I included the students' three preferred topics: interaction design, eye tracking, and data visualisation. Interaction design was spread over two lecture slots, with cognitive psychology included as a subtopic to satisfy the overall individual interest in cognitive psychology. Eye tracking was the first choice—both for groups and individuals. Since eye tracking is a specialised skill that requires a substantial amount of theoretical knowledge and practical exercise, I allocated two lecture slots for this topic. The visualisations of the individual topic rating data that students submitted as their first assignment revealed that they lacked basic chart and visualisation design skills. I allocated only one lecture to data visualisation with the idea to cover only the very basics of the topic. The UX/usability evaluation topic received the fifth highest individual score, and it is part of the core of the ACM/IEEE curriculum. So, although only two groups selected this topic, I included UX/usability evaluation to be covered in one lecture. This lecture preceded the eye tracking lectures to provide the broader evaluation context in which eye tracking is a specialised topic. HCI for business analysts was requested by only one group, but it attracted the students enough to be placed fourth in the individual ratings. Since it seemed sensible to make the last lecture a summary of the course, HCI for business analysts was given that lecture slot with the idea that

TABLE 7.3 Co-Designed Syllabus for the Remainder of the HCI Module

Slot	Topics to be covered
Lecture 2	Interaction design 1: requirements; defining the problem space; user characteristics; cognitive psychology
Lecture 3	Interaction design 2: design; guidelines; prototyping; participatory design; interface metaphors
Lecture 4	UX/usability evaluation: Overview of evaluation methods
Lecture 5	Eye tracking: Theory and practical demo
Lecture 6	Eye tracking: Group demos of homework assignment; feedback and reflection on eye tracking specifically and on evaluation in general
Lecture 7	Introduction to data visualisation
Lecture 8	Summary and examination preparation (HCI for IT managers and BAs)

it would be used to tie together all previous topics and to show how HCI overall relates to IT industry activities and issues.

At the start of the second lecture, I presented the syllabus, along with the results on which I based the selections to the students. Time was allowed for discussion, during which students clearly expressed their appreciation of the participatory design process. The students accepted this syllabus as presented.

Using the Participatory Design Exercise as a Practical Example of an HCI Technique

Participatory design was one of the subtopics in interaction design that was covered in Lecture 3. I capitalised on the students' course co-design experience in Lecture 1 to scaffold how I taught participatory design techniques. Furthermore, the students used their experience to enhance their understanding of participatory design's place in interaction design. Although their experience was in course design, and not in the design of an interactive system or an interface, it was easy to relate their experience to participatory design activities in interaction design. For example, the concept of "user centred design" could be directly related to the "student centred design" approach followed in the course design.

Evaluation of the Module Design

The next step in the process was to evaluate the course design to assess the success of the participatory design exercise and to determine how the course could be improved for the next semester. The evaluation was based firstly on implicit evidence, such as class attendance, class participation, and student achievement in formative and summative assessment, and secondly, on the results of two explicit student evaluations of the course content and delivery. The implicit evaluation is discussed in detail in Gelderblom and Van der Merwe (2015). It is difficult to link the good class attendance, high quality of assignments, and good pass rate to the participatory design effort, but, as Gelderblom and Van der Merwe report, these aspects could be attributed to the positive influence that the course co-design experience had on students' attitude and motivation. However, in this discussion I focus on the students' explicit evaluations and topic ratings, which could be related more directly to the participatory design exercise.

At the end of the course, after Lecture 7, students were again asked to rate the initial ten topics. The results of this rating were compared to the outcomes of the first rating to see how students' opinions changed after gaining HCI knowledge. The outcomes of the second rating were also taken into account when adapting the course for the next round.

First Student Evaluation

The first evaluation occurred at the end of Lecture 6 and took the form of a standard course evaluation questionnaire administered by an administrative staff member in the department. It covered three areas, namely module content, lecturer, and assessment. The criteria for the evaluation in each of these areas are listed in column 2 of Table 7.4. A five-point Likert scale was used for the closed questions, with 1 being negative and 5 positive. Students could also add open-ended comments related to each criterion. In this evaluation the questionnaire was completed by 33 of the 41 registered students. Column 3 of Table 7.4 summarises the quantitative results. The overall score for the course was 4.48, which is regarded as very high. Lecturers are expected to receive a score no lower than 3.

TABLE 7.4 Results of Standard Course Evaluation

Area	Criteria	Score
Module Content	Organisation	4.52
	Study material	4.18
	Usefulness of material for completing course	4.24
	Usefulness of course	4.33
Lecturer(s)	Interpersonal relationships	4.61
	Level of knowledge	4.79
	Attitude	4.85
	Preparation, use of media	4.82
	Learning opportunities	4.42
Assessment	Clarity of criteria	4.30
	Nature, content and method	4.21
	Fairness	4.48

The item that is most relevant with regard to the participatory design of the course is "Module Content (Organisation)." The score of 4.52 achieved here indicates that students probably thought the content was well organised, and hence that they felt positive about the way the syllabus was compiled. Each item in the evaluation questionnaire has space for open-ended comments. Since we are particularly interested in the usefulness and practical applicability of the participatory design exercise, the value of the experiential learning exercise, and the general student experience, my analysis of the written open-ended comments focused on finding information related to these.

Nineteen of the thirty-three respondents commented on "Module Content (Organisation)." Eight of these specifically mentioned their participation in the course design, noting that they enjoyed and appreciated the active role they played in the process. Several also commented that the syllabus and course organisation was much clearer because of their involvement in its design. They said, for example: "It was a great idea to get students involved in selecting areas of the subject they would like to focus on" and "I appreciate that we were actively part of deciding on the syllabus."

Seventeen students made positive comments on "Module content (Usefulness of course for career)," noting that it enabled them to "see how [HCI] would play a role" in career choices and that the course offered "elements/topics which any organisation can benefit from." Only one doubted the usefulness for his/her career, saying: "I think it is very insightful but as a B.IT student I think there are other things that will be more important."

One danger in asking students to contribute to the design of the syllabus is that students may think the lecturer is trying to transfer some of his/her duties to the students. Comments on the "Lecturer (Level of knowledge)" criterion countered this. Ten of sixteen responses mentioned that the lecturer was knowledgeable and experienced. Students expressed their appreciation of opportunities to hear about real-life design experiences as well as opportunities to apply what they were learning in hands-on activities. They offered comments such as "Opportunities to use equipment that is used in industry was fantastic" and "Work activities helped improve understanding."

With regard to general learner experience, I analysed student feedback on "Comment (Level of difficulty)," "Comment (Work load)," and "General comments." The first of these received 32 comments, and in seven of them students used words such as "fun," "interesting," and "enjoyable," in the sense that the level of enjoyment made up for the level of difficulty. Twenty-eight students made general comments, and here I learnt the most about the student experience. Twenty-three expressed clear enjoyment, for example: "I have really enjoyed the module thus far. It has made me think differently on many aspects of system design and life in general"; "So far I've been intrigued by the course. I thought it would be fun, but not so much fun. I truly enjoyed taking this course"; and "By far the best, useful and interesting subject of my whole year."

The few negative comments from students were suggestive of individual learning differences rather than emerging design themes. For example, one student felt that there was too much group work, while another felt that there was too much emphasis on specific HCI areas like eye tracking that reduced presentation of more general HCI principles. While the responses were of interest individually, no course design implications were drawn from them for this initial exploratory case.

Second Student Evaluation

The predominantly positive feedback in the first evaluation could be the result of demand characteristics response bias (i.e., the when respondents adapt their responses to fit the expectations of the researcher) (Dell, Vaidyanathan, Medhi, Cutrell & Thies, 2012). I therefore did a second evaluation in the final lecture in which I phrased the questions in a way that would compel the students to think critically about the course. I asked the following two questions:

1. List at least three things you would change about the course.
2. It seems from the evaluation that the level of difficulty of this module might be below what is expected at honours level. Please comment on this.

For this discussion, I was mostly interested in students' responses to the first question. Twenty-two students answered the question, and the responses can be grouped into three broad themes:

*   Fewer assignments—five students mentioned this. Two more asked for fewer group assignments and more individual ones. There was, however, one respondent who specifically asked for more assignments.
*   More practical work—nine students requested this, but in different ways. Some wanted practical work in class to replace the theoretical parts of the lectures. Two asked for more practical eye tracking work (although two other students specifically asked that eye tracking be omitted from the course). Two students asked for practical work that would involve programming.
*   A broader range of topics—three students asked for more HCI topics to be covered; on the other hand, one student complained about too much breadth and too little depth.

In this evaluation, there was only one respondent who referred to the participatory design activity. He/she did not appreciate the fact that students co-designed the syllabus, saying the "structure of the course should be planned out in advance by the lecturer." The question specifically asked what the student would change about the course. Therefore, since no other students mentioned the participatory design activity as something they would change, we can assume that they approved of it.

Re-Rating of the HCI Topics

The re-rating of the ten topics was done after Lecture 7. By letting students rate the ten topics again, I could deduce whether they were satisfied with their choices in the beginning of the course.

The second survey was completed by all 41 students. Eye tracking remained the favourite topic, receiving an even higher score (8.4) at the end than at the beginning (8.3). There was a significant change of opinion about UX/usability evaluation, which received an average score of 5.1 in the beginning and 7.4 at the end. This indicates that it was the correct decision to go with the ACM/IEEE guidance in this regard and include it in the syllabus. The scores for cognitive psychology and designing online communities also increased. Interaction design, which received the second highest score in the July survey (7.7), dropped notably and at the end of the course (with 6.7) was third in line after eye tracking and UX/usability evaluation. Data visualisation dropped from third to fourth position. The students clearly appreciated the eye tracking topic a lot, and since the practical eye tracking work they did related directly to UX/usability evaluation, this is could explain why the latter topic moved up in the ratings.

The three topics with the lowest scores in July were HCI and education, designing online communities, and social impact of technology. In October, HCI and education was still the least popular, then designing for special user groups, and again the social impact of technology.

Overall the second survey confirmed that the topics included in the syllabus should remain unchanged.

Conclusions

In this chapter I described a case in which participatory design was used to develop a fourth-level HCI course. The students enrolled in the course were the co-designers, and the outcomes of the design exercise were implemented in the same semester the design took place. I tackled the three challenges mentioned in the Introduction, as follows:

Fitting the participatory design exercise into the available lecture time without compromising on content covered was doable. The first two-hour lecture and an assignment were allocated to the participatory design exercise. The outcomes were immediately analysed so that the first topic could be covered two weeks later in the second lecture period. Since lectures take place once every two weeks, the lecturer could implement the outcomes on a week-by-week basis. Although I found it challenging to be developing course content throughout the semester, the pay-off for co-designing the course with students compensated for the difficulties.

The participatory design exercise also served as an experiential learning exercise whereby students learnt how to use a core HCI design technique. In subsequent lectures, the lecturer used this participatory design exercise as a practical example whenever it was relevant (e.g., when we discussed user-centred design, user experience, and, of course, participatory design).

The outcomes of two rounds of course evaluation showed that students felt very positive about the course. There was clear appreciation for the participatory way in which the syllabus was designed. Only one student commented that he or she would have preferred a predesigned course. Also, no major changes needed to be made to the syllabus for the 2015 semester, based on the outcomes of the evaluation.

In general, my experience confirmed Bovill et al.'s (2011) belief that treating students as peers who are able to provide valuable input will develop a good relationship between lecturers and students. Students seemed to communicate easily with me, and there was lots of active participation in all lectures. Their positive evaluation of my "Interpersonal relationships" and "Attitude" supports this. I attribute the success of the course to the general tone that was set by starting the course with the participatory design exercise. In 2014, 41 students were enrolled for this elective course, and this number increased to 77 in 2015. This drastic increase can be explained by the 2014 students' positive reports reaching the 2015 students through word of mouth.

Would I do it again? I was motivated to follow the participatory course design route by my insecurity in a new teaching environment and lack of experience in teaching postgraduate BCom students. The co-design exercise solved my problems and had many positive side effects, as discussed above. In 2015 I continued the participatory design exercise by reporting in the first lecture on the evaluation results of the previous class and discussing the emerging complaints with the new students. I did not change the syllabus, and in 2015 the results and evaluations again confirmed that the choices made in 2014 were successful. I now have a better understanding of the context and the mind of a BCom Honours Informatics student and do not feel that it is necessary to redo the participatory design exercise every year. If, however, I was asked to teach any course or student group that I did not have experience with, I would without doubt follow the participatory course design route again.

The only thing I would change if I did it again would be to let the students form their own groups for the group exercise in Lecture 1 and not to allow other academic staff members to participate in this exercise. In retrospect, I believe that the grouping of students with people they do not know aggravated the problem of stronger individual voices influencing the outcomes. If students were grouped with their friends, this may have allowed for better collaboration within the groups.

References

ACM & IEEE (2013). Computer Science Curricula 2013. Curriculum Guidelines for Undergraduate Degree Programs in Computer Science, December, 20 2013, at www.acm.org/education/CS2013-final-report.pdf. Last accessed 28/3/2015.

Bovill, C., Cook-Sather, A., & Felten, P. (2011). Students as co-creators of teaching approaches, course design, and curricula: implications for academic developers. *International Journal for Academic Development*, 16(2), 133–145.

Churchill, E.F., Bowser, A., & Preece, J. (2013). Teaching and learning human-computer interaction: past, present, and future. *Interactions*, March and April 2013, 44–53.

Dell, N., Vaidyanathan, V., Medhi, I., Cutrell, E., & Thies, W. (2012). Yours is better!: participant response bias in HCI. *Proceedings of the SIGCHI Conference on Human Factors in Computing Systems*, May 2012 (pp. 1321–1330). ACM.

DiSalvo, B., & DiSalvo, C. (2014). Designing for democracy in education: participatory design and the learning sciences. In *Learning and Becoming in Practice: The International Conference of the Learning Sciences* (ICLS), Vol. 2, pp. 793–799.

Fincher, S., Cairns, P., & Blackwell, A.F. (2012). A Contextualized Curriculum for HCI. Workshop summary in the *Proceedings of CHI 2012*, May 5–10, 2012, Austin, TX. pp. 2707–2710.

Gelderblom, H., & Van der Merwe, A. (2015). Applying human-computer interaction (HCI) design principles and techniques in HCI course design. In Coleman, E. (ed.), *Renewing ICT Teaching and Learning: Building on the Past to Create New Energies*. Proceedings of the 44th Annual Southern African Computer Lecturers Association Conference (SACLA 2015), 1–3 July 2015, Johannesburg, South Africa, pp. 7–18.

Jacobson, I., Booch, G., Rumbaugh, J., Rumbaugh, J., & Booch, G. (1999). *The Unified Software Development Process* (Vol. 1). Reading, PA: Addison-Wesley.

Spinuzzi, C. (2005). The methodology of participatory design. *Technical Communication*, 52(2), 163–174.

Vredenburg, K., Mao, J.-Y., Smith, P. W., & Carey, T. (2002). A survey of user-centered design practice. In *Proceedings of the SIGCHI Conference on Human Factors in Computing Systems* (pp. 471–478). Minneapolis, MN: ACM.

Wasserman, A. I. (1996). Toward a discipline of software engineering. *IEEE Software*, 13(6), 23.

Case Studies of Participatory Design in Learning Research

8

DESIGNING LEARNING PATHWAYS IN A COMPLEX LEARNING ECOLOGY

A Research-Practice Partnership Focused on Interest Brokering

Marti Louw, Nina Barbuto, and Kevin Crowley

In this chapter we describe an exploratory, design-led research project to align a top-down learning innovation and improvement agenda (to support youth-centered, interest-driven learning pathways) with the needs and interests of a local community-based creative arts and technology organization. To negotiate alignment of stakeholder priorities and values, draw on theoretical learning sciences research to inform practice, and to guide us toward productive innovation, we turned to a participatory, design-centered process to enact theory and creatively synthesize multiple perspectives for action. Our claim is that design-led modes of inquiry are especially needed to respond to ambitious visions of educational transformation and funding directives, which leave much unresolved detail to be determined and realized by local practitioners, leaders, and learners. Our case study provides one example of this kind of design-led learning innovation that builds on and extends our understanding of interest development, and describes its local application in a series of design probes to support forming and deepening interest-driven learning pathways for youth.

A growing body of empirical research takes an ecological perspective to account for the dynamic nature of learning that evolves across the multiple and diverse settings in which youth spend their time (Brofenbrenner 1979; Barron 2006; Banks et al. 2007; Bricker & Bell 2014). A related line of learning research emphasizes the critical enabling roles adult and peer relationships play in supporting youth learning and interest development (Barron et al. 2009; Weiss & Lopez 2015). Interest formation itself is highly contextual and deepens through socially supported "lines of practice" that span contexts and enable identity formation in culturally valued life activities (Hidi & Renninger 2006; Azevedo 2011; Järvelä & Renninger 2014). Rather than examining learning in episodic encounters in a particular learning setting, researchers are now thinking about designing for "connected learning" where learning experiences fit together to form coherent, interest-driven learning pathways that sustain and develop into the future (Ito et al. 2013; Sefton-Green 2016). This broader ecological view has led to calls for a more coordinated and intentional brokering of interest-based learning opportunities for youth across time and place (Rosenberg et al. 2014; Ching et al. 2015; Russell et al. 2017).

An expanded view of youths' learning lives has inspired the implementation of new intervention approaches such as a set of regional City of Learning[1] initiatives to build and study coordinated ecologies of opportunity through networked infrastructures, programs, and platforms that seek to equitably open learning pathways for youth to pursue and deepen their interests across settings (Barron et al. 2014). In our region, the learning pathways agenda has been shaped in part by a local backbone organization and associated network of organizations (Dolle et al. 2013).[2] To support this effort, a local foundation funded a university-based research team of "design fellows" to collaborate with a set of local learning providers to interpret and support efforts to create learning pathways of opportunity for youth.

Our case study focuses on one of the design fellows (the first author) who was embedded in a "community arts with technology" organization. The case describes how a participatory design process enabled a professionally diverse team to first reckon with multiple perspectives on what constitutes valued learning, and to collectively define and ground the abstract concept of learning pathways in ways that are locally relevant, valued, and actionable with respect to learning providers, youth and their families

Case Study in Design-Led Learning Innovation Research

How do families, mentors, and caring adults in youths' lives identify learning opportunities and help youth make choices that cultivate the development of their individual interests? How can we help families interpret complex citywide learning ecosystems in ways that make learning pathways apparent?

To better understand how families navigate Pittsburgh's informal learning ecosystem (the physical, social, and culturally situated sites of learning locally available) and broker learning opportunities, our research-practice partnership focused on the decision-making criteria that families and adult caregivers use when choosing out-of-school experiences for their children (Figure 8.1). In particular, we explored how parents and mentors find, value, and encourage children's participation in creative technology and maker-based program offerings. The framing of this study emerged through a participatory process where stakeholders engaged in learning design are positioned as co-creators and included from the inception of the project through data analysis, interpretation,

FIGURE 8.1 Moving from a Program-Centric to a Family-Centric View of Learning Opportunities

and dissemination activities. The founding director of a local informal learning provider (ASSEMBLE),[3] her teaching artist staff, and the volunteer board were included in problem formulation and goal setting for the design of this study, as well as in the data synthesis and presentation of findings at professional and academic conferences.

As with many nonprofit organizations, ASSEMBLE has the perennial goal of increasing the recruitment and participation of youth in its programs, and in particular reaching the underserved community in its immediate neighborhood. The organization uses its website, associated social media channels, tabling events, paper fliers, direct mailings, and word-of-mouth reputation as the primary strategies for raising awareness and interest in programming.

To address ASSEMBLE's goal of increasing and broadening participation in their programs, we wanted to better understand how families navigate the Pittsburgh learning ecology of out-of-school time (OST) programs—such as summer camps, weekend workshops, after-school activities, and family events—and select these opportunities for, and with, their children. In particular, we sought to understand how adults decide to encourage (or not) children's participation in creative technology-rich programs (e.g., robotics, digital media production, coding, and maker activities) being offered around the city.

Study Design and Methods

Our research questions and study design sprang from a collective problematizing process where the expanded research-practice team engaged in facilitated discussions over several months in order to surface organizational challenges and opportunities. Moreover, we were able to identify key problems of practice related to the regional charge to develop learning pathways as part of the Pittsburgh 2014 Cities of Learning[4] initiative. Much conversation centered on the challenge of reaching parents and recruiting underserved youth in ASSEMBLE's economically distressed home neighborhood. The team decided to focus our design research efforts on better understanding how families choose to participate in informal learning activities.

Parent Way-Finding in a Complex Learning Ecology

To reframe this challenge as a learning research design question, we developed and piloted a parent way-finding study to (1) understand how parents and supporting adults in youth lives become aware of organizationally hosted informal learning opportunities for their children and characterize their information-gathering needs and habits, and (2) identify the decision-making criteria that families use when choosing technology-rich programming with their children. We used a mixed-method approach to examine how supporting adults (i.e., parents, mentors, caregivers) find out about creative technology programs, and surveyed various pragmatic and logistical factors that might influence their decision to support a youth's participation in a program.

For the study 10 adult caregivers were recruited from two ASSEMBLE programs: "Learn to Scratch" and "Make It," both aimed at preteen audiences. These adults included parents as well as two mentors, and one parent-child combination also participated. Of the participants, four were male, six female, and four were of African American descent. These caregivers were invited at drop-off and pickup times to engage in a program flyer think-aloud & sort activity (Ericsson & Simon 1998), where they told us what they were thinking as they read through 10 short program descriptions offered by various informal learning providers around town, including museums, community organizations, arts groups, and after-school programs. Adult participants then sorted these programs descriptions into "likely," "maybe," and "unlikely" piles and described their reasoning for these selections out loud. In addition, participants responded to a semi-structured interview about their child's interest areas, how they find and select informal learning programs, and they were asked to describe their family's approach and philosophy to informal, out-of-school learning time. All the interviews were audio-recorded and transcribed. We then analyzed the qualitative data in two rounds, first with researchers and ASSEMBLE staff in a Data Synthesis Workshop using an adapted collective affinity diagramming method (Simonsen & Friberg 2014) described next, and then in a second round where the research team identified and collapsed thematic categories in the dataset (Chi 1997).

Data Synthesis Workshop

As a vital step in the co-design process, the researchers and ASSEMBLE staff worked together to review and make sense of the parent interview data. This workshop activity enabled us to listen closely to parent concerns and priorities, jointly synthesize and identify patterns in the data, and finally to discuss the implications and design opportunities. Five members from ASSEMBLE participated, including teaching artists, the director (second author), and a volunteer board member together with the research team in a three-hour workshop session. For the workshop, each participant was given an envelope containing excerpted comments from the full parent interview transcripts presented as color-coded strips of paper. Initially unknown to participants, the color codes were related to parent gender and ethnicity.

First, the group individually went through each parent interview transcript (edited only for off-topic chat and process comments) and used green dots to mark positive statements and red dots to mark negative ones. Each participant was given a set of silver stars to call out particular quotes of interest they wished to discuss with the group. This seeded the next activity, where we began a visual clustering exercise to group comments into categories, first reading them aloud, then moving them into emergent groupings and labeling them. After formulating high-level categories, we revealed the gender and ethnicity color-codes to check for any visually prevalent clusters of parent talk based on these demographic factors (see Figure 8.2).

FIGURE 8.2 Images from the Design Workshop Activity Showing the Color-Coded Transcriptions, Coding, and Examples of Shared Categories Generated during Our Analysis of Parent Talk (*continued*)

FIGURE 8.2 Images from the Design Workshop Activity Showing the Color-Coded Transcriptions, Coding, and Examples of Shared Categories Generated during Our Analysis of Parent Talk (*continued*)

FIGURE 8.2 Images from the Design Workshop Activity Showing the Color-Coded Transcriptions, Coding, and Examples of Shared Categories Generated during Our Analysis of Parent Talk

Design Research Findings and Insights

Our parent way-finding study highlighted the important enabling role adults play in supporting youth participation in informal learning opportunities. In particular, we see evidence of the "learning broker" role Barron and her colleagues characterized in their work describing the different roles parents assume when attempting to advance their children's technological fluency (Barron et al. 2009; Barron et al. 2013). These parental learning support roles include collaborating with them, learning from them, brokering outside learning opportunities for them, providing nontechnical support to them, or hiring them to do technical work. In their parent typology, a learning broker "seeks learning opportunities for children by networking, the Internet, peer networks, and other information sources. This adult signs a child up and provides necessary support for endeavor." In our interviews we saw this brokering role articulated in four ways: logistical brokering (e.g., transportation to a site, registration), financial brokering (program fees, bus fares, material costs), transactional brokering (tapping personal networks for opportunities, recommendations, reviews, and advice), and sourcing/vetting forms of brokering (searching for safe and appropriate high-quality programs, activities, and events).

In survey questions, we asked adults to weigh the relative importance of six factors influencing the selection of informal learning opportunities for their children: ease of getting there, cost of program/event, when offered (schedule), where held (location), hosting organization, and activity focus. These program factors were ranked on a scale of 1–3, with 1 being not important, 2 being somewhat

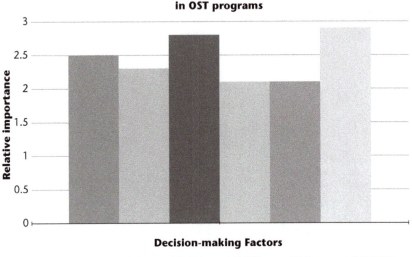

FIGURE 8.3 Relative Importance of Six Decision-Making Factors That Influence Youth Participation in OST Program Activities (n = 10)

important, and 3 being very important (see Figure 8.3). Parent participants rated, on average, all six factors as at least somewhat important, with location of the organization hosting the program scoring the lowest in terms of relative importance. Cost and ease of getting to a program ranked slightly higher in terms of relative importance. Participants indicated the most important factors influencing their support for a child's attendance in a program revolved around when a program was offered (scheduling), ease of getting there, and the nature of program activities. The program activity focus was consistently selected as very important by both parents and adults mentor participants.

Our analysis of interviews and think-alouds from the adult brokering study provided insights into why adults rated the program activity focus as very important, and shed light on the considerations parents weigh when choosing an informal learning activity for their child. Not surprisingly, we found that a common sort criterion adult caregivers use to judge the appropriateness of a creative technology program is their perception of a child's interest in the topic.

Interest-Brokering Considerations

At the heart of much of the parent talk we heard was a deep concern for cultivating children's interests through informal, out-of-school learning experiences. Parents of primarily tween-aged youth frequently mentioned they would have discussions and involve their child in the decision-making. We coded for these interest considerations and found that parents described interest in terms of four distinct dimensions: matching, exposing, expanding, and deepening.

A. Matching Interests

When reviewing program descriptions, many parents first scanned the copy for interest matches. They used words like "my kid likes or doesn't; is interested in or into" to quickly weed through program descriptions and assess programs fit for their child:

> So the first thing I always look for is anything science related because when it goes into anything just straight art related, they kind of pull back from it, but if it's tied with something science for whatever reason, that's their gateway into anything. [Father (S09) / Son, age 12]
>
> . . . Intro to Video Game Programming, um, I think just from the description, he would be interested in that. So almost no question that this matches his interests and would be worth investigating. [Father (S02) / Son, age 13]

B. Exposing to New Interests

A second form of interest brokering talk we heard from parents revolved around exposure, and the need to provide youth with opportunities to find and explore new areas of potential interest by introducing them to unfamiliar topics and contexts, and giving them access to different kinds of tools, materials, and forms of expertise. Several parents were admittedly coercive in their attempts to encourage youth to move outside their comfort zones to discover and develop new interest areas. We heard this in-vivo exposure-seeking talk most frequently with mentors and our African American parent participants:

> She says she just wants to sketch. But I want her to be exposed to a list of, a lot of different mediums, lots of different types of art. And again, I know the importance of the STEAM education initiatives and I'd like her to be exposed to that in a way that's interesting to her. [Mother (S08) / Daughter, age 12]
>
> I would love to get involved with these organizations and introduce them to the tech world, introduce them to the making world, introduce them to art, introduce them to everything. But if it's not affordable . . . [Mentor (S04) / Son, age 11]

C. Expanding an Existing Interest

A third category of interest brokering talk involved using a youth's expressed interest in one affinity area as a seed to expand interest in another. Parents talked about using a child's existing interest as a hook to pull them into trying out a related but unfamiliar activity. We also heard parents wanting to use a strong interest in one area to broaden or shore up learning in a perceived deficit area. These caregiver comments often centered on taking a youth's interest in computers or video games and trying to bend that interest toward a more "productive" or creative output through a game design or coding class, or by connecting a youth's interest in art to technology though STEAM kinds of programs.

> So this would be really interesting *Introduction to Video Game Programming* because they're interested in programming and they always talk about doing it for video game stuff. But they never make the connection between the two. So that one I'm drawn to just to give them a real sense of what it actually would take or be like. [Father (P09) / Son, age 12]
>
> She's interested in crafts, art, science, drawing sketches specifically and so forth . . . . and learn about the chemistry behind the awesome printmaking process. So it's art and science, which I think is good for her because art is just like the perfect avenue for her to start learning, you know, about more science and advanced science and technology. [Mother (S08) / Daughter, age 12]
>
> So he's interested in computers. I mean we tried to steer him towards more the producer-producing stuff, as opposed to just consuming it. [Father (S07) / Daughter age 7, Son age 10]

D. Deepening an Interest

A fourth interest brokering category of comments centered on finding ways to support deepening an area of interest. Families were looking for, and often not finding, informal learning opportunities to "level up" and build on emerging creative technology skills and talents. Parents expressed frustration at not being able to find stepping-stones on which to deepen and extend interdisciplinary digital making, coding, and technology-infused interest areas.

> [My child] has learned Scratch, that will definitely be something that we try to do continuity on things that he's already done. The question would be—whether or not it's at a new level—if it's a beginner level that he's already done, he may not want to do that and look for something that's more advanced. [. . .] So looking for the continuation of the next level up is one of the things that we look for, for sure. [Father (P09) Son, age 12]
>
> The electronics stuff there . . . you do it once and you're done with it. [Mother (S05) / Daughter, age 11]
>
> They've taken one and then another and it's been too similar to the thing they already did, so it wasn't very excited because they already learned everything they were gonna learn out of it. They needed the next level. [Father (S09) / Son, age 12]

Lastly, the data synthesis workshop marked a turning point in the embedded design fellow's relationship with ASSEMBLE, as it helped convince a somewhat skeptical staff about the value of research activities and the use of "data" and evidence to uncover new opportunities; and it helped built trust in the interpretation and authenticity of the findings. Subsequent to this workshop event, the research team was more frequently included in internal e-mail chains with staff members, and invited to a broader set of ASSEMBLE board meetings and planning activities. This trust-based relationship is vital to productive research-practice collaborations.

Design Implications and Probes

Communication Design Issues

As parents read through program descriptions several communication design issues were noted. Parents appreciated graphic treatments in the copy that boldly called out date, time, age, location, and cost information that could be gleaned in quick scan. Not all program descriptions clearly stated age ranges or limits. And when an age was listed, adults also questioned whether participation in a technology-related offering should be strictly based on age and not competency. In several cases parents had to reread copy to determine if a program was a one-off event or a series, and guess at whether "drop-in" or partial participation was allowed. To address these communication issues, providers should indicate whether a program is an open studio arrangement that can support learners at different skills and ages, or instead follows a more planned instructional sequence that requires consistent attendance for progress.

With regard to program descriptions and informational copy, the use of jargon can be a double-edged sword. Terms such as "tween," "making," "STEAM" and "hack" can be appealing, and indicative of a certain kind of cultural affiliation to those who recognize it. But several parents were put off by this jargon, and tripped on unfamiliar and insider terms that in several cases resulted in parents rejecting a potentially appropriate program for their child. Parents also honed in on the specific description of the activity to determine whether the experience described would be worthwhile in terms of offering something special or fun. Parents commented positively when activities seemed unique and provided access to novel materials, specialized tools and expertise, or offered hands-on learning opportunities not available at school or home. More than organizational reputation, university affiliated "brands," such as MIT SCRATCH and the CMU CREATE Lab's Hummingbird, were noted by several parents, and these names seemed to function locally as a seal of approval for technology education programs. Having consistent and related programming strands from one semester to the next also helps parent find and fit programs around seasonal constraints and future schedule expectations. Lastly, parents often tried to gauge the likely expertise and instructional talent of the staff who would be facilitating the programs.

FIGURE 8.4 Design Probe 1: Refining Key Information Callouts, and Reducing Jargon in Program Communications

With ASSEMBLE staff, we piloted simple design probes such as making intentional changes to copy in communication materials (web descriptions, print flyers), minimizing insider language, and clarifying jargon to improve communications with parents and students (see Figure 8.4). At staff and board meetings, we presented our findings, including the important role of interest brokering and how adults use interest matching, exposing, expanding, and deepening as key decision criteria when choosing informal learning opportunities for their children.

We then discussed suggestions for how this adult role in interest brokering might be used to improve communications and the understanding of learning pathways. Ideas generated during these meetings included communication strategies ASSEMBLE staff could engage in, such as talking directly to families about a youth's interests at community outreach events instead of just promoting the particular programs that ASSEMBLE is trying to "sell." Communications could describe how OST and enrichment activities are important for youth to exercise creativity, build technology fluency, learn hands-on skills, and deepen interests, all of which can have positive academic, civic, and vocational impacts. Other hooks and value propositions include reminding parents that ASSEMBLE is a place and a community in which to develop a creative arts, technology-savvy maker identity and network with a supportive community of practice. Communicating this character of the space, and connecting youth with local and online communities of practice, would entail rethinking communications with an intentional focus on connecting youth interest with opportunities—a move that we discuss next.

Family Engagement Design Opportunities

Starting from our adult interest brokering findings, the team set out to develop a set of design probes for ASSEMBLE's "Make It" and "Gotta Scratch" digital fabrication and media-based coding programs. We prototyped two new kinds of parent communication formats, and explored ways to connect families to future learning opportunities and events for their youth. We also worked with program facilitators on ways to flag and share relevant online opportunities to encourage youth's emerging and developing interests.

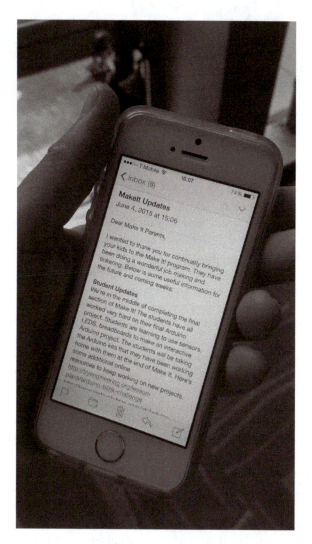

FIGURE 8.5a   Design Probe 2: *What's Up* and *What's Next* Messaging to Parents

FIGURE 8.5b Design Probe 3: Reframing Conversations around Interest Brokering at Family Engagement Events

To be good learning brokers, adults need ongoing ways to remain aware of their children's evolving interests and strengths, find resources, and develop networks of learning supports to encourage those interests and associated skills development (Rosenberg et al. 2012). They also require technology supports that fit seamlessly into the family's existing communication practices (Lewin & Luckin 2010). With this in mind, we piloted "What's Up" and "What's Next" communication probes with adults during the Make It program to offer learning supports (see Figure 8.5a). We began by surveying adults as to whether they wanted these kinds of communications, and what type of content and formats they preferred. Our goal was to brief adults in person (at pickup) and via messaging (e-mail/text) to provide insights on what children enjoyed, gravitated toward, shined at, and where they might go next in terms of other programs, resources, and events happening around town. We also e-mailed adult caretakers activity updates, and created a youth-facing blog for the program with curated, safe, high-quality online resources and community sites that instructors frequented, so that youth could continue to use the technology (e.g., Arduino kits) in new projects and find online support once the program was completed.

Another touchstone idea we used to help focus the organization's work around learning pathways was to view ASSEMBLE program experiences as part of a larger "cycle of engagement" (Goffman 1963). This perspective reminded the program design team to consider holistically not only the program activities, but also the beginning phase (awareness and attraction phases of an engagement) as well as closure and "what's next" transitional moments following an informal learning experience. This cycle of engagement framing also moved us from a provider to a learner-centric focus that strategically considers how children develop, nurture, and grow an interest over time.

We discussed goals and engagement approaches for community tabling events that would focus on learner-centric interest brokering, rather than a program recruitment frame. Our interviews suggested that matching, exposing, expanding, and deepening considerations operate as key factors adults use to select informal learning program opportunities for their youth. At outreach events, ASSEMBLE staff began to talk with parents about their youth's interests in these terms, as well as opening up discussion about learning beyond school walls (see Figure 8.5b). Other communications materials contained information and invitations to ASSEMBLE's upcoming Youth Showcase, local open studios, a Youth Maker Night event at the Children's Museum of Pittsburgh, and a sponsored invitation to a Maker Event in Detroit. The goal of these communications was to help families find places, tools, resources, and social learning environments that allow children to experiment with creative activities aligned to their interests.

We brainstormed with ASSEMBLE staff other ways to be mindful of the rhythms of family life and discussed adding calendar reminders about public school in-service days to the internal calendar, and adding reminders to start the summer camp marketing push in February, when working parents start to commit to camps for the summer. Other ideas included offering pop-up maker programming on snow days for busy working parents. We also considered more conceptual ideas such as starting to think about the organization not just as a provider of programs, but also serving as a guide and way-finding resource that supports a learner's journey. ASSEMBLE already functions to some degree in this way, with an enticing table of flyers with hip-looking events and programs, promoting not just their own programs but citywide opportunities as well (Figure 8.1). This lightly curated set of STEAM activities around town is a useful resource for youth and families to discover, and something parents told us that they wished existed more formally online in a centralized resource of informal learning opportunities and interest pathway guides.

Conclusion

Pathways in youth sports and performing arts have, in many ways, mastered the learning progression aspects of program design and parent communication with clear skill development trajectories and participation structures that grow with interest, age, and competency. However, in relation to creative digital making and technology programming, we heard repeatedly from adults that the next steps for children who had completed a program were lacking, hard to find, redundant, or did not "level up" as kids grew. Our small sample reflects what is perhaps a larger issue in youth informal learning programming: it is often fragmented, redundant, and potentially "dead ended" (Russell et al. 2017). Adults were voluble about how hard they had to work to help their children find appropriate learning pathways to deepen skills and interests. The highly structured parental approach to enrichment and the "concerted cultivation" of youth's informal learning activities also tends to correlate with higher socioeconomic status (Lareau 2003). We know from research that, when adults are able to broker learning opportunities successfully, it can be life-altering for the youth (Crowley et al. 2015). But for adults to play that critical role, culturally appropriate and socially appealing on-ramps to learning pathways must exist and be evident, when decisions are being made about where and how youth spend their time (Barron et al. 2014; Martin et al. 2016). Moreover, the adults supporting youth themselves must have "cosmopolitan" social networks in order to effectively broker diverse learning opportunities (Ching et al. 2016). This brokering of opportunity is all the more important because data shows a widening class gap in parental investment in children's out-of-school "enrichment" activities and, at the same time, a pernicious drop in the availability of school-based extracurricular activities (Putnam 2016).

"Unhiding" learning pathways will require a regional set of learning providers and communities to intentionally organize and make interest-driven learning pathways visible and navigable to youth and adults. This exploratory learning design research highlights the ways in which adult caregivers operationalize interest in terms of matching, exposing, expanding, and deepening—and use these features of interest development to way-find and broker learning opportunities for their children.

In conclusion, our work suggests three sources of design inspiration:

1. Parents and supporting adults in youth lives play a vital role in brokering appropriate learning opportunities for children.
2. Adults struggle to navigate complex and fragmented learning ecologies to find places, tools, resources, and social networks that will allow youth to experiment with creative, technology-infused activities aligned with their interests.
3. Learning brokering requires a solid, ongoing awareness and insight into a child's specific and evolving interests (and skills), as well as trusted guides to link those interests to appropriate opportunities.

Reflections Design, Learning Research, and Educational Innovation

The call for design, or design thinking, in learning research is not new. Against the backdrop of student uprisings on college campuses in the late 1960s, Joseph Schwab, a progressive 20th-century educational reform scholar and noted raconteur, expressed deep frustration with the ongoing failure of educational research to effect lasting change. He specifically blamed the fragmentary and incomplete nature of contemporary educational theories, and pointed to the inability of applied research to effect positive change. Schwab believed moving educational research and practice forward would require paying much more attention to what he called the eclectic and practical arts of deciding and doing (Schwab 1971). The "Eclectic Arts" are the means by which theory and insights are selected and readied for practical use through the arts of polyfocal conspectus, integration, and framing. By "Practical

Arts," Schwab references the arts of perception, problematization, prescription, and commitment that enable groups to decide what course of action to take. What Schwab was describing was the need for what we might call design today.

Design research and practice at its most ambitious seeks to be the integrative 21st-century discipline that combines the eclectic arts of finding, selecting, and synthesizing multiple perspectives and theories with the practical arts of seeking to perceive, formulate problems, deliberate on solutions, and take planned action (Buchanan 1992). Since Schwab's time, design as an inquiry approach, an array of methods, and a set of disciplinary commitments has increasingly surfaced in educational research discourse and practice. In the early '90s Ann Brown and colleagues began to call for situated design experiments (Brown 1992; Collins 1992; Design-Based Research Collective 2003) as a way to make learning theory more sensitive to the particulars of real-world conditions, enable a methodologically grounded process for reformulating questions, and make design changes in response to findings that emerged during the research process. The field has since continued to explore disciplinary connections between design and research (e.g., special issues of *The Journal of the Learning Sciences* [Vol. 13, No. 1, 2004) and the *Educational Researcher* [Vol. 32, No. 1, 2003]), debating the complexities, fuzziness, and slow theoretic yield of design-based research in applied settings. "Design" in learning sciences has become a term that signals a practice-oriented research agenda that will intentionally adapt and evolve in response to iterative design challenges in the learning intervention or object under study.

In 2011 Penuel and colleagues began advocating for design-based implementation research (DBIR), to address the challenges of effectively scaling successful educational programs. DBIR draws on participatory design traditions, with its roots in Scandinavian workplace democracy movements, as a means to bring about a more grounded and inclusive research process to large-scale implementation projects (Penuel et al. 2011) The DBIR model emphasizes the need to focus on "persistent problems of practice" that often thwart efforts to scale and sustain policies and programs in education. Participatory design methods and approaches are called upon to enable greater stakeholder involvement, elicit tacit issues, and give problem-solving agency to a broader set of affected actors in order improve teaching and learning as well as the culturally sensitive "infrastructuring" of learning systems (Simonsen & Robertson 2012). Equity-oriented researchers push even further, calling for the positional and relational work involved in design-based educational interventions to be made explicit so as to reveal the underlying power and racial dimensions present in research-practice endeavors, and strongly encourage researchers to be more fully open to community-valued definitions of learning (Vakil et al. 2016).

Our case study follows in a participatory design tradition and contains many of the practical theory-testing and knowledge building features associated with learning sciences research (Santo et al. 2017). However, we think of this work primarily as an example of participatory design informed by the learning sciences, or a form of research through design where the knowledge is embodied in the design (Santo et al. 2017; Zimmerman et al. 2007). Design is a form-giving mode of inquiry that strives to democratically involve users in a full innovation cycle that includes shared problem-finding (envisioning) and defining (framing) and continues through project realization and engagement in outcomes. In doing so, design shifts the role of stakeholders from informants to participants in the design research process. For research on learning, we believe that a participatory design-led approach offers a strong set of disciplinary practices to reckon with multiple value-laden learning goals, wrestle with the application of incomplete or fragmented theory, and finally to help ground sweeping visions of educational change that speak only partially to the complex, locally situated learning design problems at hand.

Acknowledgments

This design fellowship was supported by a grant from the Grable Foundation to the University of Pittsburgh. Any opinions, findings, and conclusions expressed are those of the authors and do not necessarily reflect the views of the sponsoring intuitions. We are grateful to the other design fellows, Megan Bathgate, Peter Wardrip, and Stacy Kehoe, for their camaraderie and the many rich discussions on learning pathways and research-practice partnerships; to Drs. Chris Schunn and Tom Akiva for their guidance and support; and to Dr. Lauren Allen for her close reading of this manuscript. This work would not be possible without the committed participation of our co-design partner ASSEMBLE's staff, and we are indebted to the parents who kindly agreed to participate and contribute their time and thoughts to this study.

1   https://hivelearningnetworks.org/; http://lrng.org/cities
2   http://remakelearning.org/
3   ASSEMBLE is a creative arts with technology organization that serves the community as an out-of-school time provider of o-STEAM learning programs, a youth maker space, multi-use events venue, and gallery curating the work of local artists. www .assemblepgh.org
4   Learning pathways were a feature of the 2014 *Cities of Learning* initiative in Pittsburgh; http://hivepgh.sproutfund.org/about-hivepgh/welcome/

References

Azevedo, F. S. (2011). Lines of practice: A practice-centered theory of interest relationships. *Cognition and Instruction, 29*(2), 147–184.

Banks, J. A., Au, K. H., Ball, A. F., Bell, P., Gordon, E. W., Gutierrez, K., Heath, S. B., Lee, C. D., Lee, Y., Mahiri, J. , Nasir, N. S., Valdes, G., & Zhou, M. (2007). Learning in and out of school in diverse environments: Life-Long, Life-Wide, Life-Deep. Seattle, WA: UW Center for Multicultural Education & The LIFE Center.

Barron, B. (2006). Interest and self-sustained learning as catalysts of development: A learning ecologies perspective. *Human Development, 49*, 193–224.

Barron, B., Gomez, K., Pinkard, N., & Martin, C. K. (2014). *The Digital Youth Network: Cultivating Digital Media Citizenship in Urban Communities*. Cambridge, MA: MIT Press.

Barron, B., Martin, C. K., Takeuchi, L., & Fithian, R. (2009). Parents as learning partners in the development of technological fluency. *International Journal of Learning and Media*, 1(2), 55–77.

Barron, B., Wise, S., & Martin, C. K. (2013). Creating within and across life spaces: The role of a computer clubhouse in a child's learning ecology. In B. Bevan, P. Bell, R. Stevens, & A. Razfar (Eds.), *LOST Opportunities* (pp. 99-118). Dordrecht: Springer.

Bell, P., Bricker, L., Reeve, S., Zimmerman, H. T., & Tzou, C. (2013). Discovering and supporting successful learning pathways of youth in and out of school: Accounting for the development of everyday expertise across settings. In B. Bevan, P. Bell, R. Stevens, & A. Razfar (Eds.), *LOST Opportunities* (pp. 99-118). Dordrecht: Springer.

Bricker, L. A., & Bell, P. (2014). "What comes to mind when you think of science? The perfumery!": Documenting science-related cultural learning pathways across contexts and timescales. *Journal of Research in Science Teaching*, 51(3), 260–285.

Bronfenbrenner, U. (1979). *The Ecology of Human Development: Experiments by Nature and Design*. Cambridge, MA: Harvard University Press.

Brown, A. L. (1992). Design experiments: Theoretical and methodological challenges in creating complex interventions in classroom settings. *Journal of the Learning Sciences*, 2(2), 141–178.

Buchanan, R. (1992). Wicked problems in design thinking. *Design Issues*, 8(2), 5–21.

Chi, M. T. H. (1997). Quantifying qualitative analyses of verbal data: A practical guide. *Journal of the Learning Sciences*, 6(3), 271–315.

Ching, D., Santo, R., Hoadley, C., & Peppler, K. (2015). *On-Ramps, Lane Changes, Detours and Destinations: Building Connected Learning Pathways in Hive NYC through Brokering Future Learning Opportunities*. New York: Hive Research Lab.

Ching, D., Santo, R., Hoadley, C., & Peppler, K. (2016). Not just a blip in someone's life: Integrating brokering practices into out-of-school programming as a means of supporting and expanding youth futures. *On the Horizon*, 24(3), 296–312.

Collins, A. (1992). Toward a design science of education. In E. Scanlon and T. O'Shea (Eds.), *New Directions in Educational Technology* (pp. 15–22). Berlin: Springer-Verlag.

Crowley, K., Barron, B.J., Knutson, K., & Martin, C. (2015). Interest and the development of pathways to science. In K. A. Renninger, M. Nieswandt, and S. Hidi (Eds.), *Interest in Mathematics and Science Learning and Related Activity*. Washington, DC: AERA.

Design-Based Research Collective. (2003). Design-based research: An emerging paradigm for educational inquiry. *Educational Researcher*, 32(1), 5–8.

Dolle, J. R., Gomez, L. M., Russell, J. L., & Bryk, A. S. (2013). More than a network: Building professional communities for educational improvement. *National Society for the Study of Education Yearbook*, 112(2), 443-463.

Ericsson, K. A., & Simon, H. A. (1998). How to study thinking in everyday life: Contrasting think-aloud protocols with descriptions and explanations of thinking. *Mind, Culture, and Activity*, 5(3), 178-186.

Goffman, E. (1963). *Behavior in Public Places: Notes on the Social Organization of Gatherings*. Glencoe, IL: Free Press.

Hidi, S., & Renninger, K. A. (2006). The four-phase model of interest development. *Educational Psychologist*, 41(2), 111–127.

Ito, M., Gutiérrez, K., Livingstone, S., Penuel, B., Rhodes, J., Salen, K., Schor, J., Sefton-Green, J., & Watkins, S. C. (2013). Connected learning: An agenda for research and design. Digital Media and Learning Research Hub. Retrieved from http://dmlcentral.net/wp-content/uploads/files/connectedlearning_report.pdf

Järvelä, S., & Renninger, K.A. (2014). Designing for learning: Interest, motivation, and engagement. In R. K. Sawyer (Ed.), *The Cambridge Handbook of the Learning Sciences* (pp. 668–685). Cambridge: Cambridge University Press.

Lareau, A. (2003). *Unequal Childhoods: Class, Race, and Family Life.* Berkeley: University of California Press.

Lewin, C. & Luckin, R. (2010) Technology to support parental engagement in elementary education: Lessons learned from the UK. *Computers & Education, 54,* 749–758.

Martin, C. K., Pinkard, N., Erete, S., & Sandherr, J. (2016). Connections at the family level: Supporting parents and caring adults to engage youth in learning about computers and technology. In Y. Rankin & T. Jakita (Eds.), *Moving Students of Color from Consumers to Producers of Technology* (pp. 220–244). Hershey, PA: IGI Global.

Penuel, W.R., Fishman, B.J., Cheng, B.H., & Sabelli, N. (2011). Organizing research and development at the intersection of learning, implementation, and design. *Educational Researcher, 40*(7), 331–337.

Pinkard, N. (2015, June 12). An ecological view of equity: Reframing our understanding of youth access to connected learning opportunities. Presented at the Digital Media and Learning Conference, Los Angeles, CA.

Putnam, R. D. (2016). *Our Kids: The American Dream in Crisis.* New York: Simon & Schuster.

Rosenberg, H., Harris, E., & Wilkes, S. (2012). Joining forces: Families and out-of-school programs as partners in supporting children's learning and development. *Family Involvement Network of Educators (FINE) Newsletter,* (6)2. Retrieved from www.hfrp .org/out-of-school-time/publications-resources/joining-forces-families-and-out-of-school-programs-as-partners-in-supporting-children-s-learning-and-development

Rosenberg, H., Wilkes, S., & Harris, E. (2014). Bringing families into out-of-school time learning. *Journal of Expanded Learning Opportunities, 1*(1), 18–23.

Russell, J. L., Kehoe, S. & Crowley, K. (2017). Linking in and out-of-school learning. In K. Peppler (Ed.), *Encyclopedia of Out-of-School Learning.* Thousand Oaks, CA: Sage Publications.

Russell, J. L., Knutson, K., & Crowley, K. (2013). Informal learning organizations as part of an educational ecology: Lessons from collaboration across the formal-informal divide. *Journal of Educational Change, 14*(3), 259–281.

Santo, R., Ching, D., Peppler, K., & Hoadley, C. (2017). Participatory knowledge building within research-practice partnerships in education. *SAGE Research Methods Cases.* London: SAGE.

Schwab, J. J. (1971). The practical: Arts of eclectic. *School Review, 79*(4), 493–542.

Sefton-Green, J. (2016). Can studying learning across contexts change educational research or will it lead to the pedagocization of everyday life? In L. Erstad, Ola, K. Kumpulainen, A. Mäkitalo, K.C. Schröder, P. Pruulmann-Vengerfeldt, & T. Jóhannsdóttir (Eds.), *Learning Across Contexts in the Knowledge Society.* Rotterdam: Springer.

Simonsen, J., & Friberg, K. (2014). Collective analysis of qualitative data. In J. Simonsen, C. Svabo, S. M. Strandvad, K. Samson, M. Hertzum, & O. E. Hansen (Eds.), *Situated Design Methods.* Cambridge: MIT Press.

Vakil, S., McKinney de Royston, M., Suad Nasir, N. I., & Kirshner, B. (2016). Rethinking race and power in design-based research: Reflections from the field. *Cognition and Instruction, 34*(3), 194–209.

Weiss, H. B., & Lopez, M. E. (2015). Engage families for anywhere, anytime learning. *Phi Delta Kappan, 96*(7), 14–19.

Zimmerman, J., Forlizzi, J., & Evenson, S. (2007, April). Research through design as a method for interaction design research in HCI. *In Proceedings of the SIGCHI Conference on Human Factors in Computing Systems* (pp. 493–502). New York: ACM.

9

PARTICIPATORY DESIGN WITH CHILDREN IN THE AUTISM SPECTRUM

Access, Participation, Personalization, and Sustainability

Juan Pablo Hourcade

Reports of increasing rates of autism diagnoses among children (CDC, n.d.) have brought much attention to autism conditions during the past decade (since 2006). This increased attention has also been reflected in research on child-computer interaction, with a surge in publications on the design and use of technologies for children diagnosed with autism in the 2010s (Hourcade, 2015). I was part of that wave of work, stumbling into it by accident, when a colleague suggested that I use multi-touch displays my research team had been developing to design technologies specifically for this population. That suggestion led to three years of field research at an elementary school and two after-school programs, involving 86 children diagnosed with autism. This chapter focuses on one aspect of the research: our experiences conducting participatory design activities.

I arrived at this research having previously conducted participatory design activities with elementary school children (ages 6–12), as well as older adults, primarily following Druin's cooperative inquiry methods (Druin, 1999; Fails et al., 2013; Guha et al., 2013). The obvious challenge for us was that an autism diagnosis reveals that a child has deficits in social communication and interaction, and displays restricted, repetitive patterns of behavior, interests, or activities (Autism Speaks, n.d.). In particular, the challenges that children diagnosed with autism face regarding social communication and interaction seemed like a significant barrier to conducting participatory design activities.

In spite of these barriers, we were able to make children's preferences, needs, and abilities central to our research by going beyond what may be typically considered participatory design, and pursuing deep engagement. This chapter recounts our experiences, which are by no means a definitive account of how to design technologies with children diagnosed with autism, but at the very least include an approach that worked for my team and may be useful for yours.

Background on Autism

It is very tempting to think of autism as a medical condition where there is an underlying, diagnosable cause that leads to a set of symptoms. However, autism is not like that. There is no medical test for autism. Instead, an autism diagnosis relies solely on the existence of a set of symptoms. It is very possible then that autism is actually comprised of multiple medical conditions, all of which share some common symptoms.

Whether autism is related to multiple conditions or not, what is clear is that it encompasses a very wide spectrum with an enormous amount of diversity in how its symptoms occur. Some acknowledgment of this diversity is evident in the latest diagnostic manual used in the United States (Autism Speaks, n.d.), which designates three levels of severity for autism diagnoses, based on the amount of support an individual needs. This diversity of needs, abilities, and preferences is one of the aspects that surprised me the most when I began working with children diagnosed with autism. In my experience, the differences between children with similar autism diagnoses are usually greater than the differences between typically developing children. These differences can directly affect any participatory design activity as they are directly tied to a child's ability to communicate. For example, the spectrum ranges from children who do not speak at all to children who may have difficulty taking a break from speaking.

Although children seem to be the most visible face of the diagnosis, autism is not a condition that children grow out of; for most, the symptoms persist through adulthood. Because the symptoms can make it very difficult for some children to succeed at school or to live independently as adults (Billstedt et al., 2005; Eaves & Ho, 2008; Howlin et al., 2004), researchers and clinicians have developed various interventions intended to reduce the amount of support people diagnosed with autism ultimately require (e.g., Elkeseth, 2009; Weiss et al., 2008).

Autism and Technology

Despite decades of research on interventions, and great efforts made in diagnosing autism early in life, most children diagnosed with autism cannot live independently as adults (Billstedt et al., 2005; Eaves & Ho, 2008; Howlin et al., 2004). In addition, existing therapies and interventions tend to be quite expensive, given the typical need for one-on-one sessions with clinicians and other experts (CDC, n.d.).

These shortcomings have opened the door to technology-based interventions, with the hope that they can either reduce the supports required by people diagnosed with autism, and/or lower the cost of interventions. In addition, based on my experience, I find that a significant portion of children diagnosed with autism are clearly interested in a variety of computer technologies. Others have reached similar conclusions (e.g., Johnson et al., 2013). My sense is that this may be due to computer technologies behaving in predictable ways, within certain parameters, and communicating within a narrow channel of interaction. In contrast, situations that often challenge people diagnosed with autism are those that are often unpredictable and involve communication over a wide channel (e.g., face-to-face social situations).

Technologies developed for children diagnosed with autism cover a great variety of goals and use a wide variety of hardware. Goals vary depending on the specific needs of children (e.g., learning basic verbal skills), but they have typically included

- building basic skills (e.g., Coleman-Martin et al., 2005; Faja et al., 2007; Hailpern et al., 2009; Venkatesh et al., 2013; Whalen et al., 2006),
- aiding communication (e.g., Escobedo et al., 2012; Tartaro & Cassell, 2008),
- practicing or improving social skills (e.g., Hourcade et al., 2012, 2013), and
- motor skills (e.g., Parés et al., 2005; Bartoli et al., 2013, 2014).

Platforms have spanned a diverse spectrum, such as

- traditional desktops and laptops (e.g., Bosseler & Massaro, 2003; Coleman-Martin et al., 2005; Faja et al., 2007; Hailpern et al., 2009; Whalen et al., 2006);
- motion-based user interfaces, especially for children struggling with motor skills (e.g., Parés et al., 2005; Bartoli et al., 2013, 2014; Malinverni et al., 2014);
- tabletops (e.g., Gal et al., 2009; Giusti et al., 2011);
- tablets and smartphones (e.g., Escobedo, et al., 2012; Hourcade 2012, 2013);
- large displays (e.g., Hayes et al., 2010; Hirano et al., 2010);
- tangible user interfaces (e.g., Farr et al., 2010); and
- virtual characters (e.g., Tartaro & Cassell, 2008; Alcorn et al., 2011).

Many of the technologies outlined above were designed by collaborating directly with stakeholders such as parents and assistive technology practitioners, but not necessarily the children themselves. Among the exceptions that directly involve children include the work of Benton et al. (2012, 2014), Malinverni et al. (2014), and Frauenberger et al. (2012, 2013). Benton et al. (2012, 2014) developed the IDEAS framework, which stressed leveraging children's strengths in order to enable their participation in design activities. Malinverni et al. (2014) used participatory design activities in the context of designing a game, and they found that going back to the game narrative and enabling children to refer to previous designs helped keep activities in focus. Frauenberger et al. (2012, 2013) focused on enabling children to provide feedback more easily by associating emojis with their experiences.

Background on Our Project

Together with graduate and undergraduate students, I began conducting research on technologies for children diagnosed with autism in the summer of 2009, with weekly research activities continuing through 2012. During the summer and fall of 2009, we conducted exploratory activities with a small group of local children diagnosed with autism to get a sense of whether our ideas of using multi-touch displays could lead to positive outcomes, and if so, what kinds of apps would best serve the children. In the spring of 2010, we began weekly activities with children (5–12 years old) diagnosed with autism at an elementary school and an after-school program for children (11–15 years old) in middle school (Hourcade et al., 2012). These weekly sessions continued in the spring of 2011. In the fall of 2011 and spring of 2012, we expanded to a third site, another after school program for upper-elementary and middle school children diagnosed with autism (10–14 years old). We conducted a formal evaluation of the app designs that had evolved during the project at this third site (Hourcade et al., 2013).

Early in the project, drawing from our experiences, existing literature, and available resources, we decided on a set of principles that we would attempt to follow: *access, participation, personalization,* and *sustainability*. *Access* meant designing technologies such that they could be available and accessible by the largest population of children possible. This led us to design our software for commoditized hardware, and to make it freely available. *Participation* was a core philosophy that is directly related to the overall goals of this book: we believed we could achieve better designs through participatory design with stakeholders, *including children*. *Personalization* became a clear goal after we confirmed the wide range of needs, abilities, and preferences among the children with whom we worked. Finally, we intended for our *sustainability* principle to help ensure the project continued even after we stopped working on it. Consequently, we made our software open source, and we continue to host it, along with activity guides, on a public website at openautismsoftware.org.

As we worked on the project, we also developed new perspectives on autism. Before we began interacting with children diagnosed with autism, much of what we knew about them came from medical literature. This literature focuses primarily on addressing the symptoms of autism. As we got to know children diagnosed with autism, we learned to appreciate their talents and kindness, and realized that, not surprisingly, they have much to offer to the world. As a result, we shifted our approach, focusing more on inclusion. While we still gave children with autism opportunities to improve skills necessary for long-term independence, we also incorporated the idea that typically developing children and adults should do their part and meet children diagnosed with autism halfway. For this reason, we invited children diagnosed with autism and typically developing children to work together in some of our research activities.

FIGURE 9.1   Screenshot of a Zoomable Drawing Tool That We Used Primarily for Collaborative Storytelling

Our research began with the idea that we could leverage children's interest in computers to have them engage in face-to-face activities with others. Our goal was to enable them to practice social skills as they participated in technology-mediated activities that they found enjoyable and comfortable. Our original idea was to use large, multi-touch tabletop displays, but as we began using tablets we realized they were a much more practical choice, and even had characteristics that made them more appropriate for our goals (e.g., the social aspects of passing a tablet to another child). Rather than focus on one app, we explored a wide variety of activities that lent themselves to multi-touch interactions in tablets. Our exploration resulted in the development of multiple apps, along with multiple activities that could be conducted with each app. Our approach to develop and enable multiple combinations of activities and apps yielded many options, so that we could usually find a combination that would work for an individual child or group of children.

Our apps all have simple, visual user interfaces, enable open-ended activities (there isn't one correct way of using them), and are "mistake-free" (there are no errors or wrong answers). Our most useful and popular apps included a zoomable drawing tool that we used primarily for collaborative storytelling (Figure 9.1), a music authoring tool that we used for collaborative music composition (Figure 9.2), a visual puzzle tool that we used for collaborative puzzle solving (Figure 9.3), and a picture modifying tool that we used for emotion modeling (Figure 9.4)

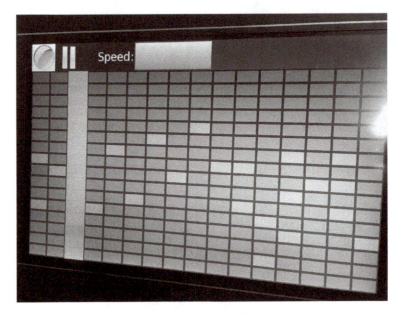

FIGURE 9.2 Screenshot of a Music-Authoring Tool for Collaborative Music Composition

(Hourcade et al., 2012). We have found that these apps can bring together children and adults, whether they have been diagnosed with autism or are developing in a typical manner.

Participatory Design Activities

We conducted participatory design activities with children diagnosed with autism in four different settings. In our first semester of work, we focused on an in-home, family setting. Our goals were both to learn about the feasibility of using multi-touch technology, and to get a sense for the types of apps that would work best. For each family, we conducted design sessions involving two researchers, one of the parents of the child, and the child. During each session, we focused on intro-ducing multi-touch tablets (iPads were not commercially available in 2009), and understanding which types of apps might be most useful. As such, these sessions fit within Druin's definition of "technology immersion" participatory design activities (Druin, 1999). Both of the girls who participated in these sessions spoke without problems, so they were able to give us useful feedback. Their parents' presence was useful in ensuring that we approached and communicated with their children in appropriate ways.

Our second and third settings were in an elementary school. One in-school setting involved a class with elementary school children diagnosed with autism who needed a significant amount of support (one-to-one adult-child ratio in the classroom). The other in-school setting involved mixed groups of children diagnosed with autism (integrated in regular classrooms) and typically developing children.

With the first elementary school group, we typically worked with one child at a time, sometimes with two (some pairs of children got along well). These sessions involved one to three researchers and a special education teacher. Typical sessions involved introducing a specific app in order to obtain information on whether it was useful, and if so, how to improve it. When children were not interested in an activity, they would quickly show disinterest or request a different activity. When they were interested, on the other hand, they would demonstrate their engagement by smiling, giggling, or using some words or vocalizations. To get more specific feedback, we would ask yes/no questions and the children would answer by pointing to yes/no signs. Some children did not feel comfortable using the tablet right away. To help increase their comfort level, we often used an app that would show fireworks following their fingers on the screen, which tended to make children feel comfortable and get them ready to use other apps. This app required minimal motor skills and provided immediate rewards through pleasant feedback. We also had to cover up lights and buttons on the tablet to help the children focus solely on the app(s).

Design sessions for the other elementary school setting, which integrated children diagnosed with autism into regular classrooms with their typically developing peers, occurred during "lunch bunches." The lunch bunches, an existing activity at the school, were created to foster inclusion. They involved two or three children diagnosed with autism inviting three to five of their classmates to lunch. The lunch bunch children would eat in their classroom while the rest of the children had lunch in the school cafeteria. This had the added benefit of enabling us to conduct design sessions in a quiet environment. As in the first elementary school's sessions, one to three researchers and one special education teacher were present. These sessions helped us develop and refine our activities and apps while inviting *all* the children's feedback. In this environment, we received about as much feedback from children diagnosed with autism as we did from their typically developing peers. Most of the feedback was verbal, but during some sessions the children used sticky notes to write down feedback that we then organized using affinity diagrams (Fails et al., 2013). Much of the verbal feedback did not require prompting, but we would ask open-ended questions if we observed children struggling or enjoying an activity (e.g., "What do you like about this activity?"). In terms of the use of sticky notes, we asked the children to write down likes, dislikes, and design ideas, one per sticky note.

Our fourth design session setting was an afterschool program where we worked with 11- to 15-year-old children. This program hosted 10 children diagnosed with Asperger's Syndrome, all of whom were able to communicate verbally. We conducted sessions with one to three children at a time (most often with two of them). These sessions typically involved two to three researchers, sometimes including a staff member from the afterschool program. Sessions were similar to those held with the lunch bunches at the elementary school, where we would present an activity and an app prototype and seek their feedback. Likely due to their older age, the children at the afterschool program had no problem suggesting changes and letting us know what they liked or disliked about our apps and activities.

Lessons Learned

As we conducted the sessions we learned several lessons outlined below. Some of these have also been incorporated into a book on child-computer interaction (Hourcade, 2015).

Deeply Engage

The first lesson we learned, which is generally applicable when designing for any population that is different from the developers, is that we benefited greatly from a deep engagement with the children diagnosed with autism, the adults in their lives, and the settings where they would use technologies. Rather than conducting only a few user sessions, we conducted participatory design sessions at two sites on a weekly basis for two semesters, iteratively developing our prototypes and activities. Only after this extensive process did we feel ready to evaluate our technology and activities. The settings in which we conducted our participatory design sessions were the places where we expected the children would use our apps on a regular basis. Knowing the physical and social environment in which our apps would be used was important. Communicating with the teachers and staff who worked with the children during every visit was also quite important in helping us achieve positive outcomes more quickly.

Involve Stakeholders

This led directly to our second lesson on the importance of involving stakeholders. We found that involving teachers and staff was important to help ensure that whatever we developed could be adopted for use in school or afterschool settings. Their help was also invaluable in helping us tune our approaches to individual children and improving the ways in which we communicated with them. In addition, we met with a parent support group at least once a semester. These meetings enabled the parents to know what we were working on and helped us answer all of their questions.

Design the Ecology

We noticed that context played a significant role in how and even whether children would participate in activities with our apps. Sometimes having a person exit the room was enough to cause significant behavioral changes. In addition,

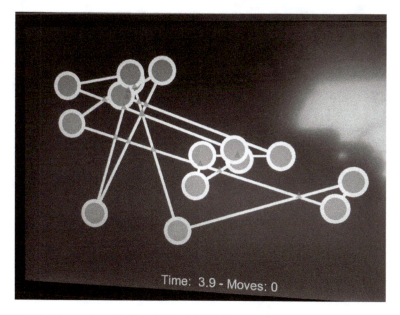

FIGURE 9.3   Screenshot of a Visual Puzzle Tool That We Used for Collaborative Puzzle Solving

we realized that developing several activities for each app afforded us extra flexibility to personalize each child's experience. The lesson learned then was that we should not just design the technology, but also design activities around the technology, taking into consideration the physical and social setting that is most appropriate.

Observe Baseline Behaviors

Learning how individual children diagnosed with autism typically behave helps us to better understand the impact that a specific activity has on them. Consequently, it is useful to observe children engage in typical activities before conducting participatory design sessions with them. In our case, when we first started working with children diagnosed with autism, we were disappointed when a few of them did not engage in activities with us for very long. We were surprised when teachers and staff told us that they actually engaged for longer than usual.

It is also useful to work with typically developing peers to better understand which behaviors may be specific to children diagnosed with autism, and which may be age-related. For example, some of the children who used our music composition app liked playing every possible note at the same time, which produced a loud, unpleasant sound. At first, we thought this behavior could be related to autism, but when we tried the same app with typically developing children of the same age, they exhibited similar behavior.

FIGURE 9.4 Screenshot of an Image-Editing Tool That We Used for Emotion Modeling

Be Flexible

While we always came to design sessions with specific goals in mind, we soon learned we needed to be flexible. This was due to variability between children as well as variability within each child. Not only did different children behave very differently, but some of the children's behaviors could change significantly from one week to the next. Our primary goal then, was to make activities as rewarding as possible for each child, given their daily realities. Even if we did not complete specific plans and objectives during design sessions, on most occasions we still learned something valuable. Another aspect that involved being flexible was learning to identify pairs of children who could work well together, or who might need to work by themselves on a given day.

Build Rapport

Just as it takes time for typically developing children to contribute in design teams, the same is true for children diagnosed with autism. However, the reasons are a bit different. Because social interactions can be challenging for children diagnosed with autism, it may take time for them to feel comfortable with researchers/designers before they can feel comfortable even using technology. It helped us to have people they trusted with us when we conducted activities in order to ease early interactions. The better the children got to know us, the more they could contribute to design and benefit from our activities.

Provide Safe Spaces

We noticed that some of the children needed to gain confidence and feel secure in their use of our technology before they could participate in activities with other children. For children who quickly disengage when in groups, it may be useful to learn more about the activities that interest them the most and work with them individually until they feel comfortable participating in these activities with other children.

Evaluate Impact over Time

Not all (and probably not most) technologies will have an immediate impact on children. Hence, it is important to see their impact over time, and to design technologies and activities to impact children over an extended period. A few sessions may not always provide designers with a good sense on whether prototypes or designs will have a positive long-term impact.

Design for Natural Contexts

Working in children's authentic contexts helped us identify technologies that were a good fit for their realities. If we had conducted sessions in our lab, we might have continued using large multi-touch tabletops. However, conducting sessions at schools and afterschool programs helped us see the advantages of using tablets, which since 2009, have proven to be more useful and popular than our original choice of platform.

Be Mindful of Skill Hierarchies

Children will not be able to use a technology if they do not have the basic skills necessary to do so. Some children diagnosed with autism have difficulty with motor skills. If this is the case, they may simply not be able to make use of the same user interfaces that their peers with typical motor development can use. Developing multiple apps enabled us to match apps to children's motor skills.

Conclusion

I hope this chapter has been worthwhile for those who want to get started designing technologies for children diagnosed with autism. The lessons that my research group learned are only the beginning. I am sure more lessons will emerge as more groups share their experiences designing for and with children diagnosed with autism.

Acknowledgments

Our research was partially funded by the University of Iowa and by the Iowa Department of Education through our university's Regional Autism Services Program, one of the child health specialty clinics. We would like to thank the children who participated in the research, their parents, and the teachers and staff at all the sites where we conducted design sessions.

Many University of Iowa students participated in the research. Thomas Hansen wrote the initial version of all the Open Autism Software apps. Natasha Bullock-Rest was crucial in developing the activities to conduct with the apps, and in identifying lessons learned from our research. Kelsey Huebner helped identify and polish the most effective activities, and helped run the formal evaluation of Open Autism Software. Stacy Williams, Elle Miller, and Lucas Liang helped process and analyze data from the formal evaluation. Ricardo Auguste and Joel Lipkowitz made improvements to the apps.

References

Alcorn, A., Pain, H., Rajendran, G., Smith, T., Lemon, O., Porayska-Pomsta, K., Foster, M.E., Avramides, K., Frauenberger, C., & Bernardini, S. (2011). Social communication between virtual characters and children with autism. In *Artificial Intelligence in Education* (pp. 7–14). Berlin: Springer.

Autism Speaks. (n.d.). DSM-5 Diagnostic Criteria. Retrieved March 16, 2016, from www .autismspeaks.org/what-autism/diagnosis/dsm-5-diagnostic-criteria

Bartoli, L., Corradi, C., Garzotto, F., & Valoriani, M. (2013). Motion-based touchless interaction for autistic children's learning. In *Proceedings of the 2013 Conference on Interaction Design and Children, IDC 2013* (pp. 53–62). New York: ACM.

Bartoli, L., Garzotto, F., Gelsomini, M., Oliveto, L., & Valoriani, M. (2014). Designing and evaluating touchless playful interaction for ASD children. In *Proceedings of the 2014 Conference on Interaction Design and Children, IDC 2014* (pp. 17–26). New York: ACM.

Benton, L., Johnson, H., Ashwin, E., Brosnan, M., & Grawemeyer, B. (2012). Developing IDEAS: supporting children with autism within a participatory design team. In *Proceedings of the SIGCHI Conference on Human Factors in Computing Systems, CHI 2012* (pp. 2599–2608). New York: ACM.

Benton, L., Vasalou, A., Khaled, R., Johnson, H., & Gooch, D. (2014). Diversity for design: a framework for involving neurodiverse children in the technology design process. In *Proceedings of the SIGCHI Conference on Human Factors in Computing Systems, CHI 2014* (pp. 3747–3756). New York: ACM.

Billstedt, E., Gillberg, C., & Gillberg, C. (2005). Autism after adolescence: population-based 13- to 22-year follow-up study of 120 individuals with autism diagnosed in childhood. *Journal of Autism and Developmental Disorders, 35*(3), 351–360.

Bosseler, A., & Massaro, D.W. (2003). Development and evaluation of a computer-animated tutor for vocabulary and language learning in children with autism. *Journal of Autism and Developmental Disorders, 33*(6), 653–672.

CDC. (n.d.). CDC, Data & Statistics, Autism Spectrum Disorder (ASD). Retrieved March 16, 2016, from www.cdc.gov/ncbddd/autism/data.html

Coleman-Martin, M. B., Wolff-Heller, K., Cihak, D. F., & Irvine, K. L. (2005). Using computer-assisted instruction and the nonverbal reading approach to teach word identification. *Focus on Autism and Other Developmental Disabilities, 20*, 80–90.

Druin, A. (1999). Cooperative inquiry: developing new technologies for children with children. In *Proceedings of the SIGCHI Conference on Human Factors in Computing Systems, CHI '99* (pp. 592–599). New York: ACM.

Eaves, L. C., & Ho, H. H. (2008). Young adult outcome of autism spectrum disorders. *Journal of Autism and Developmental Disorders, 38*(4), 739–747.

Eikeseth, S. (2009). Outcome of comprehensive psycho-educational interventions for young children with autism. *Research in Developmental Disabilities, 30*(1), 158–178.

Escobedo, L., Nguyen, D. H., Boyd, L., Hirano, S., Rangel, A., Garcia-Rosas, D., … Hayes, G. (2012). MOSOCO: a mobile assistive tool to support children with autism practicing social skills in real-life situations. In *Proceedings of the SIGCHI Conference on Human Factors in Computing Systems, CHI 2012* (pp. 2589–2598). New York: ACM.

Fails, J. A., Guha, M. L., & Druin, A. (2013). Foundations and trends® in human–computer interaction. *Foundations and Trends® in Human–Computer Interaction, 6*(2), 85–166.

Faja, S., Aylward, E., Bernier, R., & Dawson, G. (2007). Becoming a face expert: a computerized face-training program for high-functioning individuals with autism spectrum disorders. *Developmental Neuropsychology, 33*(1), 1–24.

Farr, W., Yuill, N., & Raffle, H. (2010). Social benefits of a tangible user interface for children with autistic spectrum conditions. *Autism, 14*(3), 237–252.

Frauenberger, C., Good, J., Alcorn, A., & Pain, H. (2013). Conversing through and about technologies: design critique as an opportunity to engage children with autism and broaden research(er) perspectives. *International Journal of Child-Computer Interaction, 1*(2), 38–49.

Frauenberger, C., Good, J., Keay-Bright, W., & Pain, H. (2012). Interpreting input from children: a designerly approach. In *Proceedings of the SIGCHI Conference on Human Factors in Computing Systems, CHI 2012* (pp. 2377–2386). New York: ACM.

Gal, E., Bauminger, N., Goren-Bar, D., Pianesi, F., Stock, O., Zancanaro, M., & Weiss, P. L. T. (2009). Enhancing social communication of children with high-functioning autism through a co-located interface. *AI & Society, 24*(1), 75–84.

Giusti, L., Zancanaro, M., Gal, E., & Weiss, P. L. T. (2011). Dimensions of collaboration on a tabletop interface for children with autism spectrum disorder. In *Proceedings of the SIGCHI Conference on Human Factors in Computing Systems, CHI 2011* (pp. 3295–3304). New York: ACM.

Guha, M. L., Druin, A., & Fails, J. A. (2013). Cooperative inquiry revisited: reflections of the past and guidelines for the future of intergenerational co-design. *International Journal of Child-Computer Interaction, 1*(1), 14–23.

Hailpern, J., Karahalios, K., & Halle, J. (2009). Creating a spoken impact: encouraging vocalization through audio visual feedback in children with ASD. In *Proceedings of the SIGCHI Conference on Human Factors in Computing Systems, CHI 2009* (pp. 453–462). New York: ACM.

Hayes, G. R., Hirano, S., Marcu, G., Monibi, M., Nguyen, D. H., & Yeganyan, M. (2010). Interactive visual supports for children with autism. *Personal and Ubiquitous Computing, 14*(7), 663–680.

Hirano, S. H., Yeganyan, M. T., Marcu, G., Nguyen, D. H., Boyd, L. A., & Hayes, G. R. (2010). vSked: evaluation of a system to support classroom activities for children with autism. In *Proceedings of the SIGCHI Conference on Human Factors in Computing Systems, CHI 2010* (pp. 1633–1642). New York: ACM.

Hourcade, J. P. (2015). *Child-Computer Interaction*. Publisher: Author. childcomputerinteraction.org.

Hourcade, J. P., Bullock-Rest, N. E., & Hansen, T. E. (2012). Multi-touch tablet applications and activities to enhance the social skills of children with autism spectrum disorders. *Personal and Ubiquitous Computing, 16*(2), 157–168.

Hourcade, J. P., Williams, S. R., Miller, E. A., Huebner, K. E., & Liang, L. J. (2013). Evaluation of tablet apps to encourage social interaction in children with autism spectrum disorders. In *Proceedings of the SIGCHI Conference on Human Factors in Computing Systems, CHI 2013* (pp. 3197–3206). New York: ACM.

Howlin, P., Goode, S., Hutton, J., & Rutter, M. (2004). Adult outcome for children with autism. *Journal of Child Psychology and Psychiatry, 45*(2), 212–229.

Johnson, G. M., Davies, S., Thomas, S., & Hilbert, J. (2013, June). iPads and children with special learning needs: a survey of teachers. In *Proceedings of the World Conference on Educational Media & Technology* (pp. 1022–1026).

Malinverni, L., MoraGuiard, J., Padillo, V., Mairena, M., Hervás, A., & Pares, N. (2014). Participatory design strategies to enhance the creative contribution of children with special needs. In *Proceedings of the 2014 Conference on Interaction Design and Children, IDC 2014* (pp. 85–94). New York: ACM.

Parés, N., Carreras, A., Durany, J., Ferrer, J., Freixa, P., Gómez, D., Kruglanski, O., Parés, R., Ribas, J.I., Soler, M., & Sanjurjo, À. (2005, June). Promotion of creative activity in children with severe autism through visuals in an interactive multisensory environment. In *Proceedings of the 2005 Conference on Interaction Design and Children* (pp. 110–116). New York: ACM.

Tartaro, A., & Cassell, J. (2008). Playing with virtual peers: bootstrapping contingent discourse in children with autism. In *Proceedings of the International Conference of the Learning Sciences, ICLS 2008*. Utrecht, The Netherlands: International Society of the Learning Sciences (ISLS).

Venkatesh, S., Phung, D., Duong, T., Greenhill, S., & Adams, B. (2013). TOBY: early intervention in autism through technology. In *Proceedings of the SIGCHI Conference on Human Factors in Computing Systems, CHI 2013* (pp. 3187–3196). New York: ACM.

Weiss, M. J., Fiske, K., & Ferraioli, S. (2008). Evidence-based practice for autism spectrum disorders. *Clinical Assessment and Intervention for Autism Spectrum Disorders*, 22–61.

Whalen, C., Liden, L., Ingersoll, B., Dallaire, E., & Liden, S. (2006). Behavioral improvements associated with computer-assisted instruction for children with developmental disabilities. *The Journal of Speech and Language Pathology–Applied Behavior Analysis, 1*(1), 11.

10

TEACHERS, STUDENTS, AND AFTER-SCHOOL PROFESSIONALS AS DESIGNERS OF DIGITAL TOOLS FOR LEARNING

Michelle Hoda Wilkerson

As this volume shows, researchers are increasingly involving learners, teachers, and other stakeholders in even the earliest stages of design (Bonsignore et al., 2013). However, different groups—teachers, students, administrators—within many educational systems often have different goals (Konings, 2005). For example, administrators adjusting to shifts in educational policy may wish to promote inquiry-oriented activities, whereas students accustomed to simple performance measures and direct instruction may expect to memorize and recall facts. Furthermore, since design-based projects seek to promote novel forms of learning (Cobb et al., 2003), participants may not know or share researchers' educational goals and values (Fishman, 2014). Such tensions are especially salient when digital tools for learning are at the center of design, because they often require new skills, pedagogies, and social configurations (Blumenfeld et al., 2000).

Communication and collaboration routines have been developed to address these tensions by facilitating perspective taking and negotiation among stakeholder groups (Penuel, et al. 2011) and between practitioners and researchers (Penuel et al., 2013; Voogt et al., 2015). There are models to identify potential synergies and points of tension among members of educational systems (Konings, et al. 2005) and to identify relevant social, cultural, and technical features of systems that may influence how designs are enacted (Bielaczyc, 2006). But even with these routines and models, researchers are still likely to receive varied or even contradictory feedback during the design process. Investigating how different perspectives are navigated and contribute to design decisions is rarely the focus of deliberate study (Konings, Seidel, & Merriënboer, 2014).

In this chapter, I present a retrospective case study focused on these decisions. SiMSAM (NSF IIS-1217100) is a project to develop tools, curricular materials, and theories of learning to introduce middle school students to computational modeling as a form of scientific inquiry. For three years, the SiMSAM research team has worked with youth, teachers, and informal educators across study contexts including laboratory-based workshops, classrooms, and after-school programs. Here I extend Sandoval's (2014) method of conjecture mapping to investigate the influence of these different participant groups and study contexts on our design.

The analysis revealed implicit systematic influences and decisions: we attended to youth perspectives on design of the tool's interface and functionality, teacher perspectives when developing and refining pedagogical theory, and our work in after-school environments informed our design of supporting materials and hands-on curricular activities for use with the SiMSAM tool. In some cases, different participant groups' input was well aligned, but in other cases their input conflicted and required designers to make decisions about whose input to take into account, and in what ways. Making these aspects of the design process explicit can reveal which stakeholder voices are reflected in the products of design and uncover the commitments that guide designer decision-making, and can help researchers purposefully plan future participant design involvement. These details are particularly important to document in the design of digital tools for learning: retrospectively, to uncover the values, perspectives, and pedagogical contexts within which the tools were developed; and formatively, to help designers identify which participant groups and settings may be most appropriate to leverage for a given feedback session.

SiMSAM Project

The SiMSAM Project aims to introduce middle school science students to *computational modeling*: the practice of creating and using computer simulations to elaborate and test scientific theories. The project brings together two important advances in science education. First, it builds on work that emphasizes the importance of scientific modeling in K-12 (e.g., Schwarz et al., 2009; Spitulnik, Krajcik, & Soloway, 1999; White & Frederiksen, 1998) by encouraging young learners to create, test, share, and revise their own explanations for surprising or unknown scientific events. Second, it builds on work that engages students in computational thinking and construction to explore and communicate about science (Jackson et al., 1994; Papert, 1980; Wilensky & Reisman, 2006; diSessa, Sherin & Hammer, 1993).

Inspired by these two lines of work, we are developing an integrated animation, simulation, and data analysis toolkit (SiMSAM). Young learners create stop-action movies to present theories about how unseen experiential phenomena such as smell diffusion, sound propagation, or evaporation work. They can then crop images from their animations to create a simulation. Each cropped image can be programmed to move and interact with other objects through a combination of direct manipulation and a menu. Finally, measurement tools allow users to explore the quantitative entailments of their theorized and simulated models. Our goal was to introduce simulation as expressive by tying it directly to stop-action moviemaking, a more familiar medium, and asking learners to model everyday scientific phenomena. Screenshots of the current version of SiMSAM are featured in Figure 10.1. We have also developed curricular activities and introductory materials for educators to use with SiMSAM.

The SiMSAM research team has regularly engaged in co-design and collaborative inquiry activities with youth, teachers, informal educators, and design consultants. These have taken place in workshops, professional development sessions, classroom enactments, and after-school programs (Table 10.1). We observed and captured detailed data about learning, usability, and social interactions as participants interacted with existing software, early prototypes, and our developing design. We also actively consulted with those participants for feedback on how

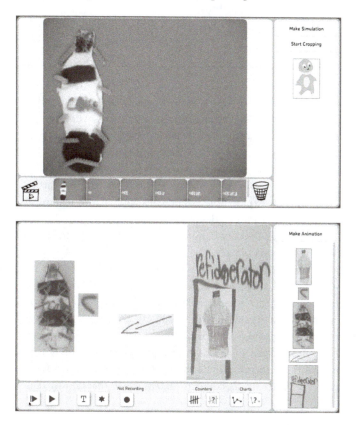

FIGURE 10.1 The Current Version of the SiMSAM Toolkit. Students create stop-action movies of scientific phenomena in the animation module (top; condensation) by taking photos using drawings and craft materials. They can then crop images from any frame of their animations; each cropped image becomes programmable objects within the simulation module (bottom).

TABLE 10.1 Overview of the First 4 Phases of Project

	Phase 1	Phase 2	Phase 3	Phase 4
Study Context	10-hour Workshop at University	15-hour Workshops at University	10-hour Classroom Enactments	10-hour After-School Outreach Club
Participant Group(s)	Youth (grade 6)	Pre-service Teachers	Classroom Teacher Students	Club Director Facilitators Youth
Data Sources	Video of Session Design Recommendations Designer Notes	Video of Session Written Work Design Recommendations	Video of Sessions Consultation with Teacher Researcher Notes	Video of Sessions Consultation with Facilitators

to improve those designs. In this way, participants are best described as design *informants* (Druin, 2002): our expectation was that each participant group would contribute "privileged observations" (Scaife & Rogers, 1999) that reflected their different roles and knowledge of the pedagogical system. This approach is similar to the informant design framework proposed by Scaife and colleagues (1997), which purposefully engages particular groups of users during particular phases of design. Our current exploration extends this approach to investigate not only how contributors might inform design at particular stages, but also what specific material, technological, social, or cultural elements of a design and its corresponding theory are influenced as well.

In this chapter, I will review four phases of research, design, and revision. The first two were internal, led by project staff at our home institution. The second two were external, conducted at educational sites where our partner educators led activities with support from the research team. Table 10.1 summarizes the study context, participant group(s) involved, and data sources collected for each; I also describe each phase in more detail in the next section. For my analysis, I use these data sources to identify (1) major changes in our design or theory across phases of the project; and (2) the participants, contexts, and/or events that informed each change.

Analytic Framework

To understand how different participant groups and study contexts influenced the design of SiMSAM, I extend Sandoval's (2014) *conjecture mapping* technique (Figure 10.2). Conjecture mapping is intended to help researchers systematically

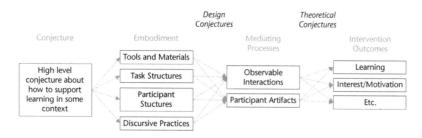

FIGURE 10.2 Overview of Conjecture Mapping Method. Adapted from Sandoval (2014).

describe the material and theoretical aspects of learning environment design—what Sandoval calls the *embodiment* of a design conjecture, and the *mediating processes* through which that design is expected to contribute to learning. Material aspects include the software, curricula, and social and discursive structures needed to enact a designed innovation. Theoretical aspects describe how specific experiences structured though that design are expected to lead to desired learning outcomes. The assumed links that connect specific elements of an embodiment to the certain mediating processes that are expected to foster learning are called *design conjectures*. The assumed links between mediating processes and outcomes are called *theoretical conjectures*.

I choose conjecture mapping as an analytic approach for three reasons. First, it allows me to examine not only the influence of participant input on the material products of design, but also on its *theoretical* products and implications: a major goal of design-based work. Second, it offers a level of specificity that allows me to isolate and trace changes in both the specific elements of an embodied design, and the corresponding theories that I expect each design element to mobilize. Third, while conjecture mapping was not originally intended to trace trajectories of design across iterations, its simple, highly structured, visual format makes analysis across iterations tractable and available for study in ways that might be difficult with longer design narratives.

Sandoval notes that while "conjecture mapping does not easily capture movement along a research trajectory, but there are a couple of ways they might be used to envision one . . . [a] longer [design] trajectory might be represented as a sequence of conjecture maps" (2014, pp. 22–23). Here, I adapt conjecture mapping specifically to examine the iterative and participatory nature of design research. I focus on how the material and theoretical products of design are affected across time and participant group. I will focus on the dimension of time by presenting iterative versions of the conjecture map for each phase of research and development, highlighting changes in the elements and links from one conjecture map to the next. I will focus on the dimension of participant group using color to identify which participant group(s) informed each change.

Tracing the Design of SiMSAM

The SiMSAM project started with a set of design and theoretical conjectures articulated in the original project proposal. The high-level conjecture described in that proposal is summarized as an effort "to bridge the gap between current theories of learning and available technologies for science education by merging an easy to use animation tool with domain-specific simulation and data analysis tools [for the purpose of] ... Providing a technological continuum from students' ideas to simulations and analysis ... Motivating the generative power of student-created models ... [and] [i]ntroducing simulation as scientific discourse" (Wilkerson-Jerde & Gravel, 2011, pp. 2–3). Figure 10.3 is a conjecture map I created from the initial intended design and conjectures described in that grant proposal. As I describe below, these conjectures and assumed pathways were quickly challenged and revised during each subsequent phase of the project.

Phase 1: Youth Design Workshops

In our first phase, we consulted with five sixth-grade girls during a multi-day modeling activity using a number of existing software tools (SAM Animation, StageCast Creator, Scratch) that had inspired our own proposed design. We used a prompt from an established scientific modeling curriculum, "How can I smell from a distance?" (from IQWST, Shwartz, et al. 2008). We asked the girls to draw, animate, and then simulate their ideas for how this happened using the available tools, and analyzed their learning and discourse throughout the activity; a detailed report of our findings can be found in Wilkerson-Jerde, Gravel & Macrander (2015). We also directly consulted with the girls about how we could improve the existing tools to better support their activities.

Both our analysis of student learning and the girls' feedback about the tools they used suggested changes we needed to make to our design. The activity prompt we provided did encourage the girls to create models based on rich existing knowledge, one of our main design conjectures for this first round of work. However, they did not engage in as much testing and refinement of their models as we expected. Our prediction was that the ability to quickly change aspects of their models, run them, and create measurements to test how well the models

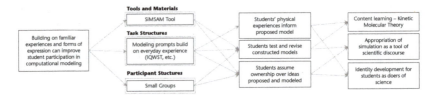

FIGURE 10.3 Conjecture Map Describing Initial Intended Project Design and Goals

reproduced reality would encourage the girls to recognize the limitations of their original models and work to improve them. Instead, they revised their models only when we directly challenged whether their model accurately reflected what they know should happen across time (smell should spread and "fade") or space (smell should be more intense at its source). We decided to add activity templates in the form of handouts that specifically focused students on how phenomena unfold across time and space.

The girls reported that they found some elements of the tools we used in the workshop frustrating to use. They confirmed that many of our intended design features, such as a drag-and-drop interface and the ability to import images directly from the animation, would improve their experience. They proposed a number of simulation functions they would like to have available in order to build the models they wanted, such as the ability to determine whether objects were overlapping one another. They also proposed interface features, such as the ability to save a simulation with a particular set up so that it could be reset and rerun. We noted these suggestions and integrated many of them into our plans for the first version of the SiMSAM tool.

Figure 10.4 presents a revised conjecture map describing how the findings and feedback we obtained from this first phase of work informed our design revisions. Items that were added or revised are highlighted in red, to indicate that they are the result of feedback or findings from youth. Dotted lines indicate a link that we expected but that did not manifest in our data, and red solid lines to indicate new links we found during this phase.

Phase 2: Consultation with Preservice Teachers

Next, we created a prototype of the integrated SiMSAM tool. We presented this prototype and draft curricular materials to preservice teachers enrolled in a STEM-focused elementary certification program. Over the course of three days, we asked participants in the program to complete an activity as if they were students. Next, we asked them to watch video from our Phase 1 workshop for additional data about how students may experience the activity. We asked the teachers to provide us with

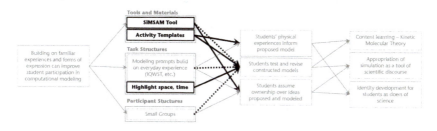

FIGURE 10.4 Revisions to Conjecture Map Based on Contributions by Youth during Phase 1

feedback about the activities themselves, including what they believed would be the most accessible, difficult, and valuable parts of the activity. We also sought feedback about the design of the tools and materials, and about what supports they would need to feel comfortable enacting such activities in their own classrooms.

The preservice teachers asserted that for the SiMSAM activities and tool to work in classrooms, students should be comfortable sharing, critiquing, and making sense of one another's work. They mentioned ways we could foster such an environment by leveraging already-existing classroom routines. For example, *gallery walks* are a common classroom activity. Students walk through the classroom, working to understand and provide feedback on one another's produced artifacts. Incorporating these preexisting routines could make SiMSAM activities more familiar and comfortable for both students and teachers, and foster the classroom cultures needed for those activities to be productive and engaging.

The teachers were uncertain, however, about their comfort level with the simulation tool and were unsure whether they would be able to support students during the activities. These difficulties with the tool's interface were in conflict with feedback from youth users, who had specifically requested many of its features and found the interface accessible during user tests. These concerns also led the teachers to question the value of computational modeling for thinking about science, given the apparent learning curve. Some teachers believed that the difficulties of the tool would prevent students from comfortably and fluently sharing their ideas. Others suggested the constraints of the tool encouraged users to focus on precise, mechanistic descriptions of the phenomenon that could be tested in ways verbal descriptions or drawings could not—indeed, one of our major goals for the project.

We addressed these tensions in two ways. Rather than edit the interface, we introduced a one-page "Tips and Tricks" document that helped teachers feel comfortable advising students on how to use the software environment. We also decided to focus more explicitly, both in our design embodiment and our theoretical considerations, on the unique benefits and limitations of computational modeling compared to other common science activities (Figure 10.5).

Phase 3: Fifth-Grade Classroom Enactment

After continued refinement of the SiMSAM tool and activities, we worked with a teacher who participated in Phase 2 to enact two-week long lessons using SiMSAM in two of his fifth-grade science classrooms. The students created and refined models to address the following questions:

- When I am thirsty in the summer, I pull a cold drink out of the refrigerator and leave it on the counter. Before long, beads of water appear on the outside of the drink. How did the water get there?
- After a rainy day, sometimes you can see puddles on the ground. Later in the day, the puddles are gone. What happened to them?

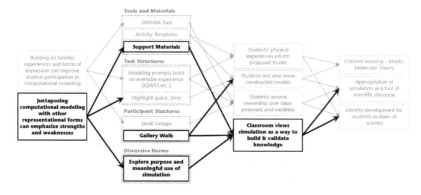

FIGURE 10.5   Contributions by Pre-Service Teachers at Design/Professional Development Workshop

We analyzed student discourse, the artifacts they produced, their interactions with facilitators, and we directly consulted students during class discussions about what types of things they wished they could do with the software but were unable to.

During these sessions, we found that the activity templates we introduced after our first phase led to some unexpected benefits. Because students created animations and computational rule sets based on the same template images, their rules could be combined or compared against one another to build or motivate classroom-level knowledge building. This led to especially productive classroom-level discussions and encouraged students to work toward group-wide consensus about what model best explained evaporation and condensation. This pushed our thinking about what mediating processes within the SiMSAM environment could lead to productive learning. Because this finding was due to feedback and findings from both the teacher/facilitators (blue) and students (red), we show it here in purple (Figure 10.6). Students also offered that while the interface was straightforward, they could not enact particular rules they thought would be important: for example, they wanted objects to spawn other objects (such as puddles creating water droplets), and they wanted to be able to change the color of objects.

Phase 4: After-School Workshops

In Phase 4, we partnered with an after-school science outreach program to conduct SiMSAM activity units at four sites. Each site met once per week, and each enactment lasted four weeks. Participating youth modeled molecular phenomena including evaporation, melting, and heat diffusion (different topics were taken up at different sites) using the latest version of SiMSAM and activity materials. The science club included educational directors and mentors—often college students—at each site, and junior mentors in their mid teens who facilitated each activity.

This new context introduced a number of new challenges. Given the information nature of the club, it was not atypical for students to "drop in" or "drop

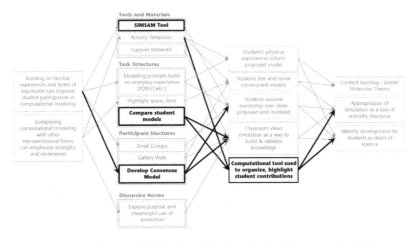

FIGURE 10.6 Contributions by Youth and Teacher during Classroom Activities

out" during activities, and many did not attend regularly. We had to develop methods to sustain youth's participation in the same, extended modeling activity across multiple weeks, offering ways for students who did not attend regularly to engage or re-engage with the scientific content without disrupting ongoing activities. At the same time, we had more flexibility and time to create hands-on supplements to the modeling activities. This led to the development of a number of new materials and social structures designed to foster and sustain inquiry across longer periods of time, and for groups that may change members over the course of the activity. We incorporated the two most successful approaches to addressing these issues into our final set of materials (Figure 10.7). First, we found it useful to have a continually present physical set up that illustrated the phenomenon at hand: a water still, tuning forks, heaters, or other materials that students could use to empirically investigate and demonstrate to one another the phenomena under exploration. Second, we found it useful to have a laptop available to show a selective number of videos—both describing the phenomenon (such as time-lapse videos of a puddle drying or ice melting)—and of students' prior animations and simulations, for youth to consult as needed.

The outreach program we worked with was also interested in working with us to develop infrastructures and pedagogical approaches that would allow them to continue using the SiMSAM activities after our research team was no longer able to support them. We created "bundles" of resources (templates, physical set ups, videos, questions and prompts), rather than the specific content-related sequences we used in classrooms, so that activities were flexible. We also created a document geared toward practitioners that briefly described model-based pedagogy and the importance of encouraging a focus on theory building and scientific mechanism during SiMSAM activities.

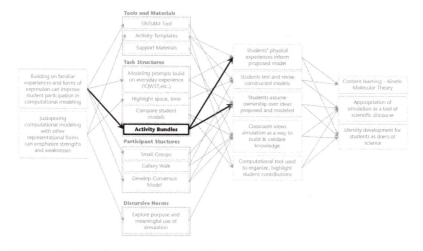

FIGURE 10.7 Contributions by Informal Educators and Mentors during After-School Activities

Discussion

Overlaying the four maps that result from each iteration of design reveals systematicities in which participant groups influenced aspects of our material design and theories of learning (Figure 10.8). Specifically, findings from working directly with youth contributed most to our design of the toolkit, and some of the task structures introduced over the course of the project. Working with preservice and in-service teachers informed our design of participant structures and some support materials. And, working with after-school groups helped us think about how to make the design of our activities more sustainable and engaging, and to develop flexible ways to disseminate the design and related pedagogical strategies.

Analyzing our design process through conjecture mapping also revealed other patterns that can be useful for thinking about and reporting design research. For example, preservice teachers during Phase 2 suggested building on existing classroom routines to encourage students to share and critique one another's work. In our conjecture map, we identified the design product resulting from this feedback to be a "Gallery Walk" participant structure. However, the suggestion from teachers was not for a particular structure, but for the design to leverage preexisting practices *in particular classrooms*. For some students, this might be presenting animations and simulations as parts of sharing circles; for others it might be critiquing one another's work using familiar discursive routines such as accountable talk. Similarly, while more specified, template- and activity-prompt-based activities worked well in time-strapped classrooms, after-school environments benefitted from empirical set ups that allowed learners to remember and revisit their explorations over extended periods of time. Explicitly allowing for such flexibility in

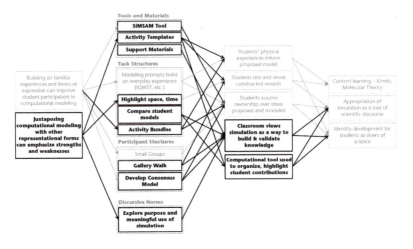

FIGURE 10.8 Contributions by All Participants during After-School Activities

design can likely facilitate the integration and productive use of digital tools for learning, especially for use at scale and across settings.

Conclusion

Applying conjecture mapping across participant groups and contexts helped us to see two more general patterns in our design approach. First, it made more evident the implicit commitments we were enacting in our design choices. For example, when testing our first iteration of SiMSAM's programming interface, we received dramatically different feedback from middle school students (who found the interface easy to use) and teachers (who found it very difficult). The interface employs interface paradigms that were familiar for our youth participants, but not for many of the teachers we worked with. Since our goal is to support youth's facility in exploring scientific ideas through computational means, we chose to prioritize their access to programming and maintained the programming-by-demonstration paradigm. This, in turn, is leading us to explore other ways to allay teachers' concerns; for example, through the development of additional support materials and social structures that allow students to demonstrate their competencies with the environment to teachers.

Second, it illustrates how important it is to involve multiple participant groups and contexts in the ongoing process of design. This retrospective clearly illustrates how we would not have been able to receive feedback about certain aspects of embodiment—notably participant structures and discursive norms—without the involvement of teachers and facilitators in our work. Similarly, we may not have created a tool that is engaging and accessible for youth had we only consulted with teachers. These emphases also provide information about which groups we may wish to consult in the future as we continue to refine particular aspects of our tool. Indeed, in a recent special issue dedicated to participatory design, it was noted that there is "a need for more evidence on how to best involve different stakeholders [in design initiatives]" (p. 3; Könings et al., 2014). As more projects utilize conjecture mapping to explore the influence of participant groups on design, we as a community can develop better approaches to co-design for digital tools for learning in complex educational settings.

Author Note

This material is based upon work supported by the National Science Foundation under Grant IIS-1217100. Any opinions, findings, and conclusions or recommendations expressed in this material are those of the authors and do not necessarily reflect the views of the NSF. Special thanks to Brian Gravel, Jason Yip, Betsy DiSalvo, and our collaborating partners. Elena Duran, Becca Shareff, Sierra Reyburn, Sydney Aardal, and Leah Rosenbaum provided helpful feedback on drafts of this manuscript. Christopher Macrander, Yara Shaban, Chelsea Andrews, Mahsa Hayeri, Vasiliki Laina, Mirjana Hotomski, Susan Bresney, Ruth Sun, and Jenna Conversano assisted with the work reported here.

References

Bielaczyc, K. (2006). Designing social infrastructure: Critical issues in creating learning environments with technology. *Journal of the Learning Sciences, 15*(3), 301–329.

Blumenfeld, P., Fishman, B. J., Krajcik, J., Marx, R. W., & Soloway, E. (2000). Creating usable innovations in systemic reform: Scaling up technology-embedded project-based science in urban schools. *Educational Psychologist, 35*(3), 149–164.

Bonsignore, E., Yip, J. C., Ahn, J., Clegg, T., & Guha, M. L. (2013). Designing for learners, with learners: Toward a theory of cooperative inquiry in the design of learning technologies. Presented at J. Rick, M. Horn, & R. Martinez-Maldonado (Orgs.), Human-Computer Interaction and the Learning Sciences. Pre-conference workshop at CSCL 2013, Madison, WI.

Cobb, P., Confrey, J., Lehrer, R., & Schauble, L. (2003). Design experiments in educational research. *Educational Researcher, 32*(1), 9–13.

Druin, A. (2002). The role of children in the design of new technology. *Behaviour and Information Technology, 21*(1), 1–25.

Fishman, B. J. (2014). Designing usable interventions: Bringing student perspectives to the table. *Instructional Science, 42*(1), 115–121.

Jackson, S. L., Stratford, S. J., Krajcik, J., & Soloway, E. (1994). Making dynamic modeling accessible to precollege science students. *Interactive Learning Environments, 4*(3), 233–257.

Könings, K. D., Brand-Gruwel, S., & Merriënboer, J. J. (2005). Towards more powerful learning environments through combining the perspectives of designers, teachers, and students. *British Journal of Educational Psychology, 75*(4), 645–660.

Könings, K. D., Seidel, T., & van Merriënboer, J. J. (2014). Participatory design of learning environments: Integrating perspectives of students, teachers, and designers. *Instructional Science, 42*(1), 1–9.

Papert, S. (1980). *Mindstorms: Children, Computers, and Powerful Ideas.* New York: Basic Books.

Penuel, W. R., Coburn, C. E., & Gallagher, D. J. (2013). Negotiating problems of practice in research–practice design partnerships. *National Society for the Study of Education Yearbook, 112*(2), 237–255.

Penuel, W. R., Fishman, B. J., Cheng, B. H., & Sabelli, N. (2011). Organizing research and development at the intersection of learning, implementation, and design. *Educational Researcher, 40*(7), 331–337.

Sandoval, W. (2014). Conjecture mapping: An approach to systematic educational design research. *Journal of the Learning Sciences, 23*(1), 18–36.

Scaife, M., & Rogers, Y. (1999). The design of children's technology. In A. Druin (Ed.), *The Design of Children's Technology* (pp. 27–50). San Francisco, CA: Morgan Kaufmann Publishers, Inc.

Scaife, M., Rogers, Y., Aldrich, F., & Davies, M. (1997). Designing for or designing with? Informant design for interactive learning environments. In *Proceedings of the ACM SIGCHI Conference on Human Factors in Computing Systems* (pp. 343–350). ACM.

Schwarz, C. V., Reiser, B. J., Davis, E. A., Kenyon, L., Achér, A., Fortus, D., Shwartz, Y., Hug, B., & Krajcik, J. (2009). Developing a learning progression for scientific modeling: Making scientific modeling accessible and meaningful for learners. *Journal for Research in Science Teaching, 46*(6), 632–654.

Sherin, B., diSessa, A. A., & Hammer, D. (1993). Dynaturtle revisited: Learning physics through collaborative design of a computer model. *Interactive Learning Environments, 3*(2), 91–118.

Shwartz, Y., Weizman, A., Fortus, D., Krajcik, J., & Reiser, B. (2008). The IQWST experience: Using coherence as a design principle for a middle school science curriculum. *The Elementary School Journal, 109*(2), 199–219.

Spitulnik, M. W., Krajcik, J., & Soloway, E. (1999). Construction of models to promote scientific understanding. In W. Feurzig & N. Roberts (Eds.), *Modeling and Simulation in Science and Mathematics Education* (pp. 70–94). New York: Springer-Verlag.

Voogt, J., Laferrière, T., Breuleux, A., Itow, R. C., Hickey, D. T., & McKenney, S. (2015). Collaborative design as a form of professional development. *Instructional Science, 43*(2), 259–282.

White, B. Y., & Frederiksen, J. R. (1998). Inquiry, modeling, and metacognition: Making science accessible to all students. *Cognition and Instruction, 16*(1), 3–118.

Wilensky, U., & Reisman, K. (2006). Thinking like a wolf, a sheep, or a firefly: Learning biology through constructing and testing computational theories—an embodied modeling approach. *Cognition & Instruction, 24*(2), 171–209.

Wilkerson-Jerde, M. H. & Gravel, B. E. (2011). *EXP: SiMSAM: Bridging student, scientific, and mathematical models with expressive technologies.* Unpublished grant proposal.

Wilkerson-Jerde, M. H., Gravel, B. E., & Macrander, C. A. (2015). Exploring shifts in middle school learners' modeling activity while generating drawings, animations, and computational simulations of molecular diffusion. *Journal of Science Education and Technology, 24*(2–3), 396–415.

11

LEARNER AT THE CENTER

Pearson Kids CoLab

Lisa Maurer and Elizabeth Bonsignore

This chapter provides the story of Pearson's Kids CoLab, from its inception to expansion. Kids CoLab is an interdisciplinary, intergenerational team that includes children (ages 7–13) as well as adult instructional designers, product developers, and learning content experts who engage in participatory design together to improve a variety of Pearson product lines. While co-design with children is typically more prevalent in academia, the benefits to industry are multifaceted, as our experience will show. I start with a brief overview of my discovery of like-minded individuals seeking ways to augment a design-based research approach. I then share some practical considerations that have been raised in our industry implementation of cooperative inquiry.

Quest for Research Expansion

In the summer of 2013, I was on a mission to find a link between my work in product design and usability research, and the learning sciences. At that time, one of my primary roles was to engage K-12 digital product teams in usability research, as part of a larger design-based research approach (Hoadley, 2002). As a former instructional designer, I wanted to find a way to more effectively bridge instructional design and usability by giving learners a more active role in the design process. As a former educator, I was already an advocate for learners, serving as an accountability partner to help teams incorporate user feedback into digital learning products and solutions. I was part of a research and development organization called the *Pearson Research & Innovation Network*, whose mission is to solve global educational challenges through research, innovation, and thought leadership. Our research center within the network covers a broad spectrum of research, spanning market research, usability, and participatory design, as well as program measurement.

For many years, we've conducted usability testing, as it is embedded in our product development cycle. With usability testing, we have interacted with children solely as research subjects. I have always sensed a gap in the depth of feedback that I could provide to product teams through this type of research. It was no problem to provide metrics around effectiveness, efficiency, and satisfaction. What I felt was missing were innovative ideas tied directly to the learning goal: new approaches to a design challenge that no one had thought of before. I was after creativity without constraints, so all options could be considered, regardless of the source—child or adult, expert or novice. I often see teams impose so many limitations through processes that aim for efficiency that they can be boxed in with their thinking. We had engaged in plenty of participatory design activities with educators in the past, but we were missing a key player in our participatory design strategy—the learner.

Efficacy at Pearson

In 2013, during the same time frame that I was searching for more meaningful ways to include the learner in our product design process, Pearson made a public commitment to efficacy. Efficacy emphasizes ways to make a measureable impact on improving someone's life through learning. Efficacy helps us ensure that we are partnering with the learner to deliver the learner outcomes we set out to achieve.

Moreover, we invite others to critique us not just by the inputs we provide to the educational system, but by the outcomes we produce (see http://efficacy .pearson.com/ for more details).

Pearson has defined four outcome categories that contribute to making a measureable impact on someone's life through learning. These categories aim to cover the entire learner experience, from the degree to which learners can access a product to complete a course to how they can apply the acquired skills and competencies to progress in life. Moreover, Pearson has identified *different types of evidence* that need to be gathered to support claims about learner outcomes, including both small- and large-scale studies as well as qualitative and quantitative data.

Ultimately, we can demonstrate the impact of our products on learner outcomes through the gold standard of research: randomized controlled trials. But what should be in place long before these large-scale trials? How can we ensure there is a foundation in place that promotes efficacy? A diverse set of iterative research and design activities is critical to support agile development teams. For example, when it comes to learner motivation and confidence, we had an untapped and potentially beneficial opportunity to directly involve learners in the design process. Before we could instantiate a truly learner-focused participatory design committee, however, I had to learn more about cooperative inquiry (Druin, 1999).

Cheese Hat Magicians

My quest to find a more explicit linkage between the learner and the design of technology to support her led me to the Computer Supported Collaborative Learning (CSCL) conference in June 2013 in Madison, Wisconsin. It was there that I found a set of like-minded individuals who were engaged in discussion about the connection between participatory design in human–computer interaction (HCI) and the learning sciences. During the CSCL conference, I discovered the cooperative inquiry method and met a group of thought-provoking researchers. Maybe it was the way they described a different way of engaging in research with children (Bonsignore et al., 2013). Maybe it was the way they asserted that *children* should have a voice in making new technology *for children*—a continuous voice from the same group of children who meet weekly at their lab to co-design new technology. Or maybe it was the cheese hats. We were in Wisconsin, after all (Figure 11.1). Regardless, I knew that Pearson needed what I saw.

In their presentation, this group shared example after example of learning solutions, spanning English Language Arts (ELA) and Science Technology Engineering and Math (STEM), all of which were designed alongside the ultimate end users, children. They shared how techniques that utilized simple office and art supplies—or "low-tech prototyping" techniques—identified child-centered user requirements and features for product teams. They also gave me a glimpse into how these groups were structured, and an account of how the child participants themselves benefitted from the active involvement in co-design activities. They even engaged in an interactive participatory design exercise with the audience to actively demonstrate the types of collaboration and facilitation skills required

FIGURE 11.1 Group Selfie of the CSCL 2013 Presenters. From left to right: Beth Bonsignore, Mona Leigh Guha, June Ahn, Juan Pablo Hourcade, Tammy Clegg, and Allison Druin. Jason Yip also presented, but is not pictured here.

to embed this paradigm shift into an organization such as Pearson (Bonsignore et al, 2013).

Who were these cheese hat–wearing research magicians? They were Allison Druin and her team of researchers at the University of Maryland Human-Computer Interaction Laboratory (Druin, 1999, 2002; Fails et al., 2012; Guha et al., 2013). That day, I decided I would do whatever it took to implement cooperative inquiry at Pearson. I promptly recruited Allison and her team to be implementation partners.

University of Maryland Summer Camp, 2013

By late summer, I had also recruited my colleague Robin Duffy (who became the eventual leader of our second Kids CoLab, Hoboken, NJ) to accompany me to summer camp for the University of Maryland's co-design team (which they call Kidsteam). The purpose of Kidsteam's summer camp is to build relationships between the child and adult design partners, and to give child designers the opportunity to get comfortable with rituals, tools, and techniques. We jumped right into the mix, dressed in jeans and sneakers (quite different from our normal office attire) and sat down on the carpet with the children and other adult design partners. In just two days, we got a true sense of how to partner *with* children to design innovative products *for* children, instead of simply working with them as research subjects. I'll never forget the "Bags-of-Stuff" activity, which flipped my definition of "new technology" on its head. By giving the children and adults open-ended art materials to build low-tech, 3-D models and low-fidelity prototypes, *anything* became possible. Total creative license without limitations enabled possibilities and directions no one had ever, or *would* ever, consider. By creating this hybrid space of part "child" reality and part "adult" reality, I realized I could bridge product teams with learners in a recurring, research-based manner. I left with a tremendous drive to establish my own co-design team as quickly as possible.

Pearson Open Houses

Our first step was to recruit children for our co-design team. At Allison's recommendation, I planned to hold a series of open houses at our Chandler, Arizona, office with families in the community. I would let them know about the opportunity for their child to participate in a unique technology design and consulting committee. We had a database of children who had participated as research subjects in usability testing from which to pull from as a start. Whereas typically parents would drop off their children at our office, this time we invited the parents to stay, observe, and even participate in the session. We wanted parents to understand the types of activities their children would be involved in, as well as to understand the commitment level required. We emphasized the triple benefits of participation. First, we shared that Pearson would benefit from working side-by-side with children on our big business challenges, and we shared that the children in the committee would see multiple benefits as well (Guha et al., 2010). Second, the children would be working in teams, not just with children of different ages, but also with adults, applying academic skills outside of the classroom and honing their presentation skills. Finally, the children would also learn about the design process. The ultimate beneficiary, however, would be the end user, the child who would someday use a product or solution designed "with kids, for kids" in their classroom.

We held three open houses from October 2013 to March 2014. In each open house meeting, we sampled a different co-design technique (Fails et al., 2012). We also worked with different product teams so we could spread the word about this new way of engaging with children in design and research.

Inaugural Pearson Kids CoLab

From those three open houses, in the summer of 2014 we formed our inaugural Pearson Kids CoLab of four boys and four girls ages 7–13 (Figure 11.2). Our goal was to have a mix of ages and genders. These children met weekly with us in our Kids CoLab at the Pearson office in Chandler, Arizona, for the entire 2014–2015 school year.

Monthly calls and two training events with the University of Maryland's Human-Computer Interaction Lab team guided our implementation. In the calls, we collaboratively planned the Kids CoLab sessions by translating research

FIGURE 11.2 Artist Rendition of the Inaugural Pearson Kids CoLab Child Co-Design Team. A framed edition of this image was hung prominently at the entrance to the Kids CoLab space, and each child also received a framed version of his/her avatar as a gift.

questions into techniques. We brainstormed strategies for eliciting creative thinking among the design partners, which included establishing a devoted space rather than a conference room that required setup and tear-down for each session. This dialogue continued when Allison Druin and Mona Leigh Guha made a trip to Pearson to co-lead a Kids CoLab session and train our adult design partners. We also toured the building, seeking out the ideal space for a permanent Kids CoLab. This hands-on training and guidance was invaluable and helped ensure we stayed true to the key design philosophies embedded in the research-based approach.

Training Adult Design Partners

A rotating cross-functional team of researchers, designers, and content experts joined the children to co-design new technology to support K-12 product development. In order to differentiate this technology committee from the typical usability studies with which product teams were most familiar, I needed to train the adult design partners who participated in the sessions. I trained every adult design partner who participated in a session. I captured several principles from the cooperative inquiry design philosophy (Fails et al., 2012; Guha, 2013) in icon form (Figure 11.3).

In essence, I emphasized that we would be design partnering with children, which required a change in our attire, mentality, and approach. We were inviting children to join our team. We would dress like them to help the children feel comfortable, and, starting very early in the process, we would collaborate and share ideas. I remember one of the first open houses in which we devoted some time to just playing with the children with items like playground balls, Hula-Hoops, and jump ropes in order to bond with them. Every adult in the room was smiling and laughing that day, and I could tell we had successfully made the first attempt to mitigate the typical adult–child power dynamics.

This isn't school even though we are ideating solutions for use in schools

We are all design partners but some are just taller then others

We dress casual like the kids to help remove the power dynamic typically in place between adults and children

We can learn a tremendous amount by starting with a blank sheet of paper

The adult and child design partners "meld" their ideas together

FIGURE 11.3 Pearson Kids CoLab Design Philosophies in Icon Form

Given that the Pearson population contains adults with varying levels of experience working with kids, a set of strategies for different scenarios evolved. On the one hand, former teachers had to adopt a co-design mentality, instead of relying on the teacher persona they were comfortable with. Still, other adults just needed to get comfortable working directly with children. We formed a set of strategies to help mitigate challenges (Table 11.1).

Creating a set of norms or "ways that we agreed to act on a normal day" proved very effective (Figure 11.4). We created them collaboratively, and once they were in place, our design partners would use the shared language with one another. For instance, "Respect the Bubble" meant "keep your hands to yourself." Our norms were a blend of behaviors that both adult and child co-design partners needed to work together effectively. Adults suggested norms to ensure basic needs were met, like "be safe," and children wanted to ensure that all ideas were

TABLE 11.1   Challenges and Strategies for the Adult Design Partner

Challenge	Strategy
The group is having a hard time getting started on a design task	Imagine that you are an "older child" and reiterate the design task by saying, "I think we are supposed to . . ."
I don't know how to add my idea to what a child already began	Don't be afraid to add to what a child began. Grab a marker or crayon and just start writing and drawing by building on the idea. By modeling that anyone can add ideas, everyone will learn to participate in this way.
Not all of the ideas are being captured in the building of an artifact	Grab a journal or piece of paper and start capturing them! As an adult design partner, part of your job is to be able to retell the flow of idea elaboration in your group. Capturing the dialogue and ideas on paper is an essential artifact.
A child is misbehaving	Having a set of group norms that are created as a group can help. This way, you can reference the norm as a way to address the behavior and state the behavior that is expected. Additionally, some children are more active than others, so giving them helper roles (ex: passing out supplies) can help them stay focused during the session. Sometimes, pulling the child from the environment for a few minutes may help if more than a role or reminder is needed.
Children are calling adults "teacher" or "counselor"	Respond with something like, "Remember, I'm a design partner just like you! We are all working together."
I don't know how to act in general	Just be yourself! Remember that children can tell when you are being authentic and when you are acting "like an adult."

FIGURE 11.4 Pearson Kids CoLab Co-Created Norms

captured somehow, suggesting, "If all else fails, write it down." This meant that the whiteboards and journals were always available to write down ideas at any time, in any circumstance. The norms were a delicate balance to reinforce the equal footing between child and adult design partners, while establishing a few interaction constraints to help promote a productive environment. For most of our child design partners, working with adults as peers was somewhat foreign, just as it was foreign for the adults to view the children as equal partners. As such, finding the right mix of autonomy, support, and boundaries required continuous calibration.

Given that our projects were focused squarely on the development of products and solutions the children would use in school, and that many of us were former teachers, I was very sensitive to Kids CoLab being equated with being in school (and all of the power dynamics that go along with a traditional school environment). However, I was truly convinced that the child design partners did not equate Kids CoLab with school when they suggested a change to our norm about not raising hands. The change the children requested was that they start raising hands to establish more order and because they felt bad for cutting off their peers. It was clear they had started to become a team (Figure 11.5).

FIGURE 11.5   Pearson Kids CoLab in Action

From Chandler to Hoboken

After a successful first year in Chandler, Arizona, we decided to expand the program and create a second Kids CoLab in Hoboken, New Jersey, led by my colleague Robin Duffy. The rationale was to increase the capacity and reach for the program, as well as to allow teams on the East Coast access to in-person participation. We also strived to target middle school products, and thus focused on recruiting fifth- to eighth-grade students, slightly older than the Chandler team.

The recruiting process for the Hoboken Kids CoLab differed, in that there was no established research database to recruit from as there had been in Arizona. Thus, the open houses were populated with families in the community recruited via a third party vendor. Many families were interested in joining, and the group was selected in accordance with the Chandler strategy, to achieve a mix of demographic characteristics.

Meanwhile, our Chandler Kids CoLab continued with the same eight children returning for year two. We established a dedicated space in the Chandler office for conducting Kids CoLab sessions. Throughout our CoLab partnership, we used the same co-design process and techniques, though we worked with different teams and on different projects. This format is typical for the cooperative inquiry co-design philosophy that we follow, in that the Kids CoLab represents a core group of child and adult co-designers who have developed a long-standing collaborative relationship and contribute to several different design projects over time (Guha et al., 2013). I touch on a few examples of the diversity of learning-design-based projects that we have undertaken in the next section.

Kids CoLab Projects

In addition to applying the cooperative inquiry philosophy with Kids CoLab, my learner-focused formula for effective digital learning was inspired by Michael Fullan (Fullan, 2013). Fullan asserted that effective digital products should be elegantly efficient and easy to use, supportive of deep learning, and irresistibly engaging (Figure 11.6). Our Kids CoLab teams have explored one or more of

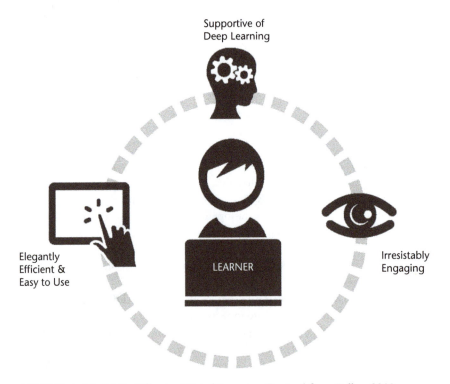

FIGURE 11.6 Model for Effective Digital Learning, Derived from Fullan, 2013

these directives across multiple sessions. No matter what the research question, we've always retained a focus on learning.

The first year, we explored needs, ideating and iteratively evaluating prototypes with increasing levels of fidelity. In addition to supporting other K-12 digital solutions, the primary focus of our co-design team in its inaugural year was the development of an early literacy mobile app with game-like features to promote language and vocabulary acquisition. We applied cooperative inquiry techniques like Bags-of-Stuff (Fails, Guha, & Druin, 2012) and found opportunities to incorporate other techniques, such as LEGO® Serious Play®, various brainstorming techniques, Innovation Games, and improvisation games. Additionally, the children on our co-design team acted as junior researchers, as they observed an Innovation Game–inspired focus group of 4-year-olds and subsequent user testing. This experience allowed the children to see firsthand the target user group (preschool children) for whom they were designing.

In the second year, we expanded the range of projects to include everything from book covers to digital character development, game features, and narratives. It was in one of these generative design sessions that a design team sketch of a flower character became an actual character in a digital learning program (Figure 11.7). Not only was it beneficial for Pearson to have direct design input from potential users, but also the child design partners were able to see their ideas being turned into a *published* product, which is a pretty powerful experience for a preteen.

Other sessions were devoted to brainstorming character backstories, game flows, and experience prototyping character animations. The ideas from these sessions enabled teams to identify stories, characters traits, and feedback messages that would resonate with learners. Throughout all our co-design sessions, we've tried to balance the need to incorporate interesting and engaging ideas, while not losing sight of the underlying learning goals.

Indeed, by partnering closely with children, we have found that sometimes engagement with learning goals can begin even before a child interacts directly with learning materials. The old adage goes, "Don't judge a book by its cover," and its relevance to learning materials should not be understated. It was through

FIGURE 11.7 One of the Characters Designed by Kids CoLab during a Low-Fidelity Prototype Sketch Session Was Incorporated into a Pearson Digital Learning Program

multiple Kids CoLab sessions of refining book covers for a math program that I learned just how important a relevant and engaging a book cover can be. If children are put off, or, worse, disgusted by the cover of the book, it is indeed a challenge to motivate them to learn that subject. In the end, Kids CoLab influenced the cover art for nine different textbook covers, across multiple grade levels.

Finding ways to balance learning goals and conventional instructional formats (e.g., arithmetic drills) with playful, seemingly silly elements that can promote engagement remains a challenge for Kids CoLab projects. Our experience underscores the complex balancing act involved in translating creative, sometimes off-the-wall design ideas into actual projects within a larger design-based, product-oriented research process.

For example, during Kids CoLab's second year, a Pearson developer requested the team's help in extending the design of a digital math game. The primary goal of the prototype design was to develop math fluency, and the developer was concerned that the content itself was not engaging enough for children to play on their own. The developers considered including scientific concepts related to plant growth as a possible extension to the main math content, so Kids CoLab devoted a co-design session to brainstorming how unconventional sources of light and water could be incorporated into the game. Ideas from both child and adult co-designers included embedding a faucet into a cactus to extract water, siphoning water from a pelican's mouth, and harnessing light from the headlights of a car. The headlight example demonstrated the ways in which child co-design partners pursued wacky, fairly unrealistic sources of light for plants. However, as we were exploring the role of engagement in the existing math game's content, these seemingly wacky ideas were translated into artwork that was incorporated into a paper prototype of the game.

During a subsequent co-design session, the child co-designers play-tested a paper prototype of the math game. A guiding research question for this session was to evaluate how the "wacky" ideas worked in the context of game-play. Throughout the play-test, the children's engagement was evident: they all smiled and laughed as they played, with one child stating, "I want to play this game at home!"

During a debrief following the play-test, the adult designer of the game prototype asked the child co-designers to share additional sources of light and water they thought might make the game even more interesting. The wackiness increased as the children brainstormed that light could be harnessed from the gleam of a very white-toothed smile or from a bald man's head. At this point, the adult designer bluntly asked the children, "Does it matter that you cannot actually grow a plant using the gleam from a bald man's head?" One of Kids CoLab designers, a 12-year-old boy, responded, "In my world, in Pretty Pony Land, you can."

This exchange between the adult prototype developer and the child co-design partner highlights the design tensions that we often face when trying to balance playful engagement with more structured learning goals and outcomes.

Because we espoused the notion that play is a form of media literacy that enables experimentation "as a form of problem-solving" (Bonsignore et al., 2016; Jenkins et al., 2009), we constantly explored ways to include children's wild and wacky sensibilities into more formal learning goals.

For instance, after the series of design sessions for the math game, we held a co-design session to explore the role of humor in learning more explicitly. Child and adult co-designers plotted the artifacts they created on a continuum ranging from "supporting learning" to "distracting from learning," and they engaged in rich dialogue about what it means to have a fun, engaging, learning experience. Specifically, by looking at the creations through this lens, we were able to parse out funny, non-educational features like a man who grows his facial hair so rapidly that he has to shave every 2 minutes, from a coach who occasionally uses silly jokes while tutoring a student. We frequently refer back to this continuum in our debriefs to help ensure that we have allowed for creativity without limitations even while keeping our learning goals in focus (and vice versa). Our overarching goal is to enable everyone on the team to continue to brainstorm wildly in blue-sky mode, then constrain these brainstormed ideas into feasible learning designs: Who says you cannot have fun while you learn, or learn when you are having fun?

Deviations from Academia

Implementing cooperative inquiry at Pearson required some minor deviations from the typical practices and protocols with the Human-Computer Interaction Lab's (HCIL) Kidsteam group at the University of Maryland. Although the age range for long-standing child co-designers on Kidsteam is 7–11 years old, the HCIL research group has collaborated with children both older and younger than this range (Bonsignore et al., 2014; Guha et al., 2004; Guha et al., 2013; Yip et al., 2012). Traditionally, cooperative inquiry's target age range for child co-designers has been 7–11 years old because children in this age range were found to be old enough to articulate their ideas, but not old enough to feel constrained during brainstorming and free-form ideation, whether due to self-consciousness associated with teenagers or due to preconceived notions of "the way things are supposed to be" (Druin, 1999, p. 596). Given that our research responsibilities encompassed the entire range of K-12 education, with many product teams devoted to the middle school level, we expanded our age range. Not only did we include a boy who was age 12 the first year, but he returned for a second year at age 13. Similar to the small but growing body of HCI design research that engages teenagers in co-design (Bonsignore et al., 2016; Danielsson & Wiberg, 2006; Isomursu et al., 2004; Read et al., 2013; Yip et al., 2012), our plan was to include older youth as we expanded our Kids CoLab, to meet our broad K-12 product range. In addition, the older Hoboken Kids CoLab team plans to grow from their initial 10- to 14-year-olds (fifth to eighth graders) to high school (14–18 year olds in grades 9–12).

Perhaps our biggest deviation involves the attendance of adults in the sessions. In the beginning, we strictly adhered to recommendations that any adult attending a session would participate fully as a design partner. This was easy to do for any in-person attendees. We even enforced this with the media, when we asked reporters to arrive in casual clothing and sit on the carpet with the children. Over time, as interest in the program grew, we began to accommodate virtual participation through web conferences for teams who were not co-located. But even then, anyone attending virtually was required to participate fully. We literally placed a tablet or laptop at the table with a small group to facilitate virtual co-design. This synchronous participation evolved out of the virtual usability sessions stakeholders had grown accustomed to. While we had a core group of adult co-design partners who collaborated regularly with child co-designers on the Kids CoLab team, our stakeholders often included Pearson developers, content experts, and market research personnel who had a vested interest in the design and development of a product, but might not participate actively throughout the co-design process. In order to save travel costs, virtual synchronous participation, although it was not without challenges, became a regular occurrence.

However, once we had six or seven interested observers who were not co-located, I had to make a choice. I decided during the summer camp to allow a group of individuals to act as "fly on the wall" observers. I introduced them at the beginning of the session, but then they remained fairly silent. I remember during one of the breaks, as I debriefed these adult observers, they had some follow-up questions for the children. We devoted some time to these questions, and I noticed that the adults were furiously taking notes. It became clear to me that they were in the midst of making some major decisions about their product. While they had pulled in multiple sources of data to inform their decisions, the Kids CoLab session was quite timely in helping advance their design process.

Later, I asked the children during lunch how they felt about having a group of adults observing, but not participating. We had a real heart to heart about it. They told me they thought it was "cool" that these adults were really listening to them and taking notes. They also stated that they liked having people "on the computer." Given the children's input, I decided that moving forward, we would allow virtual observers but still require anyone in-person to be a full design partner.

Other than these minor adjustments, our industry implementation has leveraged the research-based techniques and democratic philosophy from cooperative inquiry to include and empower our triple beneficiaries: Pearson product teams, Kids CoLab members, and the eventual end users.

Conclusion

Pearson took a stand for our industry to position the learner at the center of all that we do, to include our research strategy. We have empowered our Kids CoLab members—children and adults alike—to take a part in creating and ideating the solutions that will likely be integrated into their classrooms someday. Kids CoLab parents have remarked about how fulfilling the experience has been for their children—how they are learning, becoming leaders and improving their ability to take charge, be focused, and take initiative. Reflecting on my own roots as a former classroom teacher, the Kids CoLab journey represents the evolution of a happy marriage between a learner-focused corporate mission and a passion for positively impacting the lives of children.

Note: Shortly after the time of this writing, the original Kids CoLab program that began within the Pearson Research & Innovation Network was discontinued, due to a consolidation of research functions within Pearson. The second instance of the Kids CoLab program in Hoboken still supports the development of next generation digital learning programs.

Acknowledgments

We would like to thank the Inaugural Kids CoLab members and families, as well as Robin Duffy and her Pearson-Hoboken Kids CoLab members and families. We also thank Pearson-Chandler Kids CoLab's recurring adult design partners, Elizabeth Bercovitz, Rusty Brandt, Nick Zakhar, Tim Cothron, and Lourdes Reyes; and business sponsors, Marc Nelson and Kristin Paperman. We are grateful to our UMD mentors, Allison Druin, Mona Leigh Guha, and Tammy Clegg, as well as our Pearson R&D group contacts, Emily Lai, Kimberly O'Malley, and Ashley Peterson-DeLuca.

References

Bonsignore, E., Ahn, J., Clegg, T., Guha, M. L., Yip, J., Druin, A., & Hourcade, J. P. (2013). Embedding participatory design into designs for learning: An untapped interdisciplinary resource. In *Proceedings of the Conference for Computer-Supported Cooperative Learning* (CSCL 2013) (pp. 549–556). Madison, WI: International Society of the Learning Sciences.

Bonsignore, E., Koepfler, J., Guha, M. L., Ahn, J., & Kraus, K. (2014). Exploring teen co-design in alternate reality games for learning. CHI 2014 Workshop on understanding teen UX: Building a bridge to the future. www.chici.org/teenUX/papers/paper7.pdf.

Bonsignore, E., Hansen, D., Pellicone, A., Kraus, K., Ahn, J., Shumway, S., Parkin, J., Cardon, J., Sheets, J., Jensen, C. H., & Koepfler, J. (2016). Traversing transmedia together: Co-designing an education ARG for teens, with teens. To appear in *Proceedings of the 16th International Conference on Interaction Design and Children, IDC 2016*. New York: ACM.

Danielsson, K., & Wiberg, C. (2006). Participatory design of learning media: Designing educational computer games with and for teenagers. *Interactive Technology and Smart Education*, 3(4), 275–291.

Druin, A. (1999, May). Cooperative inquiry: Developing new technologies for children with children. In *Proceedings of the SIGCHI Conference on Human Factors in Computing Systems* (pp. 592–599). New York: ACM.

Druin, A. (2002). The role of children in the design of new technology. *Behaviour and Information Technology*, 21(1), 1–25.

Fails, J. A., Guha, M. L., & Druin, A. (2012). Methods and techniques for involving children in the design of new technology for children. *Human–Computer Interaction*, 6(2), 85–166.

Fullan, M. (2013). *Stratosphere: Integrating Technology, Pedagogy, and Change Knowledge.* Ontario: Pearson Canada.

Guha, M. L., Druin, A., Chipman, G., Fails, J. A., Simms, S., & Farber, A. (2004). Mixing ideas: A new technique for working with young children as design partners. In *Proceedings of the 2004 Conference on Interaction Design and Children, IDC 2004* (pp. 35–42). New York: ACM.

Guha, M. L., Druin, A., & Fails, J. A. (2013). Cooperative Inquiry revisited: Reflections of the past and guidelines for the future of intergenerational co-design. *International Journal of Child-Computer Interaction*, 1(1), 14–23.

Guha, M. L., Druin, A., & Fails, J. A. (2010, June). Investigating the impact of design processes on children. In *Proceedings of the 9th International Conference on Interaction Design and Children* (pp. 198–201). New York: ACM.

Hoadley, C. P. (2002, January). Creating context: Design-based research in creating and understanding CSCL. In *Proceedings of the Conference on Computer Support for Collaborative Learning: Foundations for a CSCL Community* (pp. 453–462). International Society of the Learning Sciences.

Isomursu, M., Isomursu, P., & Still, K. (2004). Capturing tacit knowledge from young girls. *Interacting with Computers*, 16(3), 431–449.

Jenkins, H., Purushotma, R., Weigel, M., Clinton, K., & Robison, A. J. (2009). *Confronting the Challenges of Participatory Culture: Media Education for the 21st Century.* Cambridge, MA: MIT Press.

Read, J. C. C., Horton, M., Iversen, O., Fitton, D., & Little, L. (2013). Methods of working with teenagers in interaction design. In *CHI '13 Extended Abstracts on Human Factors in Computing Systems* (pp. 3243–3246). New York: ACM.

Yip, J. C., Foss, E., & Guha, M. L. (2012). Co-designing with adolescents. In *Designing Interactive Technology for Teens Workshop*, NordiCHI, Copenhagen, Denmark. Retrieved from: www.chici.org/ditt2012/papers.html.

SECTION IV

Emerging Perspectives on Participatory Design and Learning

12

LEARNING AT/WITH/FROM THE EDGES

Ann Light and Jos Boys

> *The architects spent time working separately without discussion; then came together (rather late) to pool what they had learnt about their materials and assemble a structure. Their offering was ambitious: a long arcing bridge of raw spaghetti. They had extended the length of the spaghetti using a novel joining mechanism that relied on penne pasta strips to tether points where two or more strands met. The bridge didn't stand up by itself and had a tendency to spring outwards, caused by tension in the spaghetti as it was made to arc. They agreed they would have needed longer to make it stable.* (Project 1: Collaboration, Figure 12.2)

A room of mixed professionals and academic researchers had been invited to discuss "collaboration" and, as a final exercise, was asked to represent what the term meant to them, collaboratively, using only some pasta and any other materials they had to hand. They were to identify their disciplinary roots and join a table. The tags on the tables read: *architecture*; *arts and humanities*; *business and management*; *design*; *engineering*; *social science*. Each discipline produced its own version of collaboration, which was the point of the exercise.

Dialogic Accounting

In this chapter, we use examples of our separate and shared community-based participatory design practices to open up questions of what collaboration involves across and between different disciplinary contexts and in complex situations. And we use excerpts of three projects' trajectories to reveal the emergent learning that ensued. The projects that we discuss are a collaborative exploration of disciplinary boundaries, a cross-disciplinary project using participatory design (PD) to investigate a specific space, and a community-based project that critically and creatively reflected on its own PD.

Much of the learning in these projects happened in ways that no one had specifically signed up to, but, importantly, aimed neither to restrict nor to close down possibilities. We are particularly interested in making manifest the *latencies* inherent in participatory design—the nascent qualities and states that remain concealed and previously untapped, only becoming actualized and developed through design processes. This learning about ourselves, and others, speaks to the potentiality involved, not only in materially changing the world (as design is understood to do), but also in the pedagogical project of "becoming more fully human" (Freire 1993: 48).

As we understand it, latency is embodied not just in the "space" of a project, but also its participants and in its methods (Boys 2016). Latencies are inherent in all such work, but not inherently positive. We will show how such latencies can both lead to valuable developments and be fraught with difficulties, and will suggest some principles and methods for ameliorating the worst effects, while enabling productive potential to emerge. In other words, we explore the process of participatory design as one within which hidden latencies become visible and new perspectives and/or reflections emerge; this is the process by which learning "happens" or emerges. The core of this concept of "emergent learning" is that *learning emerges* through the process of unveiling latencies and the revelations that come from reflecting upon differences.

We ourselves come from different disciplines into design, one with a background in educational drama and media, the other in architectural education and practice. We find it valuable to co-explore the unspoken fissures that exist and are created when we work together and with others—to start from difference rather than to smooth it away. Indeed, it has become a tenet of our practice, to *start from difference* as a learning strategy—and to be attentive to implications throughout a project. These are not merely differences in disciplinary knowledge or subject perspective that can be resolved through some kind of process of informal consensus. They are the both explicit and implicit differences in how participants position themselves and others, and are positioned by, through "normal" social and material practices—what Wenger calls "repertoires" (1998) and Latour, "assemblages" (2005). Crucially, locating oneself (and being located) as a learner and/or teacher, researcher and/or activist, professional and/or artist, and/or other is enacted through (not separate to) our ongoing everyday encounters, settings, and artifacts. It is a relational and situated performance that dynamically creates, perpetuates, adapts, contests, and transforms those everyday social and material practices through the *spaces in-between* participants (Boys 2016).

Collaborating through Difference

"Opening up," part of Project Two: Architecture-InsideOut (AIO), *was a one-day design charrette held in Turbine Hall at Tate Modern in London. It brought together disabled artists with architects to create temporary interventions into the space that*

"spoke to" making the building more accessible, not just functionally but creatively. Each artist-architect team took a different direction, working together in more or less structured ways, some engaging the public and some not. One team decided to make a series of games, challenging the earnestness with which disability is framed in both architectural discourse and regulatory practices, and reclaiming the joys of childhood from a "normal" commonsense that always assumes being disabled is childlike. This group made swings, threw balls, climbed the walls, and left dynamic traces—footprints, wheel-marks—in patterns on the floor.

The collaboration exercise that opened this chapter, and the one described above as part of *Opening Up!* (Figure 12.1), involved cooperation through doing and reflecting. Whilst the "pasta bridge" collaboration exercise afforded participants an opportunity to stop and think about what was happening within and across each of their disciplinary groups, the "opening up" design charrette sparked cross-disciplinary pairs to act out in the world, exploring and testing various ideas about how to change that world. However, both design exercises share a similarity of framework:

- Tacit knowledge can be made explicit through the nonverbal means of making and doing (Polyani 1996).
- Ideas, methods, actions, and creations are emergent, rather than pre-framed, as Gaver suggests in exploring research through design as a pre-paradigmatic process (Gaver 2012).

FIGURE 12.1 Architecture-InsideOut (AIO) Event *Opening Up!* Turbine Hall, Tate Modern, 10 May 2008. Photography: Jos Boys

- Transformative creative work can be supported through projects that build on intuition and reason but also reveal and resist simplified and normative assumptions about the world: as Deleuze says, creating knowledge *through* action (1994, 2003).
- Cross-disciplinary collaboration is a powerful means of enabling these processes.

In each project, the balance of activities varied across and between groups. We saw differences across many dimensions: in the amount of talk, of experimental or representational making, in organizational structure, and in role division.

In the case of the collaboration exercise, these differences were a source of entertainment to the participants, as some of the activities could be seen as almost caricaturing the different priorities and ways of working that emerged from the different professions present (Figures 12.2–12.7).

The genesis of the pasta exercise was itself a collaboration. An international group of design researchers[1] was charged with running an "informative exercise on the nature of collaboration" as part of an invited workshop. I [Ann] was put in mind of a task I had given to postgraduate students studying interdisciplinarity. I had asked them to work together in groups that reflected their original degree (including computer science, psychology, and sociology) and prepare something to explain to others how they understood the terms "communication" and "information." (Inevitably, huge differences were apparent.) As we considered this activity, we saw the value in asking people to make something—it was a meeting of many presentations, and we wanted to access a different part of people's brain. The idea of pasta followed as a construction material, since it is cheap, easy to source, and entertaining as a medium. Someone else had used it to good effect before, so we used it for our segregation exercise.

Thus each "pasta" design group worked in isolation, and when we saw one another's images of collaboration, it was with heightened curiosity. As an organizer, I was not alone in wondering at how characteristic of each discipline each response in pasta felt. There were some (perhaps justified) stereotypes perceived in the responses by the groups, observed by both the presenters and other participants viewing the outcomes of the different tables.

In other words, we found that each group's pasta design was characteristic of disciplinary differences. We noticed differences in terms of style, ambitions, and degrees of abstraction. There was also a related difference in how each group spoke about their designs, such as how they had worked together in making it and how they managed relations in telling us about it. Many participants were aware of the procedural aspects of what they had produced and some were articulate about them. Willingness to talk about such dimensions and differences varied among tables. So, even the degree of reflexivity brought by the disciplines varied enormously, as did interest in social process in contrast to the design of the product.

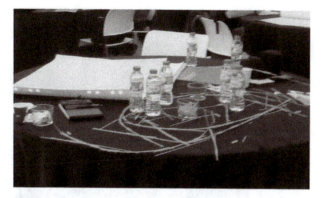

FIGURE 12.2 The "Architects' Table," with Its Cleverly Sustained Arc
Photography: Ann Light

FIGURE 12.3 The "Engineering Table": Each Piece of Pasta Is a Person or Project
Photography: Ann Light

FIGURE 12.4 The "Business/Management Table": Structures and Policies Were
Enacted with the Pasta
Photography: Ann Light

FIGURE 12.5 The "Arts/Humanities Table": Still Negotiating as the Mobile Is Being Presented to the Group
Photography: Ann Light

FIGURE 12.6 The "Social Science Table": Lively Labeling Complements the Pasta
Photography: Ann Light

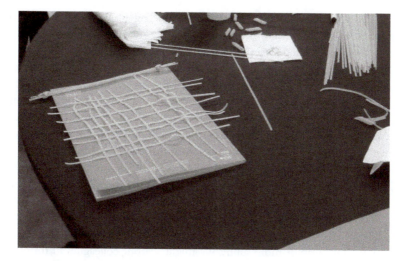

FIGURE 12.7 The "Design Table": Ingenious and Understated
Photography: Ann Light

In this, part of the *Collaboration* project, the most literal version of "a collaboration" came from the engineers (Figure 12.3), who produced a model with a formal structure that appeared to be a professional hierarchy (shaped as spokes from a central point). They could name the role of each person involved in the project it represented and give their relationship to the whole. They held a quiet discussion about what to produce. When they showed their model, one person introduced it, courteously inviting each of his colleagues to add a perspective.

On a nearby table, business and management (Figure 12.4) were putting the final touches on another structure that involved pasta people, carefully colouring the penne blue and red to show diversity.

In another part of the room, members of the arts (Figure 12.5) table, who had worked spontaneously to make a hanging mobile, were arguing vociferously about what to suspend on the last arm. One of the team held it, while the others weighed objects at their disposal and considered balance. They rounded this off with a long and unstructured theoretical explanation of what each section represented, informed by argument and lively debate even at presentation stage.

It would now be unfair to readers with a design or social science background not to share what these tables produced. In short, the urge to explain found a different outlet with the social scientists (Figure 12.6), whose work was characterized by a lot of words in the shape of a labeled exhibit and a large sheet explaining their discussion and decisions. Everyone chipped in to help describe it.

The quietest table of all belonged to the designers (Figure 12.7), who had also been experimenting with their materials. They had soaked their pasta in hot water for most of the allocated time, then wove it into a mat and made a punchy little video about their work. The artifacts were largely expected to speak for themselves, in direct contrast to the social science group. And there was an air about the table of having cleverly addressed the problem.

Apart from the joy of seeing so many people come up with markedly different ideas that we could not have predicted (but at the same time seemed so right), there is a more serious point to the observations we are making in relating this. The exercise raised many of the issues that participation introduces through polarizing positions and revealing assumptions. It was striking how levels of abstraction/literalness and planning/spontaneity varied.

Such a short exercise enables a revealing of, and opportunity to reflect on, the implicit frameworks, methods, and assumptions that people bring to participatory design. It is possible for many of us to situate ourselves on one or other disciplinary table, adopting a familiar strategy. We might any of us perform our discipline when challenged by other ways of thinking and engaging, either in this conspicuous way or more subtly. We might see our colleagues in this exercise showing us that designers are smart (and can be smug?), artists experimental, engineers logical, and businesspeople concerned with diversity and people. It was a gamble to ask individuals to work together in this way, though something interesting must surely come out of inviting people to illuminate their practice. Instead, the differences were so blatant that our positions—and the fact of our positionality (England 1994)—were held to our faces.

But such an exercise could not (and did not intend to) explore how such differences intersect throughout the duration of a collaborative project. It showed us nothing about how this might affect the quality of the process and its outcomes. We address these aspects further below. But we note that, even in these contexts, when participatory design embraces the latent and emergent—where not just outcomes but also educational "scaffolding" protocols, and procedures are co-designed (e.g., Light and Akama 2014)—then differences in both everyday unspoken assumptions and explicit subject positions can increase potency and reduce effectiveness and can lead to resonant interactions and frustrating problems simultaneously. These tensions, of course, offer an excellent forum for learning, depending on how they are made apparent. How, then, can we better understand the latencies in "participatory design"—using the term both in its general definition to mean what is *hidden but has potential*, and in its more scientific use—to describe the gaps or delays (the potential "drag" caused by duration) that happen between a starting point and an actual change occurring?

Exploring latencies is about what we have already called the spaces in-between—opening up to investigation how *potential* is released (both positively and negatively) through the embodied everyday enactments of a project as it is continuously performed through participant encounters with each other, settings, artifacts, and "normal" social practices. It is here, through *negotiating* these gaps, that learning, in its widest sense, takes place, as we each attempt to make better sense of, and survive effectively in, the world. Learning is happening across all participants, but what is being learnt—the new interpretations and perspectives that are emerging—may remain dormant, go unrecognized, be implicitly or quietly contested, or set up unspoken antagonisms. It is the very mundaneness of such activity that allows it to go unnoticed and unremarked upon, when in fact it is actually *durational work*— what has been called "problematic accomplishments" (Ryave and Schenkein 1974). It takes time and effort both to perform everyday routines as obvious and natural and to redesign or "breach" them (Garfinkel 1967: 37), as participatory design aims to do.

> The brief that has been given to the disabled artist-architects teams at Tate Modern is "welcome all ye who enter here." Some take this as an opportunity to celebrate diversity and difference, others to make a critical commentary on the inequality of access to built space.
>
> "How many ways can you get from A to B" choreographed a public mass run down the Turbine Hall's ramp, asking participants to invoke as many ways of moving as they could. (Figure 12.8)
>
> "In/Security" involved the team dressing up as security guards and creating a performance of blocking measures that temporarily restricted public movement in often surreal and humorous ways. (Figure 12.9)
>
> Each of these projects expressed a hidden latency in the space, in enabling it to be used differently (through playfully either increasing or decreasing ease of mobility).

FIGURE 12.8 Artist and Architect Collaboration Entitled "How many ways can U get from A2B?" from Architecture-InsideOut (AIO) Event *Opening Up!* Turbine Hall, Tate Modern, 10 May 2008. Photography: Jos Boys

FIGURE 12.9 Artist and Architect Collaboration Entitled: "In/Security" from Architecture-InsideOut (AIO) Event *Opening Up!* Turbine Hall, Tate Modern, 10 May 2008. Photography: Jos Boys

The approach and content of each of these works at London's Tate Modern, the method of their implementation and the organizational roles and relationships, again varied across teams. One team struggled to produce anything; one showed some discontent with the work it produced. These two groups were used to participatory design methods and worked hard together using mainly tacit and nonverbal methods—through making and doing. But their attempts to translate the latent potential of their artist-architect collaborations into an actual performance and/or artifact was "unsatisfactory." That is, they were very dissatisfied with their results. Rather than emergent ideas and prototyping productions leading to resonant, positive, and multiplying effects, there was instead a kind of dragging and interference, a diminution and lack of fit.

The "stuttering" within these projects' durations formed in the spaces in between:

- What each individual brings to the process, not just in terms of disciplinary context, knowledge, and skills, but also of confidence, power, and resilience, of expectations, perceptions, and experiences
- How each individual locates themselves within the group, takes on and negotiates a role
- The explicit rules of the game, the equivalence and equity of roles and relationships
- The complexities of designing things and processes that aim to act as a critical reaction to/commentary on/improvement to the "normal" world

We would suggest that in education, such spaces in-between may often be obscured by assumptions (and realities) about how teaching and learning "works," what roles educators and tutors take within it, and what relationships of expertise they bring to it (Austerlitz 2008). This has been particularly explored within dis-ability studies, where dis/ability tends to create just such gaps or stutters in the "normal" workings of the university (Titchskosky 2011; Price, forthcoming). These scholars show how it is often the very invisibility of the amount of work required to maintain the everyday "normal" social and material practices of higher education, that perpetuate it in one form rather than another.

In community-based projects, the framing spaces of participatory design are also often blurred, or contested. The transitory and inventive nature of much col-laboration in community and professional space contrasts with the fixity of much school and workplace infrastructure. So these different contexts can have an effect too. There may be a failure to notice that a stuttering is happening at all (or an avoidance of it) when structures are too fixed. And it may be much harder to real-ize productive potential when matters round an unexpected corner if processes are inconsistently fluid.

Principles of Resisting Definition

Fluidity, disruption and mischief were motifs of a third project (Effectiveness in Action), employed as the means of destabilizing relations (and thus allowing and enhancing the learning possible by participating) in work that the two authors embarked upon together as university researchers in collaboration with community activists. This co-research activity had the ultimate aim of using participatory design to develop (through a series of invited participant workshops) a better understanding of what underpins community-based action—why people do it and how they keep going, often against the odds. It was a slippery project, where neither mischief nor disruption was ever quite confined to the methods or learning outcomes. This time, not just "deliverables" were to be generated out of participatory design, but also the very underlying conceptual framework and language; the methods of development, implementation, and communication; and the grounds of which the project as a whole might or should be evaluated. As Bjogvinsson et al. suggest:

> Designing for, by, and with stakeholders may be challenging enough where common social objectives are already established, institutionalized, or at least seen as reasonably within reach. These social communities are sup-ported by relatively stable infrastructures. The really demanding challenge is to design where no such consensus seems to be within view, where no social community exists. (2012: 116)

In our experience, working together from locations within and across both uni-versity and social activism, it was not a failure of social commitment or lack of stable community that created stuttering, but an explicit questioning around how differences (and differential power) can act to frame public funded participatory design in one way rather than another. To give a focus to our work—and most crucially to avoid pressures to create "normal" research outputs—we committed to collaboratively editing our various insights in a material form, ultimately a book (Figure 12.10).

But even this focus was arrived at through considerable negotiation, and the resulting product was a testament to its loose and evolving structure and an emphasis on juxtaposition, not synthesis.

A first principle: Starting from difference, there is no "we." There will always be real and perceived differentials in who is seen to have the "correct" expertise: to have power and control over, and to gain most from, the participatory design process.

> *Our encounters produced a distinctive form of research. It is difficult to talk about it without referring to the collective and I am not the collective. I do not speak for others' experience. Every use of "we" is thus potentially problematic, even though a collective did form to make decisions, grouped to produce three events for fellow change-makers and brought this material together. I can only point to the plurality of the outcome and suggest that it wasn't accidental.* (Ann, excerpt from *Everyday Disruptions*, 2014, the book of the project)

A second principle: Concepts and processes are not already pre-framed. But neither do they emerge from an assumption that collaboration and participation through time (however patient) lead to consensus and a shared commonality. Rather, an attempt is made to let the latencies reveal themselves, to let them

FIGURE 12.10 *Everyday Disruptions*, 2014, Book Produced by the Effectiveness in Action Project. Photography: Ann Light

emerge in whatever miscellaneous, unexpected, and even tortuous ways and provide the grounds for learning. We might also consider Björgvinsson, Ehn, and Hillgren (2012) and DiSalvo (2012) on the agonism incipient in community relations, and Bannon and Ehn (2013), who directly challenge the merits of consensus in participatory design contexts.

> *We collaborated with many participants to learn how best to share, celebrate and commemorate our perceptions and experiences of community action. Themes came and went, drifted sideways, re-focused and then took other directions. If thoughts and discussions began to revolve around notions of reverent actions, playfulness, trust, gentle disruption and enchantment, this was without the expectation of imposing an artificial consensus. (Jos, excerpt from* Everyday Disruptions, *2014)*

A third principle (a.k.a., the "principle of loose bundles"): Starting from difference means that there can be no coherent, consistent, and comprehensive "result." Rather, the design experience and outcomes become a move in a more or less coordinated direction that can inform others in what they do.

> *This is not without tension. A balance is needed, to hold the line, to push for transformation or challenge authority with a degree of grace in the way that people come together. Obstruction and flow are both present . . . and a sense of movement towards. (Ann, excerpt from* Everyday Disruptions, *2014)*

What emerged from the particular latencies of this project, then, was a design methodology and system of managing our creative output we called the *principle of loose bundles*. This was an approach that accepted difference as a starting point; it did not try to produce consensus, but instead looked for patterns of intensity and repetition in the events and materials we produced both together and apart.

> *This looseness has itself become our method—what we ended up calling the principle of loose bundles. The multitude of diverse voices and moments generated out of project events formed our raw data. Performances, talks, songs, writings, drawings and activities were recorded. With the project team working together, we recalled what was resonant, important, relevant to each of us; selections were made and argued over; laid out into groups, and then other groups as various patterns resolved and dissolved. Out of this, particular notions slowly coalesced together and literally became loose bundles as we worked.*
> *[. . . .] Crucially, these loose bundles made sense to everyone in the project team (even if what we each see in the groupings includes different angles of emphasis and interpretation). Where pieces overlapped between bundles—which many do—we have used colour-coding to reference connections.*
> *From the beginning this project did not want to tell people what to do; or to make a handbook or toolkit for "how to do" community action; or to impose the appearance*

of a coherent structure on diverse voices. [. . . .] We hope that the principle of loose bundles, which holds onto many layers and entanglements, and does not imply either completeness or consistency, allows those many voices to communicate both our communality and our differences. (Jos, excerpt from *Everyday Disruptions*, 2014)

As noted, the project, perhaps ironically from this distance, was called "Effectiveness in Action." We were courting the unknowable and unstructured in our choice of working partners (who were organized to be fleet of foot, not representative of other people in their doings) and our methods (which evolved in answer to the question, which was evolving too), so it is no surprise that we would emerge with many different understandings of our achievements and measures of success. This too can be regarded from the perspective of education, both informal, which our work might be considered to embrace, and formal, where different forms of success are a political issue. A challenge for us is that the learning in a research project should not stay with only the participants of the project, but be available to those who have commissioned the project: in our case, the British public by proxy of the UK research councils. In many other learning situations, the only group being targeted is "learners," but this idea of a one-way street where only designated learners learn is a narrow conception of the possibilities (e.g., exploded by Freire's teacher-student and student-teachers, 1993).

Even if we allow that everyone is a student acquiring new knowhow, we can see success in a multitude of ways: as new understanding, new practices, or, more cynically, the capacity to respond to hoops by jumping through them to the approval of others.

Framing this specific plurality (and varying degrees of indifference to the need for formal learning in the shape of some research outcomes) is the wider discussion as to what might be regarded as effective participatory design—or, indeed, what might be seen as a good *co-research* and *co-design* project? This is a better question, since we had eschewed the easier option of organizing round an established heart of action, as participatory design practice must organize if it is to be participation *in* something. Our ambitions to make relations and questions from the ground up pointed towards something more balanced and equal, even as we recognized the impossibility of such leveling.

Ideas about purpose and types of outcome (and the need for a way of recognizing them) was a difference that cut through the collective in confrontational ways, not because the academic researchers were traditionally goal-oriented, but because they were perceived to be hoping for a project successful enough to capitalize upon. Despite many conversations, this area of distrust persisted, fuelled by the spectre of accountability for public money and the hard fact of different professional orientations. Success itself was contested.

Beyond that were shades of resistance to assessment that everyone shared, such as a discomfort with academic, or governmental, modes of accessing effectiveness, value for money, and performance measures (and, indeed, the industrial values of improved commercial design), instead seeking to explore questions residing under the surface: those that are not often acknowledged, those we would like to start giving a voice in some way.

> *It got me thinking about how social action often challenges what it is ordinarily "sayable," about how activists speak (and act) around and against the taken-for-granted language and concepts of contemporary society; whether insisting that landscapes are about more than just property rights, or refusing to accept that choices about social provision should be based on the free market. This kind of speaking is about opening up cracks and fissures, about revealing what is invisible or undetectable, precisely because it is being left unsaid or undone in the smooth surface of the "normal run of things." And not only have these gaps to be found, they have to be expressed in ways that are shared, resonant and robust.*
>
> *The many words [. . .] thrown up by this project—irreverent reverence, tricksterism, pleasurable insurrection, mindful audacity—begin to capture something of this resistance to not just "the way the world works" but also to the manner in which it talks and "explains" (justifies) itself to us. Not surprisingly, these modes of creative subversion also resist being pinned down, explained and analysed, in case this just becomes a return and reduction to the "normal world," a capturing and controlling through imposed "understanding."* (Jos, excerpt from *Everyday Disruptions*, 2014)

For academic researchers on the project, this elusiveness was a potential problem. The underlying co-designing structure means not just that activists are researchers but also that researchers are activists—there may be no "we," but there also is no "them and us." We accept that this may make us radicals in the sense that Freire (1993) uses it, that we see developing together as a praxis, and "reality" as "really a process, undergoing constant transformation" (1993: 56).

In its development, the project had centrally challenged any academic analytical model that demands to explain a situation coherently and comprehensively, as ultimately known and controlled, evaluated and made more effective through "solutions (principles, tool-kits, programmes). It refused the kind of "thinking about" reflection that involves a standing outside, commenting on, looking down, and distancing from the acts of lived and engaged participation that *are* the project.

What, then, can be said here? There are two intertwined challenges. As academics who are both also involved in social action, we may struggle too, sometimes with the imposed rationality of much university research, itself captured and reduced by specific ways of framing research "excellence."Yet we are—in different ways—interested in how the alternative ways of saying and doing that come out of social action are able to create ripples outwards beyond a particular group of participants. The Effectiveness in Action project wanted to take notice of and honour how people care when they undertake social action—to communicate something of what motivates and sustains us in this work to others engaged in similar activities. This celebration, through speaking up, is not so much to offer the *unknown* but to articulate the *hidden* in such a way that people nod with recognition and see their concerns presented afresh in the (un)familiar language that others can bring.

But, as well as this, we are part of various scholarly communities—also with their own ways of speaking and doing—communities that are themselves always revisiting and revising their analytical methods, and their conceptual positions in and against the normal run-of-things. How, then, can these existing academic communities learn from this community-based project's refusals, subversions, and interventions? This is to explore how we can share not only some of the ways of making "sayable" social action from its participants' perspectives, but also ask how we can engage productively as *scholars* in these processes.

Writings by Isabelle Stengers have been central to such conceptual shifts, in critically exploring how academic work might be more open, relational, and politically engaged. As she asks, how can one

> present a proposal intended not to say what is, or what ought to be, but to provoke thought; one that requires no other verification than the way in which it is able to "slow down" reasoning and create an opportunity to arouse a slightly different awareness of the problems and situations mobilizing us? How can this proposal be distinguished from issues of authority and generality currently articulated to the notion of "theory"? (Stengers 2005: 994)

To do this as academics we attempted to *stay within* the project that had brought us together (*Effectiveness in Action*), rather than stand outside at some evaluative point, so to reflect our conclusions on it. Instead, by being part of paying attention to and "getting a hold on" what is being said/done, it is possible to act not from the artificial authority of analysis and reflection, but from the pragmatic position of a "relay." The passage of relays, Pignarre and Stengers (2007) suggest, implies

> not only holding but also giving. For the relay to be taken it must be given, even if those who give know they are not masters of what they give, that when a relay is taken it is not a matter of a simple translation but of a new creation. (2007: 123)

Relaying here replaces "evaluating effectiveness." If this project's process of co-designing began with the technique of "gentle disruption" (Light 2013)—another tool that operates from the *inside* as a form of shared elucidation—it might also use this concept of "relaying" as a means of articulating the passing on of what has happened to others, as part of both a continuity and a shifting and changing, a getting hold of but not laying claim to.

Conclusion

Our coming together—Jos and Ann, in making the text here—mirrors the conception process for this chapter and the way we found we worked in the project just described. We take turns, review and build upon each turn, find ourselves moved by the turn the text has taken. Our ideas are close enough to allow us to enjoy the discrepancies, the chance to reconcile perspectives (from different backgrounds ourselves), and our interpretation of each other's language through the practices of construction. For our purposes here, we are both slightly more concerned with process than form, assembling rather than closing down.

So we do not present an a single and uncontested analysis of how participatory design might grow and change to become more accommodating of difference, the different, the differently abled, the differently minded, the edges, margins, the unknowable and not to be resolved. We do not comment on how the practice of it might police the gaps and make spaces for the unusual, the uncommented upon, the political with a little "p" and the lost nuances that fall between.

Instead, we draw attention to the three projects' trajectories as emergent learning, for everyone involved, in ways that no one signed up to. We note the latencies, the gaps and holes, tensions and misunderstandings and accept them as part of that learning, incorporating *designing* and *making* as means to think about, express and reflect on processes, status and ambitions without ever leaving the action, without always having to find words for what is best shown. And here we extend the relay and pass the baton . . .

Acknowledgments

We thank the UK's Arts and Humanities Research Council for funding *Effectiveness in Action* (grant no. AH/K006622/1), noting that the material used in reference to this project is available in the project book *Everyday Disruptions* (https://db.tt/lgeP0Uoc).

Note

1   With thanks to Laurene, Yoko, and Andrew for the chance to try this out together.

References

Austerlitz, A. (2008) (ed.) *Unspoken Interactions: Exploring the Unspoken Dimension of Learning and Teaching in Creative Subjects*. London: Centre for Teaching and Learning in Art and Design (CTLAD).

Bannon, L. J. and Ehn, P. (2013) "Design: Design matters in participatory design," in Simonsen, J. and Robertson, T. (eds.), *International Handbook of Participatory Design* (pp. 37–63). London and New York: Routledge.

Björgvinsson, E., Ehn, P. and Hillgren, P.-A. (2012) "Agonistic participatory design: Working with marginalised social movements," *CoDesign*, 8(2–3): 127–144.

Boys, J. (2016) "Finding the spaces in-between: Learning as a social material practice," in Carvalho, L., Goodyear, P. and de Laat, M. (eds.), *Place-Based Spaces for Networked Learning*. London: Routledge.

Deleuze, G. (1994) *Difference and Repetition*. London: Continuum.

Deleuze, G. (2003) "The three kinds of knowledge," *Pli: The Warwick Journal of Philosophy*, 14: 1–20.

DiSalvo, C. (2012) *Adversarial Design*. Cambridge, MA: MIT Press.

England, K. V. L. (1994) "Getting personal: Reflexivity, positionality, and feminist research," *Professional Geographer*, 46(1): 80–89.

Everyday Disruptions (2014) Northumbria University. https://db.tt/lgeP0Uoc

Freire, P. (1993) *Pedagogy of the Oppressed*. London: Penguin.

Garfinkel, H. (1967) *Studies in Ethnomethodology*. Englewood Cliffs, NJ: Prentice Hall.

Gaver, W. (2012) "What should we expect from research through design?" *Proceedings of the 2012 ACM Annual Conference on Human Factors in Computing Systems* (CHI '12) (pp. 937–946). http://dl.acm.org/citation.cfm?id=2208538

Latour, B. (2005) *Reassembling the Social: An Introduction to Actor-Network-Theory*. Oxford: Oxford University Press.

Light, A. (2013) Effectiveness in Action, Report for the Arts and Humanities Research Council, AHRC.

Light, A. and Akama, Y. (2014) "Structuring future social relations: The politics of care in participatory practice," in *Proceedings of the ACM Participatory Design Conference (PDC '14)* (pp. 151–160).

Pignarre, P. and Stengers, I. (2007) *Capitalist Sorcery: Breaking the Spell*. Palgrave MacMillan.

Polanyi, M. (1966) *The Tacit Dimension*. Chicago: University of Chicago Press.

Price, M. (forthcoming) "Un/shared space: The dilemma of inclusive architecture," in Boys, J. (ed.), *Disability, Space, Architecture: A Reader*. London: Routledge.

Ryave, A. L. and Schenkein, J. N. (1974) "Notes on the art of walking," in Turner, R. (ed.), *Ethnomethodology* (pp. 265–274). New York: Penguin.

Stengers, I. (2005) "The comspolitical proposal," in Latour, B. and Weibel, P. (eds.), *Making Things Public: Atmospheres of Democracy* (pp. 994–1003). Cambridge, MA: MIT Press.

Titchkosky, T. (2011) *The Question of Access: Disability, Space, Meaning*. Toronto: University of Toronto Press.

Wenger, E. (1998) *Communities of Practice: Learning, Meaning, and Identity*. Cambridge: Cambridge University Press.

13

PARTICIPATORY DESIGN FOR VALUE-DRIVEN LEARNING

Betsy DiSalvo and Kayla DesPortes

Designing learning experiences that initially spark students' interests and sustain their engagement throughout the educational experience is difficult. Frequently, in the learning sciences, we contextualize learning with initial interest, or hooks, that are useful to engage a specific group for a short period of time. But as John Dewey (1913) suggests, external attempts may catch someone's interest; however, holding it and engaging learners in persistent effort and identification with a topic are much more difficult. What should educators do when initial interest can be sparked, but economic, cultural, or other considerations conspire to impede sustained learning? In this chapter, we explore how participatory design has shaped our interest-driven learning experiences into *value-driven learning* experiences. Using two case studies, we demonstrate how traditional participatory design practices and a meta-design approach to participatory design can help craft value-driven learning that enables students to navigate seemingly countervailing values, nurtures their interests, and creates supportive contexts in which to pursue those interests.

Our focus has been in integrating cultural value-driven design of informal learning in computer science. Recently, in the United States, a number of initiatives have been promoted to increase K-12 computer science education. Unfortunately, the underrepresentation of women, African American, Latino and Latina, Native American, and differently abled populations, is a significant barrier to achieving "Computer Science for All" (Margolis, Good & Chapman, 2015; NSF, 2008; Peckham et al., 2007). Extensive research has studied why this under-representation exists (Margolis, 2008; Margolis & Fisher, 2002) and looked at the various approaches used for mitigating the differences (DiSalvo et al., 2013; Eglash, Gilbert, & Foster, 2013; Eglash, Bennett, O'Donnell, Jennings, & Cintorino, 2006; Kafai & Burke, 2014).

We use the term "value-driven learning," rather than "interest-driven learning" (Edelson & Joseph, 2004), to identify an approach used to design learning experiences that build upon *cultural values*, rather than the individual's identity or interest. While interests, such as music, games, or fashion, can be ways to entice young people into trying new disciplines, such as computing, Edelson and Joseph (2004) have highlighted how identifying authentic interest and sustaining interest is challenging and has not been addressed. González, Moll, and Amanti have put forth a related concept, *Funds of Knowledge*, the idea that learners bring their own personal and cultural experiences, values, and knowledge to formal instruction. However, teachers and designers of educational experiences do not listen to or leverage these cultural experiences. The result is the creation of interest-driven learning experiences that are based upon educators' best guesses, which do not sustain interest and go out of fashion quickly.

Cultural values can be defined as the ways individuals choose to act in the world based upon their family, friends, media, and other influences to which they have been exposed (Swidler, 1986). In this way, cultural values are not simply the values expressed by the student's community or the values of the individual students themselves. They are *the ways in which individuals choose to meet or reject those values and the broader values they see in their culture*. For example, a teen African American male may place a strong emphasis on the learning skills tied to employment because he perceives that his family values a man who is financially responsible for himself (B. DiSalvo et al., 2014). Whereas, a teen Latina may place a strong emphasis on training for employment because she perceives her family values her ability to financially contribute to the family (Sy & Romero, 2008). These values speak to potential motivations of *not* participating in a learning experience. An individual's values not only differ by community, but they might also differ by the populations within those communities. For example, values that are applied by relatives to Latinas (e.g., staying close to home) might not be applied to male Latinos.

In the design of learning experiences, educators often try to appeal to a specific demographic through a targeted design of curricula that creates interest-driven experiences for students, such as music (Freeman et al., 2014), e-textiles (Buechley, Eisenberg, Catchen, & Crockett, 2008), or games (Repenning et al., 2015). Whether the experience results in value-driven learning depends entirely on the students' ability to bring their own values to what they design as part of these learning experiences. It is not that these learning experiences aren't able to center on the values of the learners; it is that incorporating values into a learning experience is difficult to do. Without scaffolding their involvement in the design process, students are unlikely to bring their values to these experiences. To design for value-driven learning, we explore two frameworks used in the practice of participatory design. First, is the use of formative participatory design as a method of uncovering cultural values that learners hold, which then become the anchors for designing learning interventions. Second, is the use of meta-design principles to develop project-based learning activities that can be rooted in the values of learners and adapt to different groups and their cultural values.

Participatory Design

While the term "participatory design" is often used to describe any design process that asks users to contribute ideas about a design, we use the term in a specific manner, referring to the branch of participatory design work that can be traced to Scandinavia in the 1970s and 1980s (Ehn, 2008; Robertson & Simonsen, 2012). These early participatory design projects, focused on workplaces, were often conducted in conjunction with worker unions, and sought to bring both the knowledge of workers' practices and the workers' values into the design process, as many tasks were becoming automated (Robertson & Simonsen, 2012). In these ways, participatory design is a set of methods, a practice of engagement, and a commitment to a particular set of values—all enacted through design. Today in this Scandinavian tradition, participatory design has been extended to many different contexts, from healthcare (Sjöberg & Timpka, 1998) to intelligence analysis (Chin Jr, Kuchar, & Wolf, 2009) to government (Anthopoulos, Siozos, & Tsoukalas, 2007), and, more recently, learning sciences (Bonsignore et al., 2013; DiSalvo & DiSalvo, 2014; Yip et al., 2013).

These new domains challenge the initial goals of participatory design. Instead of directly engaging participants in a known system, they often ask participants to work on design activities that seek to inform more nebulous goals. Still, this mode of participatory design is an extension of the foundational methods, practice of engagement, and commitment to democratic values as described by Ehn in Chapter 2. The difference in our use of participatory design is that the end goal is to create an experience or event that develops the agency of participants in the design of learning experiences, rather than in the design of a product, service, or system.

Meta-Design

Meta-design is a technique designers use to create something that enables the users to act as the designers themselves. Ehn describes how participatory design activities become *meta-design*, where *infrastructuring* provides the necessary resources to prompt, support, and sustain collective and collaborative inquiry through design (Ehn, 2008). It is seen as a type of participatory design that empowers stakeholders and democratizes design, enabling a flexible environment for the users (DiSalvo, Clement, & Pipek, 2012; Ehn, 2008; Fischer, 2013; Fischer & Giaccardi, 2006; Giaccardi & Fischer, 2008). Within the educational domain, the meta-designer (frequently a teacher) creates an educational environment that enables the students to become active in directing their own learning, usually as part of a project-based learning activity. Technology within the learning environment can be designed to stimulate the students to take an active role in leading their own learning. One of the key features of meta-design is its ability to evolve and flexibly support change over time.

In designing value-driven learning, we leverage meta-design frameworks to focus closely on a structure that scaffolds students to integrate their values into the projects, creating value-driven designs that are student-led. Ehn (2008) describes four infrastructuring strategies that can be implemented in meta-design to assist users in becoming the designers. We use the following terms and definitions as originally outlined by Ehn (2008, pp. 5–6):

1. *Formats*—predefined solutions with an outline of important characteristics. These can be flexibly applied to new situations based on the users' knowledge of the process to appropriately modify characteristics.
2. *Component Strategy*—*LEGO block* approach, in which the user can build solutions for specified problems they encounter using the *components* provided.
3. *Design Patterns*—configurations that are described in terms of a contextualized problem and a solution. Based on this knowledge, the pattern can be appropriated or modified based on a new problem.
4. *Protocols*—within a social context, the defined *procedural agreements* for completing activities and/or communicating.

In computer science education, a project-based approach is often taken that shares many similarities with meta-design. These projects can range from high to low structured experiences. The structure of these curricula usually defines the learning experience's flexibility to target the students' diversity. Highly structured interventions often lack the flexibility of being able to appeal to various demographics due to an over-constrained problem space. On the other hand, when you allow the students to have free reign over the designs of their projects, they have the ability to create something that they care about. However, these low-structured interventions are usually resource intensive in terms of time and materials. Furthermore, low-structured interventions also place a large burden on the educator to assist the students and appropriately scope the projects. By using a meta-design learning experience, we scaffolded the structure and focus the students on creating something within that structure that is reflective of and incorporates their cultural values. This provides *value-driven design* that is flexible (see Figure 13.1), but can still be constrained in terms of the structure to make the interventions more scalable.

By using participatory design practices, we can better understand cultural values and how to design for cultural values. With the following two case studies, we explore more traditional approaches to participatory design to uncover cultural values in the development of the *Glitch Game Testers* and the use of meta-design frameworks for participatory design of project-based learning activities in the *Interactive Día de Muertos Puppets*.

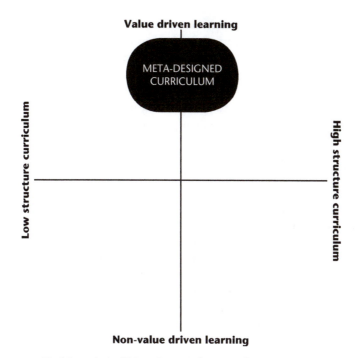

FIGURE 13.1   Ideal Location of Meta-Designed Curriculum on a Spectrum of Structure to Value Driven Learning

Case Study: Glitch Game Testers—Formative Participatory Design

We used a series of participatory design activities in the development of the *Glitch Game Testers* to better understand the values of young African American males living in economically depressed neighborhoods. The development of *Glitch* was prompted by observations, interviews, and data that indicated young African American males had a strong interest in video games, but were not leveraging that interest in computer science like their white and Asian-American male peers (DiSalvo & Bruckman, 2009). Based upon a strong association with sports and value of sportsmanship, we found African American males' general play practices with video games limited their interaction with the underlying computation of video games. To leverage their initial interest in video games, we needed to better understand their play practices, and what values might motivate them to pursue computing. We conducted a number of participatory design activities with teens in after-school programs that served economically depressed, predominantly African American neighborhoods. The goals of these activities were to develop a relationship with the teens, understand their perspectives on school and education, and find ways to design learning experiences with them that would meet their values, beyond what they found interesting or fun, to include what was important to them, as well as to their families, peers, and community. These were not co-design activities that directly asked participants how to design something. Instead, the activities scaffolded experiences that allowed the participants and designers to develop a shared vocabulary, spend time on reflecting, and speculate about the future. Below, we describe two activities, a neighborhood tour and a media literacy activity; both highlight the ways that participatory design helped us create an open dialogue and understanding of our participants' values regarding education.

Neighborhood Tour

Participatory design can help researchers establish dialogues with participants and shift power structures that might inhibit participants from sharing. In the *Glitch* program, one method we used to help us establish a dialogue was a *Neighborhood Tour*. The goal of this activity was not to design a tour with the participants. Instead, it was to learn from the process of creating a tour, and to create a more equal environment for designing because the participants were the experts in their neighborhoods. In our participatory design activities, we tried to make the activity educational or beneficial to the participants as well as the researcher. For this neighborhood tour, we provided the participants (consisting of five teenage African American males) with a camera, a handheld environmental sensor, and a set of questions about their neighborhood. Example questions were, "What is the best place in your neighborhood?" and "What is the most polluted place in your neighborhood?" At each location the participants chose, they told the researcher why the location was the "best" or "most polluted." Then, we used the environmental sensor to measure pollutants in the area. This data sparked reflection on what it meant to be the "best," because the young men chose a playground with a recycled tire surface, which emitted fumes picked up by the sensor. In contrast, we also reflected on the point that their "most polluted" area was a trash-strewn, empty field that registered few indications of pollution on our sensor. This set of activities was both informative to us, but also educational to the participants.

In addition to the specific locations, participants also showed the researcher around the more general neighborhood. The young men demonstrated the pride they felt about their neighborhood, but also expressed dismay over the gentrification that was changing the neighborhood. A number of new homes recently built had displaced apartments and homes that were previously occupied by their friends and families. In addition, they pointed out the several homes developers could not sell. These homes had broken windows, which made the students assume that people were doing drugs in those abandoned buildings. It frustrated the young men to think that drug dealers and drug users had better homes than they did.

While walking around, the few white residents that were out with their dogs or jogging would cross the street before sharing the sidewalk with the five African American male teens and a white female researcher. The residents' motivation for crossing the street was unclear, and it was difficult to determine if the participants noticed this behavior. Regardless, the experience made the white researcher (first author B. DiSalvo) more aware that racially motivated fear (Russell, 1998) was a factor that could hamper a learning environment for young African American men, and noted that this factor would need to be mitigated or addressed in a learning environment.

The neighborhood tour accomplished a number of goals. It gave the teens the power to: direct the tour and conversation, break down barriers between researcher and subject, and let them recognize they had expert knowledge and understanding of their own experience, which could help inform the design. It also attuned us to some of the value systems at play. These young men were frustrated with the rewards they perceived drug users and dealers were getting. The young men also felt they had little power to address this issue or the negative consequences of gentrification in their neighborhood. And, finally, the neighborhood tour gave us researchers a glimpse into the experience of being a young African American male, and an idea of how other community members might negatively perceive them. In these ways, the participatory design activity helped us to begin to understand the cultural values of these young men. The use of open-ended explorations was part of the design process, and helped the participants and designers understand what is valued, what is "normal," and how that might be disrupted in a positive manner. In this way, we were not trying to answer specific design issues, but we were better able to understand the design space with the participants.

Media Literacy

While a number of participatory design activities were conducted with young African American youth, one activity on media literacy provided pivotal insight into the design of the *Glitch Game Tester* program. The activity was conducted with 10 male and female participants at an after-school program. It started with an introduction to advertising, asking the participants to think about what advertisements were trying to do, and discussing what strategies they used to accomplish their advertising goals. Then, we described some of the methods used in brainstorming and pitching advertisements. Researchers asked participants to first individually, then in groups, mock up an advertisement that would encourage young people to stay in school. Finally, the whole group agreed on a strategy and produced a final advertisement together. The final mockup featured a dirty basement room with the tag line, "If you do not like to live in your mom's basement, DO YOUR HOMEWORK!!!!!!" (see Figure 13.2). In all of the advertising concepts, a focus on future economic independence was the primary concern. Other learning motivations, such as creativity, learning for the sake of learning, and living up to family expectations, were not mentioned in the discussions. Researchers gained an important insight into the values that would

FIGURE 13.2 In the Media Literacy Activity, Participants Collaborated to Make an Advertisement to Encourage Kids to Stay in School and Do Their Homework

motivate these young people to participate in learning activities. It was not about a focus on doing cool or interesting things. Instead, their values were based on pragmatic approaches to encourage economic stability. Based upon this finding and others, the researchers developed a program that not only leveraged the participants' interest in games, but one that also directly addressed participants' desire for economic stability by offering game testing jobs. These were paid positions where the participants tested real, pre-release video games. Over three years, the *Glitch Game Tester* program employed 33 young African American males. Over 60% of those males continued on to study computing or information technology in college (DiSalvo et al., 2013). The success of the project can be attributed to these two participatory design activities along with many others that helped researchers and young African American males develop and negotiate an understanding of the cultural values that would drive an educational program for computer science.

Case Study: Interactive Día de Muertos Puppets—Meta-Design

Within the Día de Muertos/Day of the Dead Puppet activity, participants were tasked to reflect on people who have been important in their lives, the cultural practices around death and mourning, and the ways they can express these complicated concepts with computer science and engineering. The students completed individual projects where they integrated microcontrollers to animate Día de Muertos puppets, which they designed themselves. The workshop was originally designed for an after-school program for middle school Latino and Latina students. However, based on that success, we implemented the activity in two semester-long, graduate-level prototyping courses (44 students total) to motivate a final project. We observed that the Día de Muertos puppets served as a meta–design, rather than as a culturally relevant or interest-driven project. The infrastructure of the puppet project allowed the students to design learning experiences in the class based upon their own cultural values. We identified how design patterns, component strategies, format, and protocol were critical in creating the scaffolding for flexible design that was still manageable for the instructor in terms of time, knowledge, and materials.

Classes began with the instructor introducing how technology was used in various art projects, and then the instructor presented artifacts, ranging from hacking toy dog robots that "sniff" out environmental threats (Jeremijenko, 2014) to web-based applications that tracked a culture of surveillance (Institute for Applied Autonomy, 2001). The initial class also introduced the cultural significance of Día de Muertos, which included images of alters, sugar skulls, and puppets that demonstrated the symbolic imagery, colors, and themes of celebration in many Día de Muertos artifacts. These various examples and representations served as *design patterns* for students to understand from a cultural perspective how symbols and designs could be used to express emotions. Students expressed surprise at the range of ways artists had used technology, and the ways that death was marked in different families and cultures.

In their first active role, students focused on a design worksheet that placed them as experts in understanding a death they experienced and their own cultural response to that death. The worksheet was a *component strategy*, which required the students to be thoughtful in identifying *components* they could use for the aesthetics and the interactions their puppet would support. The handout guided thinking about their expression with questions in five sections, allowing for room to write and draw responses: 1. *Who is someone important to you that has died?* 2. *Why were they important to you? How did their death impact you?* 3. *What is the story you want to tell about the person you are celebrating?* 4. *Symbolic Representation—What is something the person you are celebrating did in the world that mattered to you? How can you represent that physically, visually, or with sound?* 5. *Symbolic Triggers—What are the things that the person you are celebrating related to from the world around them? How can you use physical computing to symbolize this reaction with sound, touch, light, or motion data?* (see Figure 13.3) The students completed these without knowing the project's end goal. These questions were structured to be *components* that would transfer to the next activity of storyboarding.

Following the handouts, we gave the students a *format* for storyboarding to guide the design process. This helped participants move from their conceptual ideas, to the design of a puppet that incorporates programming, to the hardware they needed to animate it. The storyboard *format* involved four states: START, INPUT, OUTPUT, and FINAL. As the instructor walked participants through the sections, they could grasp the significance of the various storyboard sections and tie them directly to the four worksheet questions. Then, the students sketched out their concept on craft paper using drawing material and collage materials, such as images from Día de Muertos celebrations, microcontrollers, sensors, and output devices. The use of the four states (START, INPUT, OUTPUT, and FINAL) encouraged students to think about their puppets as interactive objects and better tie their conceptual ideas about symbolic triggers and representations into the hardware, such as light, motion sensors, speakers, or lights.

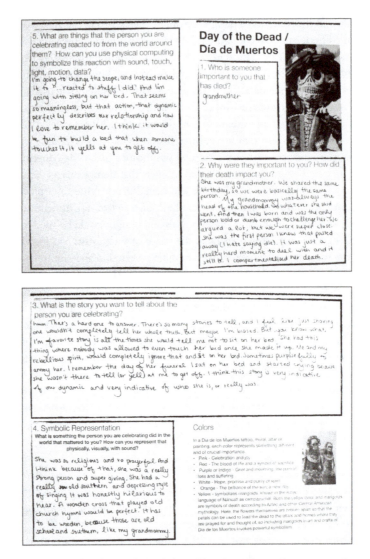

FIGURE 13.3 Example of Design Worksheet That Served as a Component Strategy in the Design of the Day of the Dead Interactive Puppets

Critiques were integrated throughout the workflow and encouraged student and educator and peer to peer dialogue, enabling an open environment for constructive criticism. Throughout the design process, the instructors visited individuals as they worked, offering critiques during the process. At the end of the design session, the participants pinned up their sketches for a group critique. These group critiques offered a chance for students to learn and be inspired by each other, gain a vocabulary for talking about technology and art, and reflect on their own ideas. For example, in critiques, the instructor pointed out that one student had not thought about the end state of interaction with their designed puppet. It prompted the other students to explore what the end state of their puppet would be. This *protocol* helped the students develop skills within the practice of critiquing and of learning from one another.

Meta-design within the Día de Muertos puppet activity created an environment for the students to actively participate in designing their learning experience. The infrastructuring strategies that were applied scaffolded the students into creating thoughtful designs driven by their values and culture, which nurtured a *community of learners in* the environments. Within the Día de Muertos, the meta-designed curriculum helped students create objects that provided the class with a starting point to have a dialogue about family, culture, and how technology can embody and represent those concepts. Stimulating students to integrate this type of meaning into their creations set a precedent in the classes for students to be more open in sharing with one another. Not only were they engaged by each other, but also the enthusiasm of the participants seemed to be enhanced by the opportunity to bring their own expertise to the process. Because each participant was an expert in their own culture and family, this was a rich ground for engaging students with the design, even when they felt the technical or creative work was outside their capabilities. Our less technically experienced graduate students were highly motivated by the project, and often spent more time on the project than anticipated, so they could *get it right*.

Conclusion

These two case studies are examples of a participatory design process in value-driven learning. Participatory design as a tool for formative understanding of the design space was used in the design of the *Glitch Game Testers* program. And, in the form of meta-design, participatory design was also used to create a value-driven learning experience with the Interactive Día de Muertos Puppets. In both cases, cultural values—not just individual values, but the values of friends and family that our teen participants had internalized—were central to the design process and designed artifacts. For the *Glitch Game Testers*, participatory design activities helped address power structures inherent in the researcher-and-subject relationship, raised the researchers' awareness of cultural issues and challenges that participants encountered, and shaped the central values of the program to focus on participants' concerns with employment and other pragmatic motivations. In the case of the Día de Muertos Puppets, the ongoing participatory design nature of meta-design allowed educators to co-create project-based learning experiences with their students. The meta-design framework helped to scaffold a design process that incorporated various cultural values and gave students the freedom to create a flexible and meaningful project, while still remaining within practical constraints such as the instructors' time, varying skill levels, and available materials. The approaches are not meant to upend the interest-driven or project-based approaches that have been well documented and successful in the past. They are a way to explore how participatory design, as a formative and meta-design strategy, can incorporate the cultural values of students, increasing the chances of sustained engagement beyond initial interest.

Acknowledgments

Thank you to the young people and students who participated with us in this work and to the faculty and youth leaders who allowed us to work with them at Georgia Tech and the Computer Clubhouse. This work was funded in part by the National Science Foundation CNS-0837733 and DUE-1431984 Awards.

References

Anthopoulos, L. G., Siozos, P., & Tsoukalas, I. A. (2007). Applying participatory design and collaboration in digital public services for discovering and re-designing e-Government services. *Government Information Quarterly, 24*(2), 353–376.

Bonsignore, E., Ahn, J., Clegg, T., Guha, M. L., Yip, J., Druin, A., & Hourcade, J. P. (2013). Embedding participatory design into designs for learning: An untapped interdisciplinary resource. In *Proc. CSCL* (Vol. 13). Retrieved from www.researchgate .net/profile/Jason_Yip4/publication/265209011_Embedding_Participatory_Design_ into_Designs_for_Learning_An_Untapped_Interdisciplinary_Resource/links/ 540543c40cf23d9765a6d9cd.pdf

Buechley, L., Eisenberg, M., Catchen, J., & Crockett, A. (2008). The LilyPad Arduino: Using computational textiles to investigate engagement, aesthetics, and diversity in computer science education. In *Proceedings of the SIGCHI Conference on Human Factors in Computing Systems* (pp. 423–432). New York: ACM. Retrieved from http://dl.acm.org/citation .cfm?id=1357123

Chin Jr, G., Kuchar, O. A., & Wolf, K. E. (2009). Exploring the analytical processes of intelligence analysts. In *Proceedings of the SIGCHI Conference on Human Factors in Computing Systems* (pp. 11–20). ACM. Retrieved from http://dl.acm.org/citation.cfm?id=1518704

Dewey, J. (1913). *Interest and Effort in Education.* Cambridge, MA: Houghton Mifflin.

DiSalvo, B., & Bruckman, A. (2009). Questioning video games' influence on CS interest. Presented at *The Fourth International Conference on the Foundation of Digital Game.* ACM.

DiSalvo, B., & DiSalvo, C. (2014). Designing for democracy in education: Participatory design and the learning sciences. Presented at the *International Conference of the Learning Sciences.* Retrieved from http://betsydisalvo.com/wp-content/uploads/2012/08/ ICLS-PD-Paper-Final.pdf

DiSalvo, B., Guzdial, M., Meadows, C., McKlin, T., Perry, K., & Bruckman, A. (2013). Workifying games: Successfully engaging African American gamers with computer science. In *Proceedings of the 44th ACM Technical Symposium on Computer Science Education* (pp. 317–322). New York: ACM. https://doi.org/10.1145/2445196.2445292

DiSalvo, C., Clement, A., & Pipek, V. (2012). Participatory design for, with, and by communities. In J. Simonsen and T. Robertson (Eds.), *International Handbook of Participatory Design.* Oxford: Routledge.

Edelson, D. C., & Joseph, D. M. (2004). The interest-driven learning design framework: Motivating learning through usefulness. In *Proceedings of the 6th International Conference on Learning Sciences, International Society of the Learning Sciences* (pp. 166–173). Santa Monica, CA: International Society of the Learning Sciences. Retrieved from http://dl.acm.org/citation.cfm?id=1149126.1149145

Eglash, R., Bennett, A., O'Donnell, C., Jennings, S., & Cintorino, M. (2006). Culturally situated design tools: Ethnocomputing from field site to classroom. *American Anthropologist, 108*(2), 347–362.

Eglash, R., Gilbert, J. E., & Foster, E. (2013). Toward culturally responsive computing education. *Communications of the ACM, 56*(7), 33–36.

Ehn, P. (2008). Participation in design things (Vol. 8). In *Proceedings of the Tenth Anniversary Conference on Participatory Design*. ACM.

Fischer, G. (2013). Meta-design: Empowering all stakeholder as co-designers. *Handbook of Design in Educational Computing* (pp. 135–145). London: Routledge.

Fischer, G., & Giaccardi, E. (2006). Meta-design: A framework for the future of end-user development. In *End User Development* (pp. 427–457). Netherlands: Springer.

Freeman, J., Magerko, B., McKlin, T., Reilly, M., Permar, J., Summers, C., & Fruchter, E. (2014). Engaging underrepresented groups in high school introductory computing through computational remixing with EarSketch. In *Proceedings of the 45th ACM Technical Symposium on Computer Science Education* (pp. 85–90). ACM. Retrieved from http://dl.acm.org/citation.cfm?id=2538906

Giaccardi, E., & Fischer, G. (2008). Creativity and evolution: A metadesign perspective. *Digital Creativity, 19*(1), 19–32.

Institute for Applied Autonomy. (2001). *iSee* [Digital]. Retrieved from www.appliedautonomy.com/isee.html

Jeremijenko, N. (2014). *Feral Robotic Dogs*. Retrieved from www.nyu.edu/projects/xdesign/feralrobots/

Kafai, Y. B., & Burke, Q. (2014). Beyond game design for broadening participation: Building new clubhouses of computing for girls. In *Proceedings of Gender and IT Appropriation. Science and Practice on Dialogue-Forum for Interdisciplinary Exchange* (p. 21). European Society for Socially Embedded Technologies. Retrieved from http://dl.acm.org/citation.cfm?id=2670301

Margolis, J. (2008). *Stuck in the Shallow End: Education, Race, and Computing*. Cambridge, MA: MIT Press.

Margolis, J., & Fisher, A. (2002). *Unlocking the Clubhouse: Women in Computing*. Cambridge, MA: MIT Press.

Margolis, J., Goode, J., & Chapman, G. (2015). An equity lens for scaling: A critical juncture for exploring computer science. *ACM Inroads, 6*(3), 58–66.

NSF. (2008). Broadening Participation in Computing (BPC) Program Solicitation. Retrieved from www.nsf.gov/funding/pgm_summ.jsp?pims_id=13510

Peckham, J., Harlow, L. L., Stuart, D. A., Silver, B., Mederer, H., & Stephenson, P. D. (2007). Broadening participation in computing: Issues and challenges. *ACM SIGCSE Bulletin, 39*(3), 9–13.

Repenning, A., Webb, D. C., Koh, K. H., Nickerson, H., Miller, S. B., Brand, C., Basawapatna, A., Gluck, F., Grover, R., Gutierrez, K., & Repenning, N. (2015). Scalable game design: A strategy to bring systemic computer science education to schools through game design and simulation creation. *ACM Transactions on Computing Education (TOCE), 15*(2), 11.

Robertson, T., & Simonsen, J. (2012). Participatory design. *Routledge International Handbook of Participatory Design* 1. New York: Routledge.

Russell, K. K. (1998). Driving while black: Corollary phenomena and collateral consequences. *Boston College Law Review, 40*, 717.

Sjöberg, C., & Timpka, T. (1998). Participatory design of information systems in health care. *Journal of the American Medical Informatics Association, 5*(2), 177–183.

Swidler, A. (1986). Culture in action: Symbols and strategies. *American Sociological Review, 51*(2), 273–286.

Sy, S. R., & Romero, J. (2008). Family responsibilities among Latina college students from immigrant families. *Journal of Hispanic Higher Education, 7*(3), 212–227.

Yip, J., Clegg, T., Bonsignore, E., Gelderblom, H., Rhodes, E., & Druin, A. (2013). Brownies or bags-of-stuff?: Domain expertise in cooperative inquiry with children. In *Proceedings of the 12th International Conference on Interaction Design and Children* (pp. 201–210). ACM. Retrieved from http://dl.acm.org/citation.cfm?id=2485763

14

CONVERSATION

Participatory Design in Research and Practice

Conversation between Allison Druin and Jon Kolko

On June 17, 2016, Allison Druin and Jon Kolko shared their thoughts on participatory design and learning in the following conversation, moderated by Elizabeth "Beth" Bonsignore. Jon is a design professional who has worked extensively with startups and Fortune 500 companies alike. He has taught design at several universities, and is currently Partner at Modernist Studio, a strategy firm in Austin, Texas. Allison is a human–computer interaction/user experience researcher whose work on co-design with children and intergenerational teams is considered seminal research in the field of design. She is currently serving as Special Advisor for National Digital Strategy with the US National Park Service. Starting from their own personal perspectives and experiences, Allison and Jon explored various aspects of participatory design and learning before circling back to closing thoughts on the multiplicity of perspectives that exist across different design contexts (e.g., academia and industry). Throughout, they touched on the following themes tied to participatory design and learning:

- Multiple personal perspectives on participatory design
- What role does the designer and design expertise play in the practice of participatory design?
- Challenges and constraints of using participatory design in different contexts
- Incorporating learning into the practice of participatory design
- Challenges of learning how to "do" participatory design
- Participatory design and social change: blending ideals and pragmatism
- Circling back to multiple perspectives on participatory design

Multiple Personal Perspectives on Participatory Design

Beth Bonsignore: What does participatory design means to each of you? Specifically, how do you think it relates to design itself, and alternatively, how does it relate to learning?

Jon Kolko: Okay. Well, for me, there are two views to participatory design and I teach them both. One is the idea that Elizabeth B.-N. Sanders champions: making rudimentary or sometimes advanced tool kits that "non-designers" can use in order to express themselves in a creative, visible fashion. These are more regimented sets of tools that use different prompts and provocations to get people to be engaged in a facilitated workshop. Another view that I am more drawn to are things like the cultural probes that Bill Gaver champions, where you go out in the field and use prompts over time to really get views into peoples' lives that you wouldn't normally get. Sometimes these are things like a disposable camera or a diary study, which encourage participation in the design process, again, by people who are "not designers."

Allison Druin: Well, for me, having been in academia most of my career, participatory design, as I have always seen it (it's now been 20 years), is about giving voice to people that have never had voice. It's the people that are not the academics. They are the people that have the needs and the frustrations that need to be heard. Any which way we can get those people heard is participatory design. What to me is so exciting is that over the last 2 decades, I've seen enormous growth in people not only acknowledging participatory design, but doing it and evolving it, and not just saying, "Just because so-and-so does this model, we have to do this model." So, it's just wonderful. In terms of learning, I've always seen that participatory design is about learning. It's about creating a community of learners. Because at the end of the day when somebody comes into my lab and says, "Hey, I need to design X," I don't know any better than anybody else that's sitting there what X is going to be. So, we're all learning together to come up with what that possibility is. Now, obviously, in more recent times, we've been able to get the participatory design acknowledged in the learning sciences so that it is seen as a powerful learning tool in formal learning, as well as informal learning. I'm very excited about that. I'm excited about the next generation of leaders in co-design that are doing that, because to me, it involves and makes that area much more powerful.

Role of Designers and Design Expertise in the Practice of Participatory Design

Jon Kolko: I don't agree with some of what Allison just said. Allison said that you don't know anything more than anyone else what the solution to a problem could be. Actually, I think that's one of the big issues with a lot of these empathetic tools: it completely discounts the knowledge and experience of the designer.

The idea, and the intent is actually that designers *do* have some preconceived idea of where they're going, because they have past knowledge and hopefully experience in whatever it is they're designing. The perspectives that they gather through qualitative research add data to that perspective. But the designer's perspective is in many ways stronger, because the people, who are theoretically the participants, doing this participatory design actually *aren't* designers. The things that these participants come up with are sometimes so crass, and so generically wrong for what the product market fit is that they're discounted entirely. The way that I view all of the work that we do around empathetic design or strategic design is that it's a combination of what you hear in the field, of what you understand from signals in the market, and of that tacit knowledge you have built up as a designer. I don't think that the combination is necessarily an equal third from fieldwork with participants, a third from the market, and a third input from the designer's experience.

As an example, the work that I did when I was at Blackboard in trying to overhaul their older products was to really focus on the opinions of the designers themselves, because I hired designers with 15-plus years of experience. We did a fair amount of qualitative research with students, mostly behavioral studies in their dorm rooms and in their homes. That research led to insights for the designers, but they then used the insights to formulate and force a design-based opinion into the products. The net affect is that the resulting opinions from designers often vastly outweigh the opinions and perspective of the participants. But to ignore the participants entirely means that you actually don't have that empathetic lens on. In most cases, I think that without participant perspectives, you're sort of counting on a strategic crapshoot. One of the things that I've noticed about entrepreneurs is that they gain that knowledge from people, and they also gain it from their sheer love and experience with whatever the topic is. That might lead to what's sometimes called an expert blind spot. But even with that blind spot, their expertise also often leads to really, really strong applicable market fit. So, in combination, those behavioral insights from participants and an understanding of market fit lead to great products.

Allison Druin: Well, this is really interesting that you explain it this way. I think we're not too terribly different in thinking about it. It's not just about what the user or the participant says. What we have always said about participatory design is that the goal is *elaboration*. It is not about my ideas trumping anybody else's ideas. It's about that I may have a great idea, and then somebody else adds to that idea, then somebody else adds to that idea. You're not sure whose idea that ultimately was, but that's the goal of it. Now, on the other hand, I don't agree entirely with you that we know where the outcome's going to be. Because at the end of the day, people come to us to do co-design because they're wide open to possibility. For an example of that—and I'm going to tell you one that's absolutely not academic just so that I can make my point here—is with Nickelodeon. We created the *Do Not Touch* button with the help of co-design. There was no way in hay

Nickelodeon was going to be creating a *Do Not Touch* button. They had come to us originally to come up with what an education app, a free educational app on an iPad would be. The designers came in with large paper and said, "Here. You can design your ideas over here, but do not touch this area over here, because these are the characters. We have to make sure the characters are highlighted." Now, that whole just *Do Not Touch* set the kids off completely. Essentially, they rebelled and created a *Do Not Touch* button. Every time you press that button, something random and ridiculous was supposed to happen. Well, not only was that embraced in the design of that educational app, but ultimately made it to the Kid's Choice Awards, made it into their TV representation. Now, their new website has *Do Not Touch* buttons everywhere. It is now even part of Nickelodeon's mission of "random plus ridiculous equals fun." So, ultimately, were we setting out to find a *Do Not Touch* button that would completely re-energize what Nickelodeon was going to be? No. Ultimately, they even got an Interactive Emmy for it. So, while I can suggest that, yes, we're supposed to be making "X," I think that co-design brings surprises and excitement to the design process that you wouldn't normally get. If I said, "Well, okay, kids. That's enough of your information. Now, we'll take it from here," it wouldn't add to the layering of ideas. I think we may agree to disagree though. [Laughter]

Challenges and Constraints of Participatory Design in Different Contexts

Beth Bonsignore: One of the interesting things about what Jon is saying is that empathetic design allows the designers to reflect on and respond to users' perspectives that they wouldn't see normally. Likewise, the elaboration process that Allison's talking about, it seems very similar because designers and participants are reflecting and responding to each other, building on their ideas. However, what are the challenges involved in trying to get learners who might not have the expertise of the designers to be more active participants in that design process?

Allison Druin: Well, it depends on the process, because for certain processes, you don't necessarily need to learn the method. You can just go. But for certain processes, you do need to learn that you do have voice in the process, and there are certain methods you have to actually learn. Then, obviously, as you're doing that process, you will be learning the content of the experience as well. With the National Park Service, many times, we've got to do some research about what that monument is, or what that National Park is, before we're actually exploring what that new design or what that new tool is going to be. So, that's definitely a challenge. Honestly, another challenge is getting people to understand what the role of a design partner could be. Many people have their own cultural norms, which are completely appropriate. So, you have to understand what those cultural norms are. You cannot completely change those norms. You have to accept that some participants are not going to be able to call you anything but your formal name. They're not going to be able to meet with you three times a week. There are a lot of different things that you have to accept that what you intended is not going to work, or you have to say, "Okay. I'm going to work in a different kind of way that will make it happen." But there's nothing better than shaping the learning experience with people that have never done co-design before. You see the light go on in learners' eyes where they say, "Oh, my goodness! We could do this with so many things," and see how they apply it, and see how it changes their formal education process into much more informal and more experiential experiences. I think what frustrates me sometimes is that, unfortunately, we come up with these sort of made-up design situations where there are so many organizations—for-profits, nonprofits, government agencies—that actually need the input and need the information from the outside world. There's no need to make up a design situation just so that end quotes "it can be a learning experience." It can be a real thing. It can be a way to help a real organization make change. To you, Jon.

Jon Kolko: I'll interpret the question as, *What are some of the challenges of doing participatory design work?* In our work, I don't see a lot of huge challenges. Our process is sort of an innovation playbook that I learned when I was at Carnegie Mellon when I was in grad school. We practiced it when I was at the global innovation firm frog design, and then my team applied it to a startup, that was subsequently acquired. Broadly speaking, it focuses on behavioral research with students, or teachers, or whomever we are designing for; the majority of my work right now is focused on students. After that research, the majority of our time is spent on synthesizing the data by ourselves. There's certainly value to bringing the end users into that process at that point; but the integration of all of the touch points that we have in various products means that you have to have deep knowledge of *all* of our products, because they all stitch together. Students don't learn on the web, and then separately learn on their phone, and then separately learn through our video conferencing application, and so on; their learning experience cuts across modalities. The products share data with one another.

So, the innovations that might come from this synthesis need to become grounded in a reality; it can't be blue sky. So that process that starts with conceptual behavioral research has to get pragmatic very quickly when you start thinking about how you're going to ship product, what are the revenue implications in making decisions, and what are the client customer satisfaction issues launching new things.

We have a very empathetic perspective in interacting with students and engaging with our users up front. But very, very quickly it becomes design-led, not user-led. It stops being democratic early in the process.

Beth Bonsignore: So, both of you come at participatory design from different perspectives. Jon has constraints related to specific products and corporations. Allison, could you discuss any constraints of working with child co-designers? Or, is it more that the design partners give you their design constraints?

Allison Druin: It's definitely where the partners take it. Now that I'm inside an organization that is doing co-design, I have many constraints in terms of doing co-design, even in the context of national parks. Where am I actually allowed to put a sticky note? Can I do participatory design inside a monument? It's really all about the context of what you have to design. Now, who your partners are in that design process may lead you to think about anything from anti-gravity machines to walkable desks with flashlights. It totally depends on who you're working with. I guess that's what makes it so interesting, because you never quite know who's going to be walking in the door to partner with you, what constraints they have, what opportunities these things lead to.

Incorporating Learning into the Process of Participatory Design

Beth Bonsignore: One of the things that we were struggling with in editing this book is the question, Why are so many different companies and educational institutions not trying to take advantage of participatory design? Or, where might be the best place to involve the user or the learner? In Jon's case, it might be his students, in Allison's case, primarily youth. Would you share a little bit about how you think the learning sciences can incorporate the philosophy, and methods, and techniques of participatory design?

Jon Kolko: I teach this process; I'll share how we teach that philosophy, and methods, and these techniques work by way of an example from my students. Lauren, Samara, and Jeff were exploring the topic of personal debt. They just wanted to understand it, but then they also wanted to find and solve a problem related to it. So, they spent a ton of time with people with debt, learning all about what it's like to have $70,000 in debt hanging over your head. They all got great quotes and insights into what that means, and were able to establish empathy with their target audience.

Then the process that my students follow is very close to what we did when I was at Blackboard, the same process I already outlined. They leverage their research to build insights, and then they quickly move to the design of something. They test their design, but they test it as a business. They don't test it as a concept. So, what these students did was they came up with this idea, a very simple idea that throughout the day, at opportune times, you'll receive an SMS on your phone asking if you want to tip yourself. So, if you go to a coffee shop and you buy a cup of coffee, with some pretty rudimentary technology like GPS, and time of day, and previous purchasing patterns, we can intuit that you're probably buying a cup of coffee. So we can send you an SMS that says, "Buying a cup of coffee? Why don't you tip yourself a quarter?" If you do it, the transaction actually happens and the money is moved from your debit account to your credit card account, and starts paying off your credit card in very, very small bits.

So, my point with the example is that we move towards a solution quickly, rather than living in Post-it note land. The students go try it. Using duct tape, smoke and mirrors, these students set up a process where they're manually sending SMS through the day to a cohort of people who have volunteered to try it. I think it was about 10 users or 12 users. They did it for approximately 3 or 4 weeks. What they saw was that people actually engaged, and over time, they paid off very small amounts of their balance. So, let's call it $12 or $16 over the course of the test.

If you then calculate that across the lifespan of a credit card and the compounded way interest grows, it actually has a substantive impact in reducing debt.

To me, the entire example is a part cultural probe and a part concept testing, because you're introducing something foreign into somebody's life, changing behavior and then understanding how it impacts the way that they live and how they think.

I guess that's a little different than what might be typically construed as participatory design, but that's the way that it plays out in our process. At the qualitative side all the way up front, they do all of those things that like handing out cameras, and taking pictures of things, and having people track, in this case, their spending over time. But they don't typically sit down and actually design the solution with the people who are going to use it. They are in control during the actual making process.

Allison Druin: In terms of the learning sciences, I think we've always been looking for that silver bullet of what's going to get those kids, or learners, excited about the possibilities of what they can understand, and how they can bring it to "real world"? The whole maker movement is born out of some of these co-design principles. As people embrace more of the maker movement, and the tools, and the processes, I hope they can move into hearing more from other people besides themselves. Because as we know, when we design only for ourselves, it's hit or miss. You know, you may get an awesome, great hit because you are brilliant. But I'm not one of those brilliant people. I know I think better when I get to elaborate off of what other people say.

Challenges of Learning How to "Do" Participatory Design

Jon Kolko: When students learn method, it's helpful for them to have a pragmatic guide on what to do, and for them to follow steps. But in reality, it doesn't work that way at all. You sort of make up your own method as you go along. I think as my students get closer and closer to graduation, we get less and less pragmatic, less and less specific in our descriptions of what we want them to do, and how we want them to do it. They start to get to an abstract but personal view of the method. And then it stops being method, and it really starts being internal process. So, when you get there, you can't be bored, because you literally have no rules.

My students, who are graduate level and between 24 and 34 years old, are typically looking to pivot their careers, to change their career trajectories. One of the things that I find interesting about these students is that, for whatever reason, they're really looking for somebody to tell them, "Just go do *this* and you will have success." The ambiguity around design really freezes them in their tracks. So, as I see them get closer to the end of the program, they become more familiar with not using predigested methods. To me that really illustrates learning in the context of this empathetic process.

Beth Bonsignore: That's great, what you've just touched on, because it sounds like the people who you're training to design with these methods are also learning what it means to *grow* through this design process. Could you talk a little more about how you help designers and others learn to use participatory design?

Allison Druin: Ideally, whether in a lab or classroom, students have a problem-centered approach to learning where you throw out a problem to them. If people don't know the process, then there's an introduction of the process. Finally, we just let people go. In an ideal situation there are also people who are experienced with the process, and we try and group those people together with the people who aren't experienced. When we do this in actual classrooms with younger kids, sometimes the teachers will feel more comfortable if we actually give them a video of the processes so that people feel a sense of, "Ah, okay. This is really not rocket science. I can do this." I mean, I think people make such a big deal about the processes, thinking that it is a really hard thing to do. The processes are not necessarily hard to do, but it is actually hard to cull the information that you want. It's hard to scope the methods and techniques to be as exploratory or as focused as you want. It does take some experience in knowing how to aggregate the information you're seeing, because you can drown in the qualitative data and not get yourself out.

Jon Kolko: To me, part of design is that it is really intuitive. But intuitive doesn't mean necessarily that you're born knowing it. Instead it is based on experience, knowing how to get to the important insights. We build almost all of the product output based on behavioral insights that are framed as provocations. In both professional life and in teaching, we really try to get to persuasive statements of truth, that are somewhat provocative and shocking, that challenge the way that people typically think about behavior so that we can build new product on top of it. That is why we start with really regimented method and move to ambiguity.

The magic happens in the most ambiguous part of all. One of my student groups once tried to do this type of synthesis work, embedded and immersed, with homeless people. My students were getting sort of a mind-meld, getting an empathetic heart-meld, if that's a phrase, with this homeless population. But it didn't actually lead to any fruitful result. I think the reason is because it's not something you can do in a few hours or a few weeks. That synthesis process takes as long as you give it, and in a context with an at-risk population like that—it can't be a petri dish. It needs to be real; it stops being research and synthesis and starts to be just *life*.

When I was at frog design, I saw one of our teams doing this really bizarre design research and synthesis. They literally lived in a house together. They brought in all of the different people who had some say in the product; I think it included end users. And they camped out in a house together for a week, sleeping over at night, and synthesizing during the day. To me, that's certainly one way to get that synthesis process immersed in a participatory style. I don't know if it worked or not. [Laughter] But that's what it takes, in my opinion, to get synthesis to become participatory or user-centered—living with the people you are trying to help. And so, practically, we don't do that. We synthesize on our own.

Allison Druin: That's interesting, because I do agree it takes stages of synthesis and aggregation. In fact, we initially aggregate sort of on the fly. It takes a fair amount of learning to be able to do that, because it's a science and an art at the same time. It's being able to sort of grab the big ideas and aggregate from a session. But it's really in the debriefing and the continued aggregation of that information the next day, then back at the company and so on that's actually where the product emerges, where the focus of the product emerges. There are times when the entire group of people are presenting, the entire group just says, *"Whoa!"* There's usually one or two aha moments in a design session. Now, whether or not the "ahas" outlive the first aggregation is another story. It depends on the priorities and the context. But, yeah. I absolutely agree.

Jon Kolko: I have sort of a love/hate with this idea of the "aha" thing. When I go out and teach executives to do this type of work, they always come up with these wild and crazy ideas that ultimately are very innovative and really, really interesting. And they are almost impossible to productize in any realistic sense. They don't fit into road maps. They're not funded. Over time, the magic of them starts to dissolve.

Allison Druin: Oh, yeah. Absolutely.

Jon Kolko: I like teaching these things. But a great idea written on an 8 ½-inch by 11-inch sheet of paper rarely sees the light of day. When it does, often it's blanded to a point where it's not very interesting, which is pretty unfortunate.

Allison Druin: Well, and it's interesting, because that's exactly why I was shocked that the *Do Not Touch* button actually succeeded so well . . . It emerged from an aha moment and never changed. I mean, it was like, "Whoa! How could that never change?" But it didn't. But it was partially because there was such a strong elaboration process during that initial design session that I believe that's why it emerged the way it did.

Beth Bonsignore: It sounds like one of the challenges with participatory design, both in the commercial sector and in more formal learning environments, is, How long can you actually practically immerse yourself with a participant, or with an end user, to learn about them so that you can get their ideas and input as best you can?

Allison Druin: I do think there are different kinds of learning. There's the learning of participatory design. There's the learning of in some sense just problem-solving and becoming a great design thinker. But there's also the learning of the content that you learn along the way because you're actually *creating.* This is where I would say a lot of the K-12 community has picked up on the maker movement and on co-design and participatory design, because it's a fabulous methodology to get at content learning without people laying down in the roads and going, "I have to memorize one more thing? Please help me." So, I think there are different kinds of learning that you can talk about. Then there is the personal growth of the students themselves from being a dependent thinker to being much more of an independent leader, where they want to take it to the next step. I think Jon described that beautifully with some of his students. So, I think that there's a whole range of where this stuff touches in terms of learning sciences. You all are just scratching the surface of it, which is wonderful.

Jon Kolko: We're about to run a summer camp doing this for teenagers. Students will learn problem-solving and gain this idea of nonlinear abstract thinking, divergent thinking, lateral thinking. Then we want them to compare that to actually *making something* that has value. Thinking and making can't be mutually exclusive. But the way that I've observed K-12 educators take to this process of "design thinking" is that they often focus primarily on the first at the expense of the second. So, there's not a sense of articulating adoption of a thing. It makes sense, because they're not companies, right? They're not trying to sell things. But the entrepreneurial part of this is important, because people have good ideas all the time. *Having a good idea* doesn't necessarily actually make change. So, teaching people how to think in more abstract ways is really valuable. But teaching them to actually do something with the thinking is more difficult. It may or may not have a place in K-12 education, but it's a really critical part of the process.

Beth Bonsignore: So, you mentioned there are two parts to the summer camp. You said the kids seem more focused on the first part and not the second. Could you say those two parts again?

Jon Kolko: In the summer camp we're running, they're going to do qualitative work: brainstorming ideas, sketching them out, learning to look at problems in many different ways during the first week. The second week, they are going to take their ideas and build something, and make sure that it has value for people. In this case, they're going to go build a board game. But they're not going to sketch it or make rudimentary examples of it, or again, make tools or probes. They're actually going to fabricate it. In that respect, it's much closer to what you would do in a more traditional design school. This is, for whatever it's worth, one of my big problems with design thinking, because it implies that there's a separation between thinking about it and doing it. The doing it really starts to, again, have that more entrepreneurial view value; does it actually have value outside of the idea itself? Does it actually have real behavioral, monetary, emotional value when it exists in the world?

Participatory Design and Social Change: Blending Ideals and Pragmatism

Beth Bonsignore: That's a great segue to a final question. Can participatory design and the learning sciences affect social change? How do you envision them working together to make change happen?

Allison Druin: Participatory design has always been a part of social change. It started out in Scandinavian countries as a part of how to bring factory workers into the discussions of the change of new technology so that these factory workers were not left out of the equation in the movement towards automation in the 1970s. It's always been about trying to bring about those possibilities.

Jon Kolko: I agree that participatory design has its roots in that. When I spent time with Pelle Ehn in Sweden, we talked about how his research was involved in that movement. But sometimes I'm really pessimistic about the way it's framed around humanitarian impact. I remember a conversation with Carl (DiSalvo) probably 10 or 12 years ago where we ended up sarcastically commenting, "Yeah, I could solve world hunger if only I had the right concept map." Problems like those, of that level of complexity, often have real operational requirements, and you aren't going to get to "solving" them at all, much less through lateral thinking or visual thinking or other phrases that you might use to frame such design issues.

Design can lead social change. But that change is rarely useful without the sort of more operational, pragmatic context of a business, a government, or whatever the existing institutional block is.

Allison Druin: Yes, I agree. You can have social change in one person, or you can have a social change in a much larger process, or in government. But giving voice to those people that will be impacted by the things that you create has got to bring about change. If it doesn't, then you're not listening hard enough, or you're not seeing well enough what's right in front of you. But is it always about how to change a government? No, probably not. But it is absolutely about change. I think that part of it makes it very difficult for people to swallow, because it feels too grandiose. They wonder, "Why are we doing such an elaborate process to get at something that's obvious here?"

Jon Kolko: Yeah, the ideas that seem obvious in retrospect are interesting when you are dealing with corporate clients, because chances are they've read *Businessweek*, or heard some speaker at a TED talk about design thinking and now they need it. They want it in their companies. The expectation is that it's going to be a silver bullet for innovation or social change in the context of their business. They want to be an Apple or socially change the way that we think about mobile phones, or some other example. But I think they don't necessarily understand *why* simple ideas pop out of a complex process. When you get to the end of the process and there's sort of something that's elegantly simple, there is sort of this sense of, "I paid for you to design *that*? Why didn't you just come up with that right off the bat?" Because it's so simplistic, typically. The solution in hindsight, obviously, is a lot easier than it is before you get started.

Allison Druin: Yes, absolutely. Absolutely I agree.

Circling Back to Multiple Perspectives on Participatory Design

Beth Bonsignore: Is there anything else that either of you wanted to add in closing, or that you were thinking while we talked?

Allison Druin: I think that confusion is an important thing to bring out. Because there are so many different roles that our users can play in the design process, it means that we may not all agree as to when to bring in that voice of the user or how to bring in that voice of the user. And that's okay, because it really is truly dependent upon the kinds of problems you're trying to solve, the kind of people that you want to work with, and the kind of time frame that you have to solve these kinds of problems, and many times the kinds of resources that you have, too. But because of that, we may label things as co-design or as participatory design in different ways. That's really okay. I do think that we have to be explicit about how we perceive what that is. From there, the sky's the limit.

I particularly liked how the conversation evolved, and I particularly liked how Jon was sort of exploring this area, because he comes at it from many different perspectives. That's important. I've been at a university for 20-something years, but now that I am out of the university and working in what I guess many would say is a client site, there are so many different ways to see the same thing.

Jon Kolko: I think some of the confusion in the beginning of our conversation was with the words used, because design strategy, design thinking, participatory design, learning science—these are all blended into one sort of gestalt way of thinking. So, when I hear these words, when Allison hears these words, when anybody else hears these words, they're obviously going to come at it with their own trajectory and baggage. It leads to a whole lot of confusion in conversations professionally, not just in conversations like this. I'll give you a very quick example. If I call myself a designer, I have a certain reaction and there's a certain expectation to the types of skills I have. If I call myself a product manager, there's a completely different expectation and set of skills. Typically, the second is much more respected in industry. When I tell people, "I'm bringing empathy or design into product management," it has a really, really different vibe than saying "I'm bringing design into the organization." The language matters a great deal.

15

ESTABLISHING CONTENT EXPERTISE IN INTERGENERATIONAL CO-DESIGN TEAMS

Brenna McNally and Mona Leigh Guha

Introduction

Children bring a unique, arguably necessary, voice to the design of their technology. Many design teams employ co-design methods, where people who are intended users of technologies—in our case, children—are brought into the design of technologies throughout the iterative design cycle. A number of these teams use the Cooperative Inquiry (CI) method of co-design (Druin, 1999; Guha, Druin, & Fails, 2013), which was specifically adapted for working with children. CI teams typically meet weekly throughout the year, maintaining consistent membership and thus building a relationship of trust and commitment between child and adult team members. These team members—including children, often ages 7–11 years old, and adults—are known as design partners. They become well versed in the co-design process and work together in a balanced partnership. These intergenerational design teams use specially developed design techniques to ideate, prototype, evaluate, and iterate diverse technologies that are meant for children. Ultimately, children become technology design experts in addition to being experts in being children.

CI teams can work on multiple projects during the same time period, meaning that not only can the technology itself change from session to session, ranging from designing websites to wearables to mobile applications, but the content areas about which the team designs also vary frequently. On a Tuesday the team may design an online computer game that supports mathematics learning for young children, while on the following Thursday they may design a mobile application that teaches second languages to children. Discussions of these and other content areas that CI teams have worked on have provoked the following question: *How can children design technologies for content areas they don't know about?* How can we expect children to design a mobile technology that teaches a second language if they don't know a foreign language, or don't know how to effectively teach language? Bringing content knowledge to the team is, indeed, critical to the ability to design appropriate technologies.

We have found three main ways to put together an effective, knowledgeable team capable of designing technologies specific to defined content goals: relying on the content knowledge of the adult design partners, relying on the content knowledge of the child design partners, or bringing in external content experts. CI design teams are often deliberately interdisciplinary, including adult design partners with diverse backgrounds ranging from child development to computer science to graphic design. The knowledge and skill sets of adult design partners can be leveraged, whether from their professional backgrounds or personal interests, to have them present content to the team when working on a related technology. Similarly, the child design partners on the team bring not only their experience in being children and in being designers, but also their content knowledge. Yip et al. (2013a) explored the notion that children who have been a part of a CI design team become design experts, revealing that children can also act as subject experts in other knowledge domains. When the team does not itself possess the necessary content knowledge, it may become necessary to bring in an external expert.

While content knowledge can be brought to the team from a variety of sources, it is important that such knowledge is introduced to the entire team before the team begins to design technologies. CI design sessions include a period of time at the start of each session for introductions to the session's topic. During this time, the content expert—whether a member of the team or a visiting partner—provides a short introduction to a topic. How much content knowledge is necessary, and what is the right amount? While this certainly varies from session to session, it is generally less than is assumed. The goal is not to create a team of content experts. What children are curious about and the ways in which they incorporate their curiosities into design features are important, often surprising, elements of technologies that support different content areas (Norooz et. al, 2015). Having a content expert present at the design session means that any critical gaps in knowledge can be addressed through asking questions.

The authors of this chapter have over two decades of experience in working on CI design teams. In the following vignettes we detail examples of how the University of Maryland's CI design team, called Kidsteam, has leveraged content knowledge to design technologies for children that address challenges in diverse content domains. We find all the sources—adult and child team members, as well as external experts—can provide the team with the content knowledge they need to design impactful and innovative technologies. For the bulk of this chapter, we share illustrative vignettes regarding the different ways in which content expertise can be shared with a design team. The vignettes we share here come from our collective experience on these teams as we reflect on the process of designing technology with children.

Vignettes

In the following vignettes we illustrate three strategies for introducing session content and describe how each strategy provides enough content knowledge to address a design problem in a variety of content areas. These vignettes highlight each of the three main approaches for bringing content knowledge to CI sessions:

1. Internal adult design partners
2. Internal child design partners
3. External experts

Internal Adults Providing Content Expertise: Quadcopters

Through a series of design sessions, we had our team consider new ways to use quadcopters. Since neither the children nor most of the adults had experience flying quadcopters, it was essential to have a person who was experienced in this field at the session. An adult design partner had learned how to fly and modify quadcopters as a personal pastime. She introduced the content to the team by bringing in a quadcopter that the design partners could practice flying. She also set up a demonstration that allowed the team members to see on a screen what was being recorded from the camera mounted on the quadcopter. These introductory activities, which were quite extensive, provided hands-on experience with what a quadcopter could do and allowed team members to witness the variety of sensors that could be attached to a quadcopter, such as photo and video.

In a follow-up design session the next week, the design team was asked to determine how they would use photographs collected by a quadcopter to create a map. The quadcopter was not brought to this session; instead, a discussion about the previous session was held to reactivate the knowledge. The team generated a diverse set of ideas, such as monitoring a neighborhood over time to obtain a historical record of changes and automatic systems that set flight paths so quadcopters do not need to be flown manually.

Lessons Learned: The personal interests of design partners can be leveraged as content expertise for the design projects. Content knowledge does not need to come from explicit experts to provide the design team with enough content knowledge to design. Content knowledge gained from prior sessions can be reactivated in later sessions to continue a design project.

Internal Children Providing Content Expertise: Children Leading Children

Some child design partners have chosen to design their own technologies, bringing their own ideas and prototypes to the design team for iteration. These children collaborate with an adult design partner to develop their own design sessions, making decisions that range from the design technique that should be used to who should work together in design groups to how to describe and discuss the content of the day's session with the rest of the team. The children themselves are the content experts for these sessions, making key decisions on the relevant pieces of content knowledge that are required for all team members to contribute to their designs.

One child began her session with a discussion, asking each member of the team what they "think of math" before leading them in a design task to evaluate a paper prototype for a math website she had designed (Yip et al., 2013b). The question about what team members "think of math" was important not only to get the team thinking about math, but also to make sure the team could address the math content she had included in her prototype. More recently, all children on the design team have been given opportunities to bring technologies they are personally designing to Kidsteam. One pair, for instance, has been working together on recipe blog for kids. As a result, they began their most recent design session with the team by discussing what blogs can be used for and what common ingredients are.

Lessons Learned: Children may possess enough preexisting knowledge to act as the content experts during design sessions.

Internal Children Providing Content Expertise: Storytelling

Many of the technologies that our team has created over the years address how children want to read or tell stories. From the International Children's Digital Library (http://en.childrenslibrary.org/) to StoryKit (http://tinyurl.com/j76eoal), many of the technologies that our team has created deal with sharing stories. When the team creates technologies such as these, child design partners typically already have enough expertise in how stories are shared to begin designing the technology. For example, in designing the International Children's Digital Library (ICDL), the team worked for years to design a multilingual, online space where children could explore and read books (Druin, 2005). As the children's previous experiences included visiting libraries and reading books, they were able to begin designing without additional specific content support. The ICDL grew and spawned the idea for StoryKit, a mobile application that enables children to tell and share their own stories. As with the sessions for the ICDL, all the child design partners had relevant personal experience in the content area. Because one of the explicit goals of StoryKit was to support sharing stories, this personal experience was brought directly to co-design sessions when family members (or other trusted adults) of the child design partners were asked to join the StoryKit design iterations (Bonsignore et al., 2013). There was very little need to provide additional content knowledge.

Additionally, during some design sessions the team collaborated with librarians and educators. While external stakeholders can provide content expertise—which we detail below—children on the team already had the base level of content knowledge in these areas to begin to design the technology, and therefore provided their expertise in conjunction with other adult team members.

Lessons Learned: Some content is known intrinsically by the team, including the children, well enough that further content expertise may not be required for designing.

Internal Children and Adults Providing Content Expertise: Connected Chemistry

Both children and adults were asked to provide content expertise on a project that investigated the design of an online chemistry program for high schoolers. For these design sessions, we formed a new team by asking teenagers to be our design partners, as the typical, younger partners were not yet of the age for which the curriculum was intended (Yip et al., 2012). The teenagers who were asked to join this team had expertise in one of two areas: they were either past child design partners with design expertise, or they were students who had experience with high school chemistry. Adult members of the design team included a past chemistry teacher as well as adults with no chemistry experience.

The technology being designed included a website in which chemical reactions were to be visualized and simulated on screen. It would not be possible to design these simulations without someone in each group who understood, at least at a basic level, what the chemical reactions were. In creating small groups, we worked to be sure that each group had a balance of teenagers with design experience and teenagers with varying degrees of chemistry knowledge. Having this diversity of content and design expertise has been shown to be effective when designing (Yip et al., 2013a). By ensuring that people with the content knowledge of chemical reactions were in each group, designers who did not have this knowledge, including the adults in the room who did not have a chemistry background, could ask either the teenagers or the former chemistry teacher when they needed more information.

Lessons Learned: Content knowledge can come from both child and adult design partners. Content should be cognitively appropriate for the age of the children. Teenagers are also able to design technologies after this kind of content introduction. When the team demonstrates that design expertise is as valuable as content expertise, a team can function well, with each member contributing uniquely.

External Adults Providing Content Expertise: Thermography

When Flir Systems (www.flir.com) released a thermal camera that attached to cell phones, thermography became substantially more accessible to children. This visual means of investigating heat transfer properties, such as conduction and radiation, seemed promising, but would children be interested in it? If interested, how would children envision using thermographic cameras? To investigate these questions, Kidsteam invited a researcher who was also a certified thermographer to describe how thermal cameras work and to participate in the design session. The visiting expert began the session with a 10-minute explanation about how heat transfer works, followed by a discussion on visible and nonvisible light, and finally how thermal cameras detect infrared wavelengths to determine heat transfer. The team was shown a short slide-show of thermal images to practice recognizing what the images meant (e.g., footprints across a carpet, a building where some windows look warm and others look cold, a hand touching a cold window and leaving a mark behind). For the rest of the design session, children were given thermal cameras to use while they rapidly brainstormed the many ways they would want to use a thermal camera, largely conceiving applications for learning, safety, and personal use.

A month later, after the session data had been analyzed, we held two follow-up sessions based on ideas the team had previously brainstormed, one on creating a mobile science application and another on creating art installations, each including the thermal camera. Each of these sessions was conducted without the thermal expert present. To reactivate the content knowledge about thermography that would be required for the design activities, at the beginning of each of these sessions the children were asked to describe how thermal cameras worked, which they did enthusiastically and correctly.

Lessons Learned: An external expert can describe their area of expertise to the team—both adult and child members—in a way that enables effective designs. The transfer of content knowledge extends past a single session and can be reactivated during follow-up sessions.

External Adults Providing Content Expertise: United States National Park Service

Our Kidsteam has enjoyed a long-standing relationship with the United States National Park Service. Over the course of more than a decade, Kidsteam has worked on projects ranging from the Webrangers website (www.nps.gov/webrangers/) to the Every Kid in a Park program (www.nationalparks.org/ook/every-kid-in-a-park). When designing technology that complements and enhances a child's experience in a national park, and/or affords some aspect of the live experience for a child who cannot get to a national park, the children and adults on Kidsteam often do not have the content knowledge necessary to design the technology. Thus, when working on content for the National Park Service, rangers and other employees of the National Park Service have brought the content knowledge necessary for the session and have participated in the design sessions as design partners. Often, a ranger skilled in storytelling would begin a session by telling brief stories about the content, always including some visual aids to help ground the designers in the content. The focus of these sessions encompassed a wide range of topics, from historical topics such as the Underground Railroad to current issues such as hiking safety to general content such as pumas. In such cases, the ranger remained at the session as an active participant, answering content questions that arose while designing.

A recent discussion with one of our long-term collaborators from the National Park Service illuminated how an external partner perceived these sessions. Wyndeth "Wendy" Davis, at the time the National Park Service Service–wide Education Coordinator, spent many years with Kidsteam, and often brought and presented the content knowledge needed for sessions. Wendy found that Kidsteam designers needed only the "basic story" in order to design technology, and that they could very often relate to experiences, such as home, family, and fairness, within the content, even if they did not have a full understanding of the entire story told at the National Park. She often found any misinterpretations and questions the children had during the design process to be helpful, because if design partners had content-based questions or misinterpretations, it was also more likely to be true of children in general. Acting as a content expert, Wendy was available during the design sessions to clarify any issues.

Lessons Learned: Content experts external to the design team can become a part of the team as they bring and share content knowledge. Good storytelling is an effective way to impart content knowledge to the team. If the external experts are amenable to and active in the co-design process, the team benefits.

Discussion

The examples presented here illustrate how children can be involved in the design of innovative technology even if they do not, from the outset of the design process, possess the content knowledge to be incorporated into the technology. In CI, children and adults work together on teams. One of the many benefits of this intergenerational configuration is that while children sometimes have the content knowledge needed, many times an adult from the team or a visiting adult may possess and can share the necessary content knowledge. This not only ensures that the content knowledge is present on the team, but also allows children and adults to shift the source of expertise.

Sometimes the process of designing technology, which includes incorporating relevant content, is mistakenly conflated with the design of curricula that uses the technology. CI design teams typically design the technology, or tools, that children are interested in using, not the curricula of which these tools may be a part. Using Connected Chemistry as an example, the CI team focused on designing the visualizations and the interfaces for the simulations on screen. University professors and chemistry teachers worked out the curricular questions and lesson planning for the curriculum that employed the tools that the team helped to design.

Designing curricula and designing a tool to be used within the curricula are interdependent but distinct challenges.

Additionally, the CI method mirrors many of the interdisciplinary design processes that most adult professional designers follow to balance content and design experience. When professional designers work in industry as experts in the design of technologies, they are not experts in every domain area. Web designers can design web pages for science-based nonprofits, large retail companies, and homework help because they understand web design and have developed the skill sets to address web design challenges. To address content requirements, design firms often contract and consult with others who possess the content knowledge needed to create their next assignment. Other design processes, such as Contextual Inquiry, do not rely on all designers to become experts in content and instead rely on context expert users (Beyer and Holtzblatt, 1997). Similarly, design partners on Cooperative Inquiry teams—both adults and children—are able to address technology design challenges across many content areas, because they have developed the skill sets to do so. In both cases, whether the designers are adults or children, they should consult with content area experts as needed during the design process.

Finally, an unintended positive consequence of CI is that, while children start as nonexperts in the content during many design sessions, there is evidence that they may learn about the content through their active participation in the design process (Guha, 2010). For example, during an interview about her experience as a design partner at the end of a year of design, one child recalled learning about oceans while working on a project with the National Park Service. Though the express intent was not to teach the children on the design team about the ocean, through working on the design of a website about a shipwreck, this child design partner recalled months later that she had learned about oceans. Because of the many benefits of co-design, which appear to include content knowledge but also have the potential to extend to other skills such as communication and collaboration (Guha, 2010), we see great potential for including co-design methods, such as Cooperative Inquiry, in the design of children's technology as learning opportunities.

During this chapter we have provided examples of how children can be an active part of the design of their own technology, even if they do not possess all the content knowledge to be included in the technology from the outset of a design session. By overcoming the expectation that children require such expertise to contribute to the design of a technology, the viewpoint of today's children can be heard in the designs of their technology. Similarly, this encourages adults from diverse backgrounds to participate, avoiding the expectation that adults try to design technologies as though they are the current generation of children. The intergenerational, interdisciplinary, and flexible makeup of the team leads to the establishment of the content expertise necessary for any given design challenge.

Acknowledgments

We thank our adult design partners, including Jason Yip, Jerry Alan Fails, Tammy Clegg, Beth Bonsignore, Beth Foss, Matthew Mauriello, and Wyndeth Davis, for their thoughts on this chapter. We also thank our many child design partners for years of exciting co-design.

References

Beyer, H. and Holtzblatt, K. (1997). *Contextual Design: Defining Customer-Centered Systems.* San Francisco, CA: Morgan Kaufmann.

Bonsignore, E., Quin, A. J., Druin, A., and Bederson, B. (2013). Sharing stories "in the wild": A mobile storytelling case study using StoryKit. *ACM Transactions on Computer-Human Interaction*, 20(3): 1–38. doi:10.1145/2491500.2491506

Druin, A. (1999). Cooperative inquiry: Developing new technologies for children with children. *Proceedings of the SIGCHI Conference on Human Factors in Computing Systems: The CHI Is the Limit* (pp. 592–599). New York: ACM.

Druin, A. (2005). What children can teach us: Developing digital libraries for children, with children. *Library Quarterly*, 75(1): 20–41. doi:10.1086/428691

Guha, M. L. (2010). Understanding the social and cognitive experiences of children involved in technology design processes. PhD dissertation, University of Maryland.

Guha, M. L., Druin, A., & Fails, J. A. (2013). Cooperative inquiry revisited: Reflections of the past and guidelines for the future of intergenerational co-design. *International Journal of Child-Computer Interaction*, 1(1): 14–23. doi: 10.1016/j.ijcci.2012.08.003

Norooz, L., Mauriello, M. L., Jorgensen, A., McNally, B., & Froehlich, J. E. (2015). BodyVis: A new approach to body learning through wearable sensing and visualization. In *Proceedings of the 33rd Annual ACM Conference on Human Factors in Computing Systems* (pp. 1025–1034). New York: ACM.

Yip, J. C., Foss, E, & Guha, M. L. (2012). Co-designing with adolescents. *Proceedings of the Designing Interactive Technology for Teens Workshop at NordiCHI*. October, Copenhagen, Denmark. New York: ACM.

Yip, J., Clegg, T., Bonsigore, E., Gelederblom, H., Rhodes, E., & Druin, A. (2013a). Brownies or bags-of-stuff? Domain expertise in cooperative inquiry with children. *Proceedings of the 12th International Conference on Interaction Design and Children* (pp. 201–210). New York: ACM.

Yip, J. C., Foss, E., Bonsignore, E., Guha, M. L., Norooz, L., Rhodes, E., McNally, B., Papapdatos, P., Golub. E. & Druin, A. (2013b). Children initiating and leading cooperative inquiry sessions. In *Proceedings of the 12th International Conference on Interaction Design and Children* (pp. 293–296). New York: ACM.

SECTION V

Concluding Thoughts and Moving Forward

16

LEARNING IN PD

Future Aspirations

Elizabeth B.-N. Sanders

Overview

This chapter describes my learning path as a participatory design (PD) research practitioner and teacher. It is written from an autobiographical rather than an academic perspective. The thoughts expressed here have been informed primarily by my practical, real-world experiences. This practice let me experiment with tools, techniques, and methods for participatory designing. During many years as a practitioner, I also read and contributed to the academic conversations about design research and PD that were going on around me.

I recently joined an academic institution, and now I am in the position of exploring how best to set up and support PD learning environments for my students. I am conducting this exploration from within a small design department at a very large American university. I continue to work part-time as a practitioner but usually in an advisory role rather than as a project manager.

My learning path evolves into a dream about where we can hopefully find ourselves in the future. It is a future where we will be able to collectively make the world a more convivial place in which to live. By "we" I refer not only to designers, but also to all the people who will inhabit this future. I call this future *collective dreaming*, a space in which everyday people are empowered to play out the futures that they imagine. I won't attempt to describe the content of this dream. Instead I will suggest methods and means for designing and design researching that may be able to get us there if we share a participatory mind-set. Once we get there, we can imagine, embody, and reflect on the future consequences of our decisions.

My learning path has been an example of hands-on, project-based learning in real-world situations in the workplace (Packer and Maddox, 2014). It has been a very good way to experiment and to learn. I want to be able to offer similar learning situations to my students.

My Learning Path in PD

I was not educated in Design. I earned undergraduate degrees in Psychology and Anthropology and then went on to complete a PhD in Experimental and Quantitative Psychology with the understanding that this education would prepare me for a career in academia. However, my first job was in an industrial design firm in 1981, where I was positioned as "an experiment in interdisciplinary design." The firm was just beginning to explore the impact of bringing disciplines other than design into designing. The experiment was to see what the intersection of design and psychology/anthroplogy would bring.

I first started practicing PD (or co-designing) as an intuitive response to challenges in practice in the early 1980s. I was not aware at that time that there was a field called participatory design going on in Europe. Keep in mind that this was before the Internet as we know it today. The designers at the firm were more than willing to collaborate with me when the "consumer" was a preschooler or an adult living with a chronic illness. For instance, on a preschool project, I invited the preschoolers to co-design with me, and created new methods to engage them in imagining and discussing a "talking teacher toy." I engaged preschool teachers and parents as well. However, the designers of my firm remained confident that they could adequately represent all other types of consumers for the products and environments they would design.

Years later, I learned that there was a practice called participatory design and sought to explore more, beginning with Pelle Ehn's (1988) dissertation. I continued to learn about participatory design by doing many small experiments over time. For example, on every new client project I would use methods that I had used previously but I would also try to introduce one new method, tool or technique. I didn't tell the client that I was doing this. In this way, my repertoire of tools, techniques, and methods for participatory design grew. Ultimately, as my repertoire evolved, my firm's designers took notice and invited me to join them in collaborations with all kinds of "users," on a much wider range of design challenges.

Throughout 30 years in practice, I have had the opportunity to explore and apply participatory design methods in most of the design disciplines, including industrial, communication, interaction, interior space, architecture, service, and social design. Unfortunately, most of this work has been proprietary. During my time in practice I was also involved at a university on a part-time basis, teaching required courses in Design Research to undergraduate and graduate design students as well as serving as a committee member for many MFA and PhD students at a number of different universities. In addition, I continued to learn from and contribute to the growing academic discourse on design research and PD practices.

From Practitioner to Teacher

Four years ago I joined the university as a full-time faculty member. This move has enabled me to conduct more small experiments. I will always be an experimental psychologist. I continue to teach courses in Design Research to undergraduate and graduate students as well as an interdisciplinary co-design studio at the graduate level. The undergraduates learn to practice research methods for design in a studio format over two semesters. The first semester focuses on foundational skills that are applied in team-based evaluative research projects. The second semester focuses on participatory design practices that are applied in the front end of the design process. The second semester, students are encouraged to conduct hands-on experiments with the design languages and materials of participation. They work on interdisciplinary design teams and often with clients or sponsors from outside communities.

The graduate students learn in collaboration with students from disciplines all over the university, a situation that mirrors the interdisciplinary world of professional practice. In the interdisciplinary co-design studio, graduate students are challenged with co-designing with people whose life situations are unlike their own. For example, last year students co-designed with the elderly, and this year they will be co-designing with young people living with a chronic illness as well as with others in their "circle of care."

At the university I have had the opportunity to become involved in several large research projects that would not have been possible with clients in industry. For example, I have been able to explore how the design of spaces, places, and materials can help to stimulate and support collective creativity and innovation. In a series of participatory design workshops, participants (teams who worked together as well as people who came together over a shared interest in creativity) were first asked to share photos and thoughts about their personal creative spaces, places, and materials. They were then assigned to small interdisciplinary teams and invited to create full-scale spaces to support and facilitate their collective creativity. They were provided with a very wide range of props and materials to use for creating the spaces. After they had made and presented their spaces, they were given the opportunity to work collaboratively in them. The ease and speed with which people were able to make spaces that could facilitate their collective creativity was remarkable. Inspired by the experience, several of the teams returned to their workplaces and changed them completely.

A second project, conducted in collaboration with faculty and graduate students from Engineering and the College of Medicine, is examining the needs of the wide range of people who work in, reside in, or visit hospital patient rooms. First we explored the separate needs of 23 different types of stakeholders who work in hospital rooms, from physician to sitter (Lavender et al., 2015). Next, we created a full-scale hospital room with Velcro walls and included all the components that are needed in a room, from the hospital bed to light switches. We then invited 25 mixed stakeholder groups to create the hospital room in which they want to work, using this model. They can position and reposition hundreds of room components. Even the bathroom and all its components move. The only fixed relationship is that the door to the hallway is opposite the window wall. After stakeholders configure their hospital room, they are asked to test it by enacting the tasks they would do in the room. They can make quick refinements to the room on the spot since all the components move. Participation has been phenomenal. For example, 115 healthcare providers and hospital staff as well as 61 former patients and family members have so far taken part in the Velcro hospital room study. We are now in the process of analyzing the results to determine underlying commonalities and points of conflict.

The move from paper-based and small-scale 3D participatory toolkits (e.g., Sanders and Stappers, 2012) to full-scale, 3D materials and environments has been particularly exciting. I have seen first hand that not only can people work collectively to make their own creative spaces and workspaces, but the resulting full scale prototypes serve very well as the stage for experiential scenarios of future use. The creation of full-scale, 3D environments sets the stage for collective dreaming where people can then act out the futures that they imagine.

What I Have Learned So Far about Learning in PD

A few things about learning in PD are particularly relevant to the direction I will describe next. I have learned that students are more open to learning about co-designing than faculty are. Some faculty still resist integrating PD perspectives into their work because they feel their special skills, abilities and roles are being taken away from them. This mind-set presents a major barrier for moving toward collective dreaming in the future.

I have observed that interest in the collaboration between industry and academia has been rapidly increasing. Consequently, informal learning on real projects is becoming easier to arrange and to facilitate today. Many possibilities are emerging that empower students to learn about PD through hands-on, project-based learning in real-world situations.

I have learned that apprenticeship is the best way for people to learn about PD. However, this approach is difficult to establish in large academic institutions where student-to-faculty ratios are high. Students respond very well to the prospect of doing real projects and make the best progress when they are given opportunities to work with outside clients. However, it is risky for industry partners to allow undergraduates to work on real co-design projects over the course of a single quarter or semester, since there are no guarantees about what the results will be.

Framework for Looking Ahead

Based on my experiences as both a professional practitioner and design research educator, I propose the following framework to structure our way forward toward collective dreaming. The framework resembles a matrix, but the columns are actually a timeline reflecting a progression from design, to co-design, to collective dreaming. The progression does not imply that older approaches will disappear. All the approaches, and likely others, will coexist over time. These approaches were introduced in "Three Slices in Time: From Designing to Co-designing to Collective Dreaming," co-written with Pieter Jan Stappers (Sanders and Stappers, 2014).

	Designing ▶	Co-designing ▶	Collective dreaming ▶
Mindset	Designing for...	Designing with...	Designing by...
Types of audiences	...customers ...consumers ...users	...participants ...communities ...organizations	...people
Design intention	Consuming Using	Improving Engaging Provoking	Imagining Vizualizing Enacting Reflecting
Future reach	Next generation	Mid-term futures	Longer-term futures
Maps		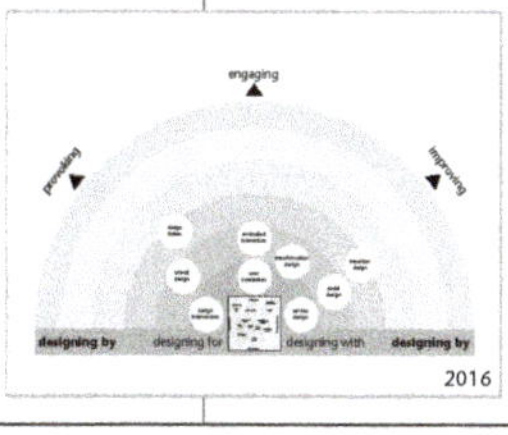	

FIGURE 16.1 A Framework Showing the Transition from Designing to Co-Designing to Collective Dreaming

The two small maps in the last row show what was happening at the transitions between approaches (e.g., at the border between designing and co-designing). The 2006 map (Sanders, 2006) reveals that designing *for* people and designing *with* people were beginning to be recognized as two distinct domains. It also reflects the emergence of design-led thinking and making in the design research landscape. The 2016 map shows that the 2006 map has been positioned as the core set of approaches and methods that now informs and inspires a much wider array of approaches with far broader intentions.

I'll start with a look to the recent past, that is, the phase called designing. Looking backward a bit affords us a contextual landscape to build on and also facilitates our perception of patterns of change. Designing refers to traditional approaches to design, in which the designer is considered the expert whose job it is to *design for* people, who are viewed as and referred to as customers, consumers, or users. The intention of designing is to support people's consumptive behaviors and use experiences by designing, developing, and producing products, services, and environments. The orientation toward the future is generally aimed at the next generation of these products, services, and environments.

2006 Map: At the Border between Designing and Co-Designing

The 2006 map was an attempt to organize and simplify the approaches to design research that were being practiced and discussed at the time. It was a

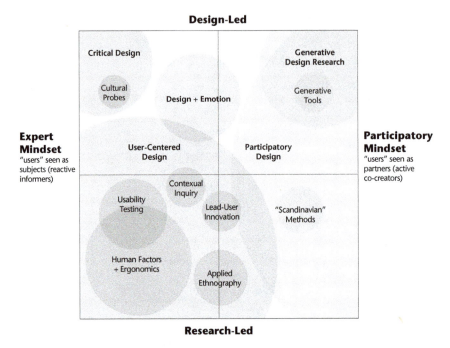

Design-Led

Critical Design

Cultural Probes

Design + Emotion

Generative Design Research

Generative Tools

Expert Mindset
"users" seen as subjects (reactive informers)

User-Centered Design

Participatory Design

Participatory Mindset
"users" seen as partners (active co-creators)

Contextual Inquiry

Usability Testing

Lead-User Innovation

"Scandinavian" Methods

Human Factors + Ergonomics

Applied Ethnography

Research-Led

FIGURE 16.2 The 2006 Map of Design Research and Practice at the Border between Designing and Co-Designing. Sanders (2006)

time of conflict and confusion, with people and organizations arguing over what was the right way to do design research. The intent of the map was to visualize the field in a way that might lead to useful conversations. The map accomplished that and has become an effective introduction to the traditional design research landscape for students and beginning practitioners. The map highlights a distinction between the expert mind-set and the participatory mind-set, with very little overlap between them. Another key attribute of the map is the recognition of the emergence of design-led approaches in addition to more standard research-led approaches to design research. But this map is now 10 years old, so let's move on.

Co-designing refers to the practice of *designing with* people. In this approach, the people to be served by design are considered the experts in how they want to live, work, and play in the future. The designer takes on the role of facilitator, focusing on supporting the creativity of their design participants. People who become a part of the co-designing process are generally referred to as partners and participants in the process, particularly when the focus of the effort is in the conception and ideation stages, where the purpose of the design research is to figure out what to design. Co-designing often takes place in communities of practice, which can range from small groups such as a family to large groups such as an organization or a city. Co-designing is oriented toward *improving and empowering.* The outcomes of co-designing tend to be both tangible (e.g., new products and services) and intangible (e.g., ownership of and pride in the tangible outcomes).

The 2016 Map: At the Edge of Collective Dreaming

As shown in the framework, the 2016 map sits at the border between co-designing and collective dreaming. In this new map the 2006 map serves as the central core upon which concentric rings of design and design research practice flow out into the more distant future. The rings represent not only "increasing scales of time, increasing scope of context, but also increasing levels of complexity, and increasing impact of the future consequences of design" (Sanders, 2016). The move from co-designing to collective dreaming is needed to address the complexity and interconnectedness of the world we live in today.

There are three basic directions of intent on the 2016 map: engaging, improving, and provoking. The middle direction of intent points to design for engaging. Here, we might use design/design research to engage people for the purpose of entertainment, learning, and/or consumption. Traditional approaches to designing fall along this slice of intent. Interaction design is in the innermost ring, with embodied interaction in the next ring moving out into the future.

The second direction of intent points to design for improving. Approaches along this direction are likely to embrace a participatory mind-set. Changes have been taking place that have positively impacted our ability to invite

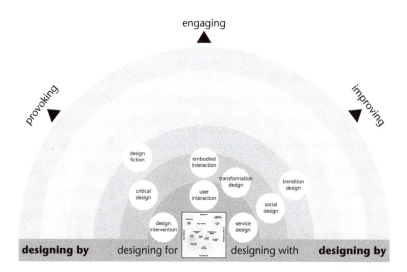

FIGURE 16.3 The 2016 Map of Design Research and Practice at the Border between Co-Designing and Collective Dreaming. Sanders and Stappers (2016)

everyday people into the design process as co-designers. First, we have social communication technologies for connecting people. Most people have access to these technologies and know how to use them. Second, more and more people share a participatory mind-set. This is especially true of younger generations (Jenkins et al., 2006). Finally, and at long last, consumerism is slowly deflating. It appears to have hit a peak and is now declining as we enter the "sharing economy" (Hamari et al., 2015; Benkler, 2004). Approaches that are positioned in the direction of improving include service design and social design. Transition design (Irwin et al., 2015) also appears to be on the trajectory that is aimed at improving. Transformation design sits between the improving and engaging slices.

The third direction of intent points to design for provoking. For example, we might provoke people to think about or act upon what they see. Sometimes we provoke people in order to incite change. The approaches that are positioned in the direction of provoking include design interventions, critical design, and design fiction (Dunne and Raby, 2013; Johnson, 2011). This slice of the map is exploding, with new and hybrid approaches that reach farther out toward the speculative future. Several examples are introduced below. The range and diversity of these approaches suggest that the intentional spaces for design will also be multiplying in the future.

Experiential futures refers to a "practice that deliberately attempts to explore the places where language alone cannot. At once an emerging form of foresight practice, design work and political action, an experiential scenario is the manifestation of one or more fragments of an ostensible future world in any medium or combination of media including image, artifact and performance" (Candy, 2010).

Anticipatory ethnography (Lindley et al., 2015) combines design fiction and design ethnography. It claims to "operationalize design fiction" as it "looks at design fiction artifacts and applies ethnographic techniques to them in order to produce actionable insights." However, as the authors admit, it is too early to see whether anticipatory ethnography can deliver on the promise of actionable insights.

Speculative interventions, on the other hand, are not done *for* design. "Speculative interventions are a mode of inquiry through design . . . for making manifest contemporary conditions and articulating issues *through* design" (DiSalvo, 2014). Perhaps speculative interventions are leading to another intentional slice?

Collective Dreaming: A View to the Future

The outermost ring in the far future reaches of the 2016 map represents the space for collective dreaming. Whose dreams are we talking about in collective dreaming? On the one hand, we could be referring to the dreams

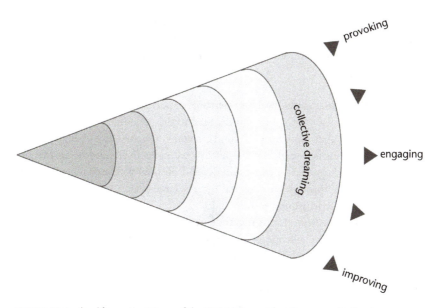

FIGURE 16.4 An AlternativeView of the 2016 Map with a Focus on Collective Dreaming

of designers and futurists. Most advocates for the design for provoking slice see themselves as the dream builders. On the other hand, we can also refer to the collective dreams of *all* people. This is a more extreme form of collective dreaming, one in which designing is done not just with the people but *by* the people. I argue that we need to explore the more extreme forms of collective dreaming now.

In collective dreaming, everyone can have the opportunity to play out (enact) imaginary scenarios in real or virtual 3D space. However, they will first need to be supported in their ability to imagine and visualize future environments and situations in which such enactments can take place. And they will need to be able to try out what they make to decide whether they want to live this way in the future. This is where new roles for designers will emerge. Designers in the future will make the tools and materials for nondesigners to use to express themselves creatively and collectively. Designers will help to make sense of and give shape to the collective dreams of people.

Collective dreaming is a place and a space for everyday people to play (i.e., visualize and enact) the futures that they imagine. We will need to create new methods to help us reach the goal of extreme collective dreaming. We will need to create methods where people can tell future stories collaboratively, where they can visualize future scenarios collectively, and where they can enact future scenarios together with others. We will need to create full scale, kinetic, 3D toolkits to support collective, embodied cognition and creativity.

Others are dreaming about collective dreaming today. Stuart Candy, Director of the Situation Lab and Assistant Professor of Strategic Foresight and Innovation at OCAD University in Toronto, and Fellow of the Long Now Foundation, writes:

> It is true that at some level, our personal experience can be only ours. But I no longer fear that we are condemned to dream alone.
>
> I think that humanity is fundamentally psychedelic—quite literally: mindmanifesting—and that the history we collectively choose to live out in years and decades to come will depend on how well we cultivate public imagination, through experiential futures, large-scale participatory simulations, transmedia games, and the like.
>
> I believe we can dream together, now. And I suspect that to the extent we rise to the challenge of good governance for the 21st century, that's exactly what we will be doing on a regular basis. (Candy, 2015)

Alfonso Montuori, Principal of Evolutionary Strategies, and Professor in the Transformative Inquiry Department at California Institute of Integral Studies writes:

> The new collaborative creativity may be one way of beginning to stimulate the collective imagination. As the changes in creativity in the 21st century suggest, the generation of images of the future will not be confined to a priestly class of artists and futurists. The new, participatory, grass-roots creativity can be mobilized for the creation of better futures. Envisioning the future has historically been a task left for artists or futurists. . . . The time has come for a process of grass-roots philosophical futurism. . . . Very important in this process of envisioning petits recits is ensuring the participation of groups that have been traditionally under-represented in the discourse of the future, including women, so-called "minorities," and young people, and the emphasis that this should be a creative process—not a deterministic techno-forecast, but a creativity as ethical aspiration and ethics as creative aspiration. (Montuori, 2010)

Final Thoughts and Questions

I believe that we can dream together now, too. We can invite everyday people to take part in the imagination and anticipation of future scenarios. We can create and use methods of *participatory design fiction* to reach toward collective dreaming. I am not talking about situations where designers and futurists create future scenarios/environments for others to experience and think about. I am talking about *extreme collective dreaming* where *all the people* can collaboratively imagine, create, and then enact their own future scenarios. People are able to do this. I have seen it happen in the two research projects discussed earlier: co-creating creative spaces and the Velcro hospital room.

We now have the means to embody immersive environments in real, virtual, and hybrid spaces. It is only a matter of time before we can invite everyday people into the collective creation of future scenarios/environments. Everyday people are ready for collective dreaming, making, and enacting.

Designers are moving from being designers of stuff to being facilitators of the imagination of others to being the makers of toolkits for collective dreaming. Are we, as designers and futurists, ready to embrace the mind-set needed to faciliate and support extreme collective dreaming? Are we willing to invite *all the people* into making sense of and shaping their own futures?

References

Benkler, Y. (2004) "Sharing nicely": On shareable goods and the emergence of sharing as a modality of economic production. *Yale Law Journal, 114*, 273–358.

Candy, S. (2010) The futures of everyday life: Politics and the design of experiential scenarios. Unpublished doctoral dissertation, Department of Political Science, University of Hawaii at Manoa. http://scribd.com/doc/68901075/Candy-2010-The-Futures-of-Everyday-Life

Candy, S. (2015) Dreaming together: Experiential futures as a platform for public imagination. In Durfee, T. and Zeiger, M. (Eds.), *Made Up: Design's Fictions*. Zurich: JRP Ringier/Art Center Graduate Press.

DiSalvo, C. (2014) Speculative interventions as inquiry. In *Speculative Interventions: The Research Network for Design Anthropology*, August 14–15, 2014, Copenhagen, DK.

Dunne, A. and Raby, F. (2013) *Speculative Everything: Design, Fiction and Social Dreaming*. Cambridge, MA: MIT Press.

Ehn, P. (1988) *Work-oriented Design of Computer Artifacts*. Arbetslivscentrum.

Hamari, J., Sjöklint, M., and Ukkonen, A. (2015) The sharing economy: Why people participate in collaborative consumption. *Journal of the Association for Information Science and Technology*, http://doi.org/10.1002/asi.23552

Irwin, T., Kossoff, G., Tonkinwise, C., and Scupelli, P. (2015) Transition design: 2015. White paper from Carnegie Mellon University's School of Design.

Jenkins, H., Clinton, K., Purushotma, R., Robinson, A. J., and Weigel, M. (2006) *Confronting the Challenges of Participatory Culture: Media Education for the 21st Century*. Chicago: MacArthur Foundation.

Johnson, B. D. (2011) *Science Fiction Prototyping: Designing the Future with Science Fiction*. San Rafael, CA: Morgan & Claypool.

Lavender, S., Sommerich, C., Patterson, E. S., Sanders, E. B.-N., Evans, K., Park, S., Umar, R., and Li, J. (2015) Hospital patient room design: The issues facing 23 occupational groups who work in medical/surgical patient rooms. *Health Environments Research and Design Journal, 8*(4), 98–114.

Lindley, J., Sharma, D., and Potts, R. (2015) Operationalizing design fiction with anticipatory ethnography. *Ethnographic Praxis in Industry Conference Proceedings, 2015* (pp. 58–71). doi:10.1111/1559-8918.2015.01040

Montuori, A. (2010) Beyond postnormal: The future of creativity and the creativity of the future. *Futures*, *41*(2), 221–227.

Packer, M. J. and Maddox, C. (2014) Mapping the territory of the learning sciences. In Sawyer, R. K. (Ed.), *The Cambridge Handbook of Learning Sciences*. New York: Cambridge University Press.

Sanders, E. B. -N. (2006) Design research in 2006. *Design Research Quarterly 1*(1), 1–8.

Sanders, E. B. -N. (2016) Where are we going? An aspirational map. In Joost, G., Bredies, K., Christensen, M., Conradi, F., and Unteidig, A. (Eds.), *Design as Research: Positions, Arguments, Perspectives* (BIRD Series). Basel: Birkhäuser Publishers.

Sanders, E. B. -N. and Stappers, P. J. (2012) *Convivial Toolbox: Generative Research for the Front End of Design*. Amsterdam: BIS Publishers.

Sanders, L. and Stappers, P. J. (2014) Three slices in time: From designing to co-designing to collective dreaming. *ACM Interactions*, November–December 2014. http://dl.acm .org/citation.cfm?id=2670616

17

CONVERSATION

Tensions and Possibilities between Learning and Participatory Design

Conversation with Yvonne Rogers,
Christopher Frauenberger, and Chris Quintana

On July 8, 2016, Yvonne Rogers, Christopher Frauenberger, and Chris Quintana engaged in a cross-continental conversation via Skype about the challenges and opportunities facing both designers and learning scientists as they strive to integrate participatory design approaches into their projects. Yvonne Rogers is a human–computer interaction (HCI) researcher whose work has contributed to the development of new theories (e.g., external cognition) and revolutionary methodologies (e.g., "in the wild" studies). Christopher Frauenberger is also an HCI researcher, but his work has focused primarily on the design of technologies with and for autistic children. Chris Quintana is both an HCI designer and an education researcher who has led the development and evaluation of software tools and frameworks that promote the scientific inquiry practices of middle school students. Moderated by Elizabeth "Beth" Bonsignore, they explored the following themes:

- Personal vignettes of participatory design and its relation to learning
- Tensions between design and learning: differing degrees of control
- Diverse definitions for participatory design
- Potential of participatory design methods when designing for learning
- Opportunities for closer collaboration between learning scientists and participatory designers

Personal Vignettes of Participatory Design and Its Relation to Learning

Beth Bonsignore: How did you become involved with using participatory design?

Christopher Frauenberger: I came to participatory design after my PhD, when I started working on the ECHOES project, which was a learning environment for autistic children. There was a strand called "Participatory Design" that I was hired to work on. As I got more and more into it, it became my main motive of research and my main way of operating in science. I do most of my stuff in participatory ways. A lot what I do now is, I think, gravitating to a more Scandinavian kind of understanding of participation and participatory design. So, it's becoming a bit more ideologically framed rather than purely pragmatic. I think that's been a result from seeing a lot of things going wrong in ECHOES, because there was a fundamental misunderstanding there. We were trying to create a learning environment for autistic children where one strand of the work was participatory design and another strand of work was learning activities. I don't think that you can meaningfully separate those two things, and a lot of the struggles that we had in the project reflected this. I think the misunderstanding was that learning scientists do the learning, and the participatory design people beautify the system so that children would engage with it. But it's much more interwoven. The learning activities and the design are fundamentally linked, so they shouldn't be developed in two different strands. What I'm doing now, in terms of participatory design, is exploring alternative futures, empowering people. What that entails is learning a lot about children's life worlds. I think that children who work with us learn a lot about design, and they learn that alternative futures are possible. So, I see it very much as a dialectical process at the moment.

Chris Quintana: My interest in participatory design began in grad school. The research group I worked with was starting to design software in one of the local high schools as part of their research on project-based science education. During that time, the group, which included my advisor, Elliot Soloway, Mark Guzdial, and Ken Hay, worked on an article that came out in *Interactions* on learner-centered design. The article addressed some of the things we had learned and needed to spotlight, from a design perspective, when creating educational software. While our group worked on learner-centered design throughout, one of the issues that emerged for us is that the design and use of educational software has a diversity of audience, with diverse stakeholders and diverse users of the software. From that starting point, we began our new ScienceWorks research project with more diligence about getting the perspectives from high school students, from high school teachers, and also, from our partners at the School of Education. We tried to bring all of those perspectives together within the design team to design the software we were developing. So, not only were we trying to integrate the perspectives of what I'll call the users, the high school kids and the teachers, but we were also trying to integrate the perspectives of the educational researchers. We didn't want to have this divide between the technology design team and the educational team. We tried to avoid the situation that I think Chris F. alluded to.

I think we carried that idea throughout the project, in trying to get ideas and perspectives from all of the different people involved. I think sometimes we were a little weak in terms of how I see participatory design could be used. While we worked well to get the perspectives of all these stakeholders, I don't know that we were always as successful in trying to build a coherent, consistent team that is constantly bringing in these perspectives. I think there's a difference between having a team where you have kids, educators, designers, and the researchers all constantly together on the team. I think that's a different situation than talking to those people at different times throughout, while not necessarily having them as a consistent part of the team. That part still remains a struggle for us. However, I think the *spirit* of trying to get all of these people's ideas, and to use those ideas in the design of the software, that is something that we're still doing today.

Yvonne Rogers: I'm not someone who's from participatory design or from the learning sciences. So, I don't have that starting point. I'm very much someone who's building innovative technologies or prototypes as a way of exploring what's possible with technology for supporting and facilitating new ways of learning. We're very much of the view that, as designers and creators, we can come up with prototype designs, and then we will run workshops and sessions with children, with educators, or with different stakeholders to get their input, and to invite them to critique or to suggest. This has worked very well for us. So, I've never really been someone who is a firm believer in participatory design because of the reasons that Chris and Chris have just mentioned.

I think the most valuable way in which you can work with people is to get their contribution at different stages, particularly as technology gets more sophisticated. So, if you were developing a website, it might be you can have participation, but when moving into more complex technology, such as technology tied to the Internet of Things, to expect our participants to have the knowledge of what to do with these new technologies at every level is probably going too far. So, what we do now is we've been developing a toolkit to support computational thinking. The toolkits we have been developing comprise tangible sensing cubes such as *MakeMe* and *ConnectMe*. We run a series of workshops with different kinds of children at different ages, getting them to think about what they might do with this toolkit. We teach them some concepts, but then get them to think what's possible and how they might expand it. I probably have quite a different approach in that regard. It's probably more sort of a traditional interaction design approach than a participatory design one.

Christopher Frauenberger: I've got two things to say, one to you, Chris. To me, participatory design is fundamentally *more* than getting everybody's perspective to do something with it. An interesting aspect, and a real potential of participatory design, is not just eliciting requirements or perspectives, but actually to create something totally new through collaboration. That has to do with empowerment; it has to do with enabling people and giving them the scope to do things on their own. On the other hand, I have to agree with Yvonne. We shouldn't expect participants to be designers, and we shouldn't expect them to understand the design space of the Internet of Things or other design spaces that we explore.

From my experience, I've worked with autistic children between 6 and 8 (years old). Very obviously, they're not designers, and they have no idea about . . . I mean, they love soldering. Everybody brings quite different skills to the table. A lot of learners, or a lot of children in my case, bring expertise in their own life worlds to the table. So we can ask: What is meaningful to them? What are potential roles for technologies?

We do build technology with them, but it's quite clear that we have the expertise to do that. At that end, I think a lot of the work is done by us. But we get children to tell us stories about magic things or use metaphors for technology to tell us what they think is meaningful to them in their lives and what technology could do. That connects to learning in a very, very interesting way, because this is what experiential learning is all about. If something is relevant and meaningful to you, you ask the right questions and you've got the motivation to learn, and you remember, and you learn. I think we've known this for a long time. For 100 years people have been saying that learning is social. Learning is embodied. Learning is experiential and situated. I think all these things are there in participatory design. So, there is an awful lot of common ground. But I want to fend off the notion that participatory design is only an attempt to elicit perspectives and then do something with it. Participatory design, for me, goes further than that.

Chris Quintana: I would agree with that. I think that's one reason why the ScienceWorks project I mentioned was frustrating. I had this feeling that we didn't go far enough with the idea of participatory design. In the end, the project remained within this more limited realm of just trying to get ideas from the kids, from the educators. I wonder if one reason was just because from an educational standpoint there was a pretty firm idea from the team of, "Here's the kind of thing we want to build *already*. Let's just try to involve these different people as we design it." We weren't going to venture too far off from that initial design concept. So, there were fewer degrees of freedom. Perhaps that's why we kind of stayed in a more limited implementation of participatory design. We certainly got good feedback from the kids. We got very useful ideas from everyone. But we still had a preconceived idea of the kind of thing that we were going to build.

Yvonne Rogers: I think there is a role for participatory design. I think what Christopher (Frauenberger) mentioned about experiential learning, certainly you can use participatory design to shape and to frame different kinds of learning. But if you are trying to design a *specific* technology, which is what I'm doing, to teach something; and it could be ecology, it could be physics, it could be computing or coding, or the Internet of Things; then I think we have to have some more knowledge and understanding of what we're trying to teach them. So, that's where I think it can be *not* necessarily a good use of our time, or the children's, if you have lots of workshops too early. The children say lots of great, crazy, creative things, but it doesn't really help us with building this technology and constraining it. I think there is a place for it. I think Chris F. eloquently described how it could be useful.

But in what we're doing as technology designers, trying to come up with new, exciting, great ways to encourage learning of specific topics, it's more difficult to use that approach. Having the children come in at different points, to comment on, or use our technology probes in various ways, to make suggestions that we haven't thought of, that's great.

Tensions between Design and Learning: Differing Degrees of Control

Christopher Frauenberger: I really agree. Maybe this is at the core of why participatory design and the learning sciences haven't overlapped as much as one would expect. It reminds me a little about the debate about the difference between action research and participatory design. I think the difference lies in the intent. While in action research, the intent is about changing an existing social situation, in participatory design the intent is directed towards actually designing an artifact, so a design outcome. Here, I think I see a parallel in ways that there's a shared value base. But the intent in the learning sciences is towards the learning, while the intent in participatory design goes towards the artifact. A lot of learning scientists might be reluctant to take up participatory design in earnest because they would need to give up some control over the learning. That might be a good thing or a bad thing, depending on where you're coming from. But just as Yvonne said, if you're trying to create something for a specific learning experience, you *can* use participatory design to maybe come up with something within that frame. But the more you go towards participatory design, the more you would need to give up the idea that you can control the scope of your idea. So, if you really give participants scope for challenging your goals, then I think learning scientists may begin to struggle. Learning scientists maybe feel more protective about their intents to create something that has specific learning goals. In contrast, participatory design—if you take it to the extreme—would say everything is up for discussion and we will just create what we want to create in an alternative future. So, there is this tension there. I think maybe along this dimension you can move up and down, between total control over the learning and full participatory design ideals. There's always going to be a bit of a clash of agendas.

Chris Quintana: You raised a good point there. The projects I've been involved in are more along the lines of what Yvonne just described. So, this idea about the control, there may be something to that. I think in the learning sciences; people don't really talk about participatory design. You hear more about design-based research, or recently design-based implementation research, which have a lot in common with participatory design *in spirit* because they support the idea of bringing together different stakeholders. But you're right. The stakeholders are brought together around a specific design idea to support a specific type of learning, and the work becomes, "Let's design *that* thing." There's less freedom to bring people together to say, "What is it that we want to design?" and possibly run the risk of getting away from that initial idea. So, I think the intent is different when you're talking from a learning sciences perspective about design-based research versus taking participatory design to its extreme. In many learning sciences projects, for example, let's say we want to teach chemistry to sixth graders, and here's what we want to teach. So, let's design the artifact around that, and we're not going to have a ton of wiggle room in terms of changing the core of what we want to teach. Now, the trick is, how do we design something that supports that specific learning goals, but in ways where the team shapes the artifact from the ground up, rather than simply giving feedback on an artifact that is already somewhat determined? Although feedback that includes stakeholders like learners and teachers in the process can contribute to the design, it's still somewhat predetermined for specific learning goals. This sounds different than what you've just described about kind of taking participatory design to its . . .

Christopher Frauenberger: Fundamentals.

Chris Quintana: Fundamental idea, yeah. Yeah. I think it *is* different. When I talk to people in the learning sciences, comparing these ideas of design-based research and design-based implementation research, I've posed sometimes the idea, "Well, there are some similarities here to participatory design." Sometimes I get agreement and sometimes I get vehement disagreement. So, within the learning sciences, I'm not sure there are any firm ideas about what participatory design is or whether people use it. I don't hear the term participatory design as much in the learning sciences, as in say, the field of human–computer interaction.

Diverse Definitions for Participatory Design

Yvonne Rogers: Depending on which camp you're in, and how strong you feel about your methodology or approach, whether it's design research or action research (and all of the other 57 varieties of how we do something), you feel more passionately or less so. I'm much more opportunistic: Let's see if it works. Let's see what we can get as we get the kids to run around and see if they can come up with things. I'm very pragmatic in how I approach things and who I work with. But in some perspectives or approaches, particularly participatory design, and perhaps the learning sciences, there's much more of, "This is the way we do things. This is what we call things. This is how we work." So, I think it depends on your philosophy as to what you think works best in order to achieve what you're trying to do. So, within participatory design, at least my understanding of people who work in it, there's a very strong sense of what you do, how you do it, and how you work with people. That's very important, but I'm a bit more open-minded about what I can get with the resources, availability, the hope, and the ambition of our research.

Christopher Frauenberger: Although, I would say that even in participatory design, there's a real broad range of interpretations. There's a quite traditional and weirdly geographic, distinction between more pragmatic interpretations in the States, and very ideological interpretations in Scandinavia and Europe. Obviously, you're sitting somewhere in between, quite physically.

Potential of Participatory Design *Methods* When Designing for Learning

Christopher Frauenberger: So, beyond the field's particularities in terms of the ways we work and what we call things, there's some good overlaps that could be exploited. We've so far only talked about participatory design as a means to actually design some learning tool or some artifacts within the learning context. But participatory design would actually be able to offer quite a lot of expertise and insights in *methods* that you could directly use as a learning activity. A lot of the methods in participatory design are about engaging people, are about creating some room or scope for them to think about what is important, and teaching them some of the skills that might be necessary, and then getting back some of the ideas that they have. I'm thinking, for example, of fictional inquiry as a standard method in participatory design. To a learning scientist, that's not big news. If you pack something into a good story, people learn quite easily. People are engaged and find it useful and meaningful. Then they learn about chemistry, because it's been packed into a story about, I don't know, world peace and atomic bombs. Just on a methodological level, there is an interesting overlap where participatory design has something to say about engagement and motivation that would be interesting for the learning sciences. It's not just about designing your artifacts.

Pragmatically, I agree that you have to move between extremes as you see fit in terms of what you try to achieve in a certain project. There's nothing wrong in particular with having a strong idea and being clear about the scope of the impact the participants can have. In ECHOES, for example, we had a big clash because we thought we had a bigger scope. The learning scientists would only give us very little. So, there was an internal struggle for impact. That was an interesting debate we had. In the end, we saw our participants reduced to telling us things like, should it be flowers or balls? That's not participatory design, to my mind. You could possibly look at it as learner-centered design, but that's a longer story.

Chris Quintana: I agree when you say that the learning sciences could benefit from looking at more of the methodologies used; not only with participatory design, but also with standard user experience design and HCI methods. In the learning sciences, although we talk a lot about design-based research, there hasn't been as much of an overlap between learning sciences and HCI as I would like.

There's still a lot of room in the learning sciences to draw from methods used in HCI—specifically, in participatory design. Recently, you're starting to see a little bit more movement in that direction with the learning sciences, where we recognize a need to talk more deeply about design and participatory design. I think there's a lot that the learning sciences can still draw from HCI, in thinking about different kinds of design methods.

Opportunities for Closer Collaboration between Learning Scientists and Participatory Designers

Beth Bonsignore: You've talked about methods, and you've talked about building the team of stakeholders together. So, do you think there are particular points during the design process, or specific techniques that learning scientists and participatory designers should share?

Yvonne Rogers: I agree with Chris (Quintana's) point that the learning sciences could benefit from HCI methods. This can be in terms of asking, how do you engage users as you explore various methods? Fictional inquiry is one method; body-storming is another. There are lots of creative methods that the HCI community has come up with in the last 5 to 10 years besides lab-based studies. We've been doing some large classroom studies, where we will come with our half-baked technologies or some of our prototypes and run more "in the wild" studies where we video kids, large groups of kids using our technologies. From that, we've started to think about how we operationalize learning in a different way than it has been traditionally operationalized. We have been looking at the collaborative and experiential aspects. For example, the last paper that we presented at Interaction Design and Children (IDC) started a conversation about different ways of measuring learning in the classroom that are a bit more "in the wild," rather than before and after, pre/post-test. As we start to come up with technologies that aren't just a simulation or an app on a PC, but involve embedding technology in the environment, we need to think in different ways about: What is the experience for kids when they use this? What are they learning? What's the process of making and designing that they're doing? How can we measure learning? It's a challenge for the learning sciences, HCI, and participatory design to rethink what we thought we had nailed in regards to learning. Because, I think learning *does* change. So, I don't think it's necessarily a case of one field or area taking from another. I think we should try and work out how we all address these new challenges afoot.

Christopher Frauenberger: I think there are two major points at which collaboration between participatory design and learning sciences might be most beneficial. One is at the earliest point of framing what learning means, which is much earlier than any of the learning technologies actually are thought about. I think it would be an amazing opportunity to really do participatory design at the earliest stage of any project, to see: What is it that children find meaningful? In which ways could you think about learning experiences? What are their ideas? Then building concepts from there. I'd agree that then there's a point where interaction designers and learning scientists go off for a little while and do their thing. But then again, I think in evaluation, or in trying to figure out what the learning experiences really are, there again, a lot of participatory design methods could help and get the voice from participants into that evaluation. I agree it's a very complicated thing to assess learning, because the broader you look at learning, the fuzzier and more complicated it gets to evaluate. But participatory design has never been renowned for rigorous evaluation. I think it is a bit of a problem. But maybe it can bring different voices to the evaluation as well.

Another point of intersection is methodology, where a lot of the methods could actually be turned into learning experiences. That is, participatory design as a way of learning for children. It's something quite powerful, and it connects to the whole FabLearn and digital fabrication movement where you see that a lot of the participatory design processes now being applied to digital fabrication and making are fundamentally connected to learning in an important way. So, I think there's an interesting circle there. And, yes, I also agree that it should go both ways. I don't think that this is one field giving to the other. I think it should be a very interesting conversation, and participatory design certainly can benefit from a lens on learning to understand what it does.

Chris Quintana: I think that cycles back to an earlier point you made, too, that within the learning sciences there may be this idea or concern of giving up control on what learning is. What you just described could move in a direction where learning scientists have to be open to rethinking what we think learning means, or thinking about learning in different ways. I see, sometimes, there can be a resistance to that. So, trying to employ these methods in the two ways that you've described would be quite interesting. I'd also like to see more talk about design methods in the learning sciences world. A lot of times in learning sciences contexts when we talk about design, it's at a very theoretical level. We don't talk about more pragmatic methods, and how we could use them in learning sciences.

I also agree that it goes both ways. HCI participatory design folks can learn a lot about different ways to talk about learning, different ways to evaluate learning, and stuff that the learning sciences does more of. So, bringing these two communities together is something I'd like to do more. I'd like to do more talk around what the learning sciences can learn about design and design methods from HCI, and what HCI can learn about how we talk about and evaluate learning in different ways, that it's not just the effects of a technology in pre- and post-test kind of approaches. But it's trying to think about effects with technologies that we are seeing *along the way*: What changes are we seeing? What changes aren't we seeing? What are we seeing learners do with these technologies? That's the kind of intersection I would like to see more of.

Beth Bonsignore: How could we then get more learning sciences and participatory designers or HCI designers together to talk about which methods and where in each of their design processes they could involve each other's techniques, theories, or perspectives?

Yvonne Rogers: I don't think you can force it. As I said, people need their identity. Sometimes it's hard to see someone else's perspective or try and integrate it. So, rather than getting everyone into a room and presenting the facts, I think it will come through a "grand challenge" or a need that's perceived or conceived by policy. For example, there could be a grand challenge saying that there are new things that children need to learn about digital literacy and so forth. How can we address this *globally?* And there could be a new funding initiative that requires both fields to come together. That would be more attractive than saying, "Let's hold a workshop and see if we can get people to talk to each other from different fields." As an aside, I was helping to run a workshop on being "super-human." We were trying to get people from human intelligence and machine intelligence to come together. We found it almost impossible to get people from both camps to talk at the same venue. That made us realize you can't force it. But you can maybe make it attractive through some higher-level call that gets the learning sciences and design or participatory design fields to tackle the same problem.

Christopher Frauenberger: Yeah. These cross-disciplinary collaborations are really difficult to foster besides grants or funding calls. I think that one approach would be to actually open up publishing venues to the respective groups. Perhaps a special issue in co-design on learning would do some good in that direction, because then participatory design people would start thinking, "What *is* learning?" Then they go and talk to their learning scientist neighbor, and in the best circumstances probably they would write a paper together. Similarly, if the learning scientists' community would find scope for a special issue on participation or participatory design in one of their journals, that would create a need for learning scientists to engage with participatory designers. Just reporting on these discussions probably would do the trick. But, yeah. I agree. You can't force it or you might end up with very poorly written articles on either side. It is needs-driven. We will hopefully come to a point where there is an evident need for participation in learning or learning in participation. Then these things will happen.

18

NEXT STEPS

Betsy DiSalvo, Jason Yip, Elizabeth Bonsignore, and Carl DiSalvo

This book began with the idea that participatory design (PD) was being used as technique in the field of the learning sciences with more frequency. As both participatory design and the learning sciences grew in the number of researchers, we observed interdisciplinary dialogue occurring in conferences such as Interaction Design and Children (IDC), Special Interest Group on Computer-Human Interaction (SIGCHI), Computer-Supported Collaborative Learning (CSCL), and the International Conference of the Learning Sciences (ICLS).

However, as we started compiling this book, gathering these chapters together, and conversing with researchers from both the fields of design and the learning sciences, we observed far more divergent ideas about participatory design than we had anticipated. Both disciplines have a rich history that includes their own practices, theories, and methods, and yet we observed very little discussion occurring between scholars and practitioners in the learning sciences and those in participatory design. Although more researchers are coming together in conferences and publication venues, we do believe both groups are not actually engaging in shared dialogue. For instance, we did not see agreement as to what constitutes participatory design in the learning sciences, what the role of learning is in participatory design (and vice versa), and what participatory design methods and techniques are important for learning considerations. The conversations between designers and learning scientists particularly highlight how these different perspectives can be challenging for people working at the intersection of learning sciences and participatory design.

Initially, we had hoped to gather some of the best practices where these two fields meet. Instead, we uncovered a set of challenges that need to be addressed if participatory design is to be used by learning scientists in a manner that supports the values that have emerged from the history of participatory design as a practice. From the perspective of design, these chapters highlight the need to better understand, accommodate, and integrate research on the diverse ways people learn. From the perspective of the learning sciences, these chapters highlight the opportunity to more fully engage the methods of participatory design in order to work more closely with the range of participants that shape learning, including students, teachers, administrators, parents, and other community members.

Despite some of the differences, we do see potential that this work between the two fields can address four strategic issues. First, we need to better identify the shared perspectives, values, and politics between the two fields; the ways in which we might use these share perspectives as a foundation for participatory design practices involved in learning; and where and how those values and perspectives diverge. Second, we need to address the challenges of working across the two disciplines, explore how these challenges might be mitigated, and transform them into opportunities for more productive participatory design outcomes. Third, we must actively seek ways for the field of participatory design to adopt inclusive practices that accommodate and celebrate the diversity of learners that the field of learning sciences works with and promotes every day. Finally, we see potential for learning sciences studies to serve as contexts in which researchers from both fields can employ and extend participatory design techniques that inform our understanding of the perspectives of a wide range of participant stakeholders (children, parents, teachers, librarians, administrators, policy-makers, et al.).

Shared Perspective/Politics/Values

At first blush, the shared perspectives of participatory design and the learning sciences seem readily apparent. Both fields value inclusivity, sharing an ideological stance that champions giving a voice marginalized communities, and that actively engages those who are often the most impacted by design decisions, regardless of context. Both fields also share values tied to democratic access to fundamental resources, such as education and accessible tools. Yet, implicit tensions emerge when examining the chapters in this book that should be addressed openly to enable the learning sciences and participatory design fields to work together in more explicit, truly interdisciplinary partnerships.

While the learning sciences does promote more accessible and inclusive learning environments, there is an unspoken assumption in much of its work that learning needs to operate within existing structures of formal education. In many cases, these formal educational structures are based upon institutionally prescribed, authoritative constructions and constraints that both contain, and are required to demonstrate specific outcomes, implicitly placing certain types of behavior and learning goals as more valuable than others. In contrast, the practice of participatory design as it is imagined from the Scandinavian perspective looks to design the structure of a system through the participatory process, including participants, such as workers, who have historically not had a voice in the design of the system they work under. We see a number of ways to address this these tensions.

First, we ask, *"What are participants learning in the participatory process and how do they benefit by participating?"* We see evidence of empowerment, such as Chapter 6 (Polman et al.), in which teachers participated in the design of learning experiences whose initial conceptions were given to them by academics. The teachers' participation gave them the agency and authority to shape their students' learning experiences in ways that could both meet their needs and build upon their strengths, rather than depending solely on the initial academic designs. Or in Chapter 12 (Light and Boys) where participatory design disrupts the understanding of mobility, and in the many examples of children's empowerment in learning that they can be the designers of learning experiences throughout the book. In Chapter 15, McNally and Guha share several lessons learned and pragmatic approaches for incorporating content expertise in participatory design projects such that all participants, regardless of their initial knowledge and experience, can contribute to, and learn from, the design of technologies and experiences that span many diverse content areas. In all three of these chapters, participant learning in participatory design is not just about improving design skill sets, but also about a shift in identities as designers.

This leads us to ask, *"Who we are educating with participatory design?"* Is the purpose of participatory design the edification of the designers of the learning experience, pedagogical theorists and experts, teachers, administrators, communities, or can the participatory design process also be an integral part of the learning experience for learners? Who are we inviting to participate in our participatory design in learning efforts, and whose values and institutional or societal structures are we prompting these participants to design toward? The questions that comprise this strand can inspire learning scientists and designers alike to reflect upon the values that we bring to our design and learning work and help mitigate any implicit power dynamics among learning sciences researchers, designers, and participants.

Our chapters and conversations offer several touch points that shed light on the many facets of cultural and individual values that can positively influence an introspective approach to inclusive, expansive learning and participatory design efforts. In particular, DiSalvo and DesPortes's chapter on value-driven learning underscores an ideal that as we engage in participatory design for learning with individuals from different cultures, ethnicities, and socioeconomic sectors, we must remain sensitized to values and perspectives that can attune us to our own blind spots regarding what and who we *★think★* we are trying to design *for* and *with*: *"the neighborhood tour attuned us to some of the value systems at play . . . [and] gave us as researchers a glimpse into the experience of being a young African American male and how other members of the community might perceive them in negative ways"* (Chapter 13, emphasis added). Similarly, Hourcade (Chapter 9) came to realize throughout his team's multiyear efforts of engaging in participatory design with children diagnosed on the autistic spectrum that he and his colleagues had much to learn about the perspectives and needs of their child co-designers, but they relished finding ways to stay flexible as they adapted and accommodated PD techniques for a wide range of autistic behaviors and skill levels. Uchidiuno and colleagues (Chapter 5) emphasizes how children and parents come together from diverse perspectives and experiences to shape design of learning technologies. Future work in participatory design and learning will need to address not only who comes together to design, but how does inclusion become a focus. Can neurotypical children work together with neurodiverse children to create an inclusive learning environment? Can policy-makers work together with classroom teachers and students together to craft agendas for learning?

Finally, we must ask, *"Is the role of participants the same when designing for learning?"* The structure of schools and the requirement for meeting certain learning objectives challenges many of the values of participatory design. Similarly, the contemporary market imposes demands on product and service development cycles that thwart a sustained commitment to participatory practices and value. While many would suggest that changing these structures and requirements is not possible and possibly not desirable, if we follow the historic development of participatory design, as Ehn laid out in Chapter 2, from the teachings of Paulo Freire, then disrupting these structure and requirements is the fundamental charge of participatory design. Indeed, to assume that we cannot change our environment (whether that is a market, a school, or, increasingly, the collapse of education into market economy thinking) is antithetical to the very foundation of design that assumes that other situations are possible and achievable. How can we as learning scientists, working with the value systems and structures of various different cultures, both respect those cultures and look to disrupt them with radical design methods? A number of cases in this book address this tension, but in Chapter 8, Louw et al. explicitly identify these conflicting value systems and speak to ways that participatory design can navigate these relationships—serving the values of multiple stakeholders. As they state:

> Our claim is that design-led modes of inquiry are especially needed to respond to ambitious visions of educational transformation and funding directives, which leave much unresolved detail to be determined and realized by local practitioners, leaders, and learners.

In his conversation with Allison Druin, Jon Kolko touched on the challenge of findings ways to use expansive participatory design techniques for ideation within the time-sensitive, market-driven constraints of a corporate, product-focused environment. Relatedly, when conversing about the constraints of more traditional educational approaches and learning outcomes, Christopher Frauenberger and Chris Quintana considered the relationship between the learning sciences and participatory design efforts along a continuum rather than an either/or:

Chris Quintana: Stakeholders are often brought together around a specific design idea to support a specific type of learning, and the work becomes, "Let's design that thing." There's less freedom to bring people together to say, "What is it that we want to design?"

Christopher Frauenberger: [T]here is this tension there. I think maybe along this dimension you can move up and down, between total control over the learning and full participatory design ideals.

Working Together

The authors in this book demonstrate how participatory design in the design of learning experiences is often taken on as an interdisciplinary effort, where an expert in one field, design or learning sciences, integrates the other discipline into their work. However, there remain few examples where learning scientists and designers partner closely and equally. We suggest that to move forward in integrating participatory design and the learning sciences, the time is ripe for more in-depth cross-disciplinary work, with the full expertise of both fields brought together on projects. This poses a number of challenges and potential opportunities for unique collaboration.

Before exploring how these two fields can work more closely together, we must first understand what they have to offer each other. In Chapter 13, Betsy DiSalvo and Kayla DesPortes describe how the use of participatory design helped to inform the designers of learning experiences about the values of participants, shaping the educational program to not only capture the interest of young people, but also to sustain that interest over time. In Chapter 11, Maurer and Bonsignore identify how industry has found value in using participatory design methods with a sustained cohort of children and adult co-designers who strive to carefully align engagement with more structured learning sciences' outcomes as they develop new educational products. And in the case study in Chapter 7, Gelderblom outlines the use of project-based learning theory that is deeply informed by ongoing participatory design with a class. But these are limited cases, and all of them call for a deeper exploration of ways to legitimize each field to the other, and to bring the theory and rigor of each field to inform the other.

The first of these explorations asks, "How can we encourage learning scientists and educators to engage the design field, and to recognize that design and participatory design are disciplines in their own right, with rigor in practice that should be attended to?" To answer this question, we believe that the learning sciences must first acknowledge that the field of design exists and it is not simply a byproduct of their research. As Christopher Frauenberger notes in his conversation with Yvonne Rogers and Chris Quintana (Chapter 17), participatory design is *"not just about designing your artifacts"* or developing "some learning tool [to fit within] the learning context"; rather, *"there is an interesting overlap where participatory design has something to say about engagement and motivation that would be interesting for the learning sciences"* (emphasis added). By looking more closely at design research and theory, learning scientists can benefit from existing approaches that not only balance input from participants and designers alike, but also encompass the perspectives and input of a diverse range of stakeholders. Examining previous work on participatory design can help learning scientists with techniques for eliciting input, working with various participants, and interpreting findings. As Liz Sanders points out in Chapter 16, she initially developed techniques for participatory design as an individual, slowly adding more tools with each new project. Learning scientists need not start from scratch; instead they can take advantage of, and build upon, previous work from the field of design.

The second question we should ask is, "How can we encourage the participatory design field to be more cognizant of the history and theories of the learning sciences to help inform and assess the learning aspects of participatory design ventures?" Designer-led case studies often recognize that learning is an implicit and important aspect of the design process, and such case studies are an integral part of design instruction; however, researchers may be glossing over opportunities for deeper inquiry into the mechanics and inner workings of learning processes and behaviors, while some designers may not consider learning theory at all. Learning theory can help to inform the structure of participatory design activities and contribute to designs overall, by providing theories of motivation, techniques for scaffolding a design experience, and approaches for engaging participants in metacognition. Moreover, being cognizant of theories of learning and empirical studies of learning requires a sustained engagement, because these theories develop overtime and empirical studies shed light on new, emerging contexts. It is not enough to simply reference Lave and Wenger (1991) or use terms such as *scaffolding* when referring to learning and design. What's needed is a deeper commitment to understanding the evolving field of learning, not out of some sort of deference to that field, but out of respect to those we are designing with and for. This by no means is a trivial task. As Yvonne Rogers states:

> It's a challenge for the learning sciences, HCI, and participatory design to rethink what we thought we had nailed in regards to learning. Because, I think learning does change. So, I don't think it's necessarily a case of one field or area taking from another.

Finally, we suggest asking both fields of participatory design and learning sciences consider the following questions: "Is there a unifying theory of PD for learning? Does PD need a theory of learning and design?" While the learning sciences uses phrases such as *Design-Based Research* and the field of participatory design uses the term *learning* without much thought to the deeper theories behind design or learning, the continual interaction between the two fields calls for us to ponder the potential of unifying theories that can contribute to our understanding of inherent linkages between the two fields, or offer explanatory power regarding reasons why design and learning are used together so frequently. Moving forward, we envision opportunities for researchers from both fields to answer these questions and others, such as: do we see ways to demonstrate that participatory design is a strong methodological candidate for design in the learning sciences? Or is participatory design viable to the learning sciences because it involves stakeholders in a democratic fashion? As the world becomes more interdisciplinary even as it grows more rich in diversity, will the perspectives of PD and learning sciences become more divergent or convergent? As learning is being moved to large scale platforms, such as online classes, will there be a place of participatory design or is PD always a small scale endeavor for local environments? How will this impact of technology and others change how we think about engaging participants in design?

To answer these questions, we argue it seems necessary to make learning science research and participatory design research more accessible to researchers in each field. Do we begin with seeking to publish in each other's venues, with cross-disciplinary workshop, or are there other ways to promote and sustain an active, continuous exchange between the fields? How do design and learning theories come together and influence each other? So while we first embarked upon this book to demonstrate the interdisciplinary ties between participatory design and the learning sciences, our greatest finding from the readings is that the two disciplines have only just begun to scratch the surface of understanding and respecting each other. We walk away from this book with more questions than answers. Much of the history of both fields is based upon democratic and pragmatic goals to give more opportunities for people to participate in their own learning and reality. Moving forward, if we can find convergent theories and practices, the fields of participatory design and learning science can better serve the motivations of their foundations.

CONTRIBUTOR BIOS

June Ahn is an associate professor of Learning Sciences and Educational Technology at New York University, Steinhardt School of Culture, Education, and Human Development. He conducts research on the design, implementation, and evaluation of learning technologies. He is interested in designing and understanding sociotechnical systems—or how social, cultural, and institutional factors intersect with the affordances of new technologies to create enhanced and equitable learning opportunities for all learners. Dr. Ahn has conducted research on the use of social media for learning, alternate reality games and playful learning, and the use of analytics for research-practice partnerships with school districts. This work has been supported by grants from the National Science Foundation and the Institute of Education Sciences.

Nina Barbuto is the Director and Founder of Assemble. Nina's passion for art, new media, and social learning led her to found Assemble, a community space for arts + technology, in 2011. On her own, Nina works in a variety of media including architecture, film, sound, and installation and often explores the idea of recycling noise into a system or elevating the vernacular to the spectacular. Nina holds degrees in architecture from Southern California Institute of Architecture and Carnegie Mellon University, where she is also adjunct faculty.

Austin Beck is a graduate research assistant at the University of Maryland's College of Education and the College of Information Studies, focusing on learning technology policy and design research.

Elizabeth Bonsignore is a postdoctoral researcher at the University of Maryland's Human-Computer Interaction Lab and College of Information

Studies. Her research focuses on the design of technology-mediated social experiences that promote new media literacies, arts-integrated science learning, and participatory cultures for youth. This work involves close co-design partnerships with children and teens (7–17 years old). She is particularly interested in the role that multimodal, interactive narratives play in helping underrepresented youth engage in lifelong learning. She has contributed to several National Science Foundation–funded projects on the design of alternate reality games and social media technologies for learning.

Jos Boys is a visiting professor in Learning Landscapes at University of Ulster, UK, and a part-time design tutor at Regent's University London, UK. Dr. Boys trained in architecture and has worked as a journalist, teacher, researcher and design practitioner. She has taught architecture and interior design for many years, both in the UK and abroad. She has also been an academic developer, instructional designer, and learning spaces design consultant, most recently at the University of New South Wales in Sydney, Australia. Her research focuses on the social aspects of architecture and interior design; and on relationships between pedagogy, material space, and technologies in higher education. This is underpinned by a design and artistic practice centered on working with community and disadvantaged groups. She is especially interested in how design intersects with gender, class, race, and disability; and in finding creative forms of collaboration with non-designers.

Tamara Clegg is an assistant professor in the College of Information Studies and the Department of Teaching and Learning, Policy and Leadership at the University of Maryland. Her work focuses on developing technology to support life-relevant learning where children engage in science in the context of achieving personally relevant goals. She seeks to understand ways such learning environments and technologies support scientific disposition development. Tamara's work is funded by the National Science Foundation, the Institute of Museum and Library Studies, and Google.

Kevin Crowley is a professor of the Learning Sciences and Policy at the University of Pittsburgh, where he also directs the University of Pittsburgh Center for Learning in Out-of-School Environments (UPCLOSE). He works in partnership with museums, community organizations, and other informal educators to develop innovative out-of-school learning environments. Crowley's group conducts basic learning sciences research in informal settings and develops new theories of how people learn about science, technology, engineering, and art. Crowley has a PhD in psychology from Carnegie Mellon University and a BA in psychology from Swarthmore College.

Kayla DesPortes is a Human-Centered Computing PhD student at Georgia Institute of Technology specializing in Learning Sciences and Technology.

She works in the Culture and Technology Lab (CAT Lab) advised by Betsy DiSalvo. Her work centers on exploring learning and collaboration in maker activities combining electronics and computer science. She investigates learning sciences theories in order to design effective curriculum that can engage a diversity of students. Her work on curriculum is complemented by her work designing prototyping tools to improve the effectiveness of the educational experiences.

Betsy DiSalvo is an assistant professor in the School of Interactive Computing at Georgia Institute of Technology. At Georgia Tech she directs the Culture and Technology Lab (CAT Lab), which focuses on understanding how culture impacts the use and production of technology and how those understandings can shape learning for groups that are traditionally underrepresenting in technology fields. DiSalvo's previous project, the Glitch Game Testers, has been one of the most successful programs to engage low-income African American males with computer science. Currently, she is partnering with the testing group, ACT Inc., to understand how to leverage parents in improving educational outcomes for low-income populations. In addition, she is the principle investigator on a National Science Foundation (NSF) award to better understand maker culture in the classroom and co-investigator on an NSF-funded project to understand the cultural implications of the New York City CS4All initiative in K-12 schools. DiSalvo holds a PhD from Georgia Tech in Human-Centered Computing.

Carl DiSalvo is an associate professor in the School of Literature, Media, and Communication at the Georgia Institute of Technology. At Georgia Tech he directs the Public Design Workshop: a design research studio that explores socially engaged design and civic media. DiSalvo's scholarship draws together theories and methods from design research and design studies, the social sciences, and the humanities to analyze the social and political qualities of design, and to prototype experimental systems and services. His first book, *Adversarial Design* (2012), is part of the Design Thinking, Design Theory series at MIT Press. He is also a coeditor of the MIT Press journal *Design Issues.* DiSalvo's experimental design work has been exhibited and supported by the ZKM, Grey Area Foundation for the Arts, Times Square Arts Alliance, Science Gallery Dublin, and the Walker Arts Center. DiSalvo has a PhD in Design from Carnegie Mellon University.

Allison Druin is a professor in the College of Information Studies and a researcher in the Human-Computer Interaction Lab (HCIL) at the University of Maryland (UMD). She is currently serving as a visiting scholar and special advisor for national digital strategy at the US National Park Service. For over 20 years, she has led intergenerational design teams of children and teens, computer scientists, educators, families, and more to develop new educational technologies for young people with co-design methods. She has served as the CHI 2016 co-chair for the premiere ACM conference on Human-Computer Interaction, chief futurist for

UMD's Division of Research, the director for the HCIL, and was named an ACM Distinguished Scientist in 2014, cited for her global reach and real-world impact.

Pelle Ehn is Professor Emeritus at the School of Arts and Communication, Malmö University, Sweden. He has for more than forty years been involved in the research field of collaborative and participatory design and in bridging design and information technology. Research projects include DEMOS from the 70s on information technology and work place democracy, UTOPIA from the 80s on user participation and skill based design, ATELIER from turn of the century on architecture and technology for creative environments, and during the last decade Malmö Living Labs, an open environment for democratic design experiments. His often collaborative publications include *Emancipation and the Design of Information Systems* (1974), *Computers and Democracy* (1987), *Work-Oriented Design of Computer Artifacts* (1988), *Manifesto for a Digital Bauhaus* (1998), *Design Things* (2011), *Making Futures* (2014) and *Democratic Design Experiments* (2015).

Christopher Frauenberger is a senior researcher at Vienna University of Technology, Austria, and principle investigator of OutsideTheBox–Rethinking Assistive Technologies with Children with Autism (http://outsidethebox.at). He holds a PhD in Computer Science from Queen Mary, University of London, UK, and subsequently worked as a postdoctoral fellow at Sussex University, UK. In his academic research he focuses on exploring interactive technologies in the context of people with disabilities. This includes designing auditory displays for the visually impaired, investigating nonverbal communication in people with schizophrenia, and technologically enhanced learning environments for autistic children. Methodologically he is committed to participatory design approaches and often reinterprets collaborative techniques from other fields in his work. He is an associate editor of the *International Journal of Child-Computer Interaction* and a member of the ACM SIGCHI Ethics Committee.

Engida H. Gebre is an assistant professor of Learning Sciences and Technologies at Simon Fraser University, Canada. His research focuses on data literacy, representational competence, and active learning environments for youth engagement. He obtained his PhD in Learning Sciences from McGill University, Canada.

Helene Gelderblom is an associate professor in the Informatics department at the University of Pretoria, South Africa, where she teaches courses in programming and human–computer interaction and supervises masters and doctoral students. Her research focuses on the use of eye tracking in usability and UX studies, designing for special-user groups, and on the design of technology for education.

Mona Leigh Guha has years of experience working with both children and adults. She is currently the director of the University of Maryland's Center for

Young Children, a center dedicated to educating preschool and kindergarten children, providing professional opportunities for both preservice and veteran teachers, and supporting research on how children develop and learn. Mona Leigh was the interim director of the University of Maryland's Human-Computer Interaction Lab, an interdisciplinary lab of more than 50 faculty, staff, and students from multiple colleges. Mona Leigh was also managing director of KidsTeam, a team of adults and children who work together to design innovative technology for children. Her research has focused on working with young children as design partners and investigating the cognitive and social experiences of children who participate on a design team. Previously, Mona Leigh was a classroom teacher in the Maryland public schools. She received her PhD from the University of Maryland in Human Development (2010). She holds an MS from Johns Hopkins in Early Childhood Special Education, and received her BS in Early Childhood Education from Lock Haven University.

Christopher Hoadley is Associate Professor in the Educational Communication and Technology Program, the Program in Digital Media Design for Learning, and the Program on Games for Learning at New York University. His research focuses on collaborative technologies, computer support for cooperative learning (CSCL), and design-based research methods, a term he coined in the late 1990s. Hoadley is the director of dolcelab, the Laboratory for Design of Learning, Collaboration & Experience. He was an affiliate scholar for the National Academy of Engineering's Center for the Advancement of Scholarship in Engineering Education (CASEE) and was awarded a Fulbright for 2008–2009 in the South Asia Regional program to study educational technologies for sustainability and empowerment in rural Himalayan villages. From 2013 to 2016, he was on loan to the National Science Foundation as a program officer. Hoadley previously chaired the American Educational Research Association's Special Interest Group for Education in Science and Technology (now SIG: Learning Sciences), and served as the first president of the International Society for the Learning Sciences.

Juan Pablo Hourcade is an associate professor in the University of Iowa's Department of Computer Science, UI3 associate director for Informatics Education, and a member of the Delta Center. His main area of research is human–computer interaction, with a focus on the design, implementation, and evaluation of technologies that support creativity, collaboration, well-being, healthy development, and information access for a variety of users, including children and older adults. Dr. Hourcade is in the editorial board of *Interacting with Computers: Foundations and Trends in Human-Computer Interaction*, and the *International Journal of Child-Computer Interaction*. He is editor of the Universal Interactions forum for *interactions* magazine.

Angela M. Kohnen is an assistant professor of Literacy in the School of Teaching and Learning at the University of Florida. Her research focuses on the teaching of writing and writing-related professional development. She earned her PhD in Education from the University of Missouri–St. Louis.

Jon Kolko is partner at Modernist Studio, and the founder and director of Austin Center for Design. He was previously the vice president of design at Blackboard, the largest educational software company in the world. He joined Blackboard with the acquisition of MyEdu, a startup focused on helping students succeed in college and get jobs. His work focuses on helping design students develop autonomy through making. He is the author of four books: *Thoughts on Interaction Design*, published by Morgan Kaufmann; *Exposing the Magic of Design: A Practitioner's Guide to the Methods and Theory of Synthesis*, published by Oxford University Press; *Wicked Problems: Problems Worth Solving*, published by Austin Center for Design; and *Well Designed: How to Use Empathy to Create Products People Love*, published by Harvard Business Review Press.

Ann Light is Professor of design and creative technology at the University of Sussex, where she leads the Creative Technology Group. She is a design researcher interested in social wellbeing and sustainable futures, the politics of participation, and the long-term social and cultural impact of digital networks in post-industrial and developing regions. Her background includes consultancy to design start-ups, drama teaching, and a number of interdisciplinary academic roles across computing, drama, communication, and design. She has worked with arts and grass-roots organizations and marginalized groups on five continents, in local, transnational, and international development settings, publishing on design of social process, social innovation, and cross-cultural methodology.

Marti Louw directs the Learning Media Design Center at Carnegie Mellon University, with appointments in the Human Computer Interaction Institute, Robotics Institute, and Entertainment Technology Center. She is the assistant dean of curriculum and faculty in the Integrative Design Arts & Technology (IDeATe) network, and teaches in the Master of Educational Technology and Applied Learning Sciences (METALS) program. As a design-based researcher, she seeks to enact theory through project-based implementations that creatively bridge learning science research and design practice from initial conceptualization through realization and assessment with stakeholders. Her research focuses on how design as an integrative form of systematic inquiry across disciplines can be used to develop technology-enhanced learning environments that are socially constructed, personally relevant, and emancipatory. Louw holds a MDes in Design from Carnegie Mellon University.

Lisa Maurer is an independent consultant specializing in training and collaborative design. Her passion to involve all key users in the design of the solutions that touch their lives inspired her to bring Cooperative Inquiry to Pearson's product development process, where it continues to thrive. Today, Lisa is squarely focused on helping organizations implement change initiatives through experiential learning and coaching. Lisa holds a BS in Sociology from Northern Arizona University, Post Baccalaureate teaching certification, and a master's in Educational Psychology from the University of Iowa.

Rosemary McBryan Davidson is the STEM Coordinator for St. Joseph's Academy in Saint Louis, Missouri. She has been a classroom science teacher for over 40 years, with recognitions as a Woodrow Wilson Fellow, American Chemical Society Teacher of the Year, Science Teachers of Missouri Teacher of the Year, and Tandy Scholar. Her interests include the development of science journalism and data journalism practices for high school classroom use. She completed her doctorate at the University of Missouri–St. Louis.

Brenna McNally is a PhD candidate in Information Studies at the University of Maryland's Human-Computer Interaction Lab. Her research investigates Participatory Design practices with children and the ways in which mobile technologies can promote learning opportunities. At the University of Maryland Brenna is the research coordinator for Kidsteam: a co-design team that works with children to design technologies that support children's learning and play. Brenna received her MS in Human-Computer Interaction from the University of Maryland in 2012 and her BA in Telecommunication–Digital Media, Art, and Technology from Michigan State University in 2008.

Kelly Mills is a PhD student in the College of Education at the University of Maryland, College Park. She is advised by Dr. Diane Jass Ketelhutt, and conducts research about science education and technology. She is currently exploring how students communicate scientific ways of knowing through social media.

Daniel Pauw is a PhD student in the College of Information Studies at the University of Maryland–College Park. He is advised by Dr. Tamara Clegg while researching how to support informal science learning. He is currently investigating how mobile technology can support interest-based science learning and collaboration.

Joseph L. Polman is a professor of Learning Sciences and Science Education, as well as associate dean for research, in the School of Education at University of Colorado Boulder. He designs and studies project-based learning environments for youth in schools and community programs, and his work has been funded by numerous federal agencies and private foundations. He received his PhD in Learning Sciences from Northwestern University.

Chris Quintana is an associate professor in the School of Education at the University of Michigan. His research lies at the intersection of education and learning sciences, human–computer interaction, and computer science. Much of his work focuses on software-based scaffolding for middle school science students, including the development of scaffolded software tools and learner-centered design processes. His recent *Zydeco* Project investigated how mobile devices (e.g., smartphones and tablets) and web-based technologies can connect science classrooms and museums to expand science learning opportunities while exploring the opportunities and challenges of developing learning activities that integrate formal and informal learning environments. Recent related work includes the study of wearable technologies (e.g., smartwatches) used by K-12 teachers in their classrooms to help monitor student activity, and software development to support students with different inquiry-based practices. He is also interested in developing technology-enhanced physical learning environments, and "design thinking" and design processes in learning contexts. Chris received his BS in Biological Sciences from the University of Texas at El Paso, and his MS and PhD in Computer Science and Engineering from the University of Michigan.

Yvonne Rogers is a professor of Interaction Design, the director of the University College London's Interaction Center (UCLIC) and a deputy head of the Computer Science department at UCL. Her research interests are in the areas of ubiquitous computing, interaction design, and human–computer interaction. A key theme is how to design interactive technologies that can enhance life by augmenting and extending everyday, learning and work activities. Central to her work is a critical stance toward how visions, theories, and frameworks shape the fields of HCI, cognitive science, and Ubicomp. She has been instrumental in promulgating new theories (e.g., external cognition), alternative methodologies (e.g., in the wild studies), and far-reaching research agendas (e.g., "Being Human: HCI in 2020" manifesto). She is the PI at UCL for the Intel Collaborative Research Institute on Urban Internet of Things, a joint collaboration with Imperial College, Intel, Future Cities Catapult, and London Legacy Development Corporation. She was awarded a prestigious EPSRC dream fellowship for rethinking the relationship among aging, computing, and creativity. She is a visiting professor in the Psychology Department at Sussex University, UK, an honorary professor in the Computer Science department at the University of Cape Town, South Africa, and was awarded a Microsoft Research Outstanding Collaborator Award for 2016.

Elizabeth B.-N. Sanders is the Founder of MakeTools, LLC, where she explores new spaces in the emerging design landscapes. As a practitioner since 1981, she introduced many of the methods being used today to drive design from a human-centered perspective. Liz joined the Design Department at The Ohio State University (OSU) as an associate professor in 2011. At OSU she invites students to use co-designing to address the significant social, economic, and environmental challenges we face today. Liz's current research focuses on co-design processes for innovation, intervention, and transdisciplinary collaboration. Liz has a PhD in Experimental and Quantitative Psychology and a BA in both Psychology and Anthropology.

Judith Uchidiuno is a PhD student in the Human Computer Interaction Institute at Carnegie Mellon University. She is advised by Amy Ogan and Ken Koedinger, and conducts research on making Massive Open Online Courses (MOOCs) more accessible for students who speak English as a second language (ESL). She is currently investigating different quantitative and qualitative metrics to identify students who need language interventions, and understanding the needs of ESL students to drive MOOC language intervention design.

Michelle P. Whitacre is an assistant professor in the School of Education at Lindenwood University. Whitacre has worked as a high school science teacher and instructional coach, and was a NSF CADRE (National Science Foundation Community for Advancing Discovery Research) Fellow. Whitacre's research interests focus on investigating how teacher learning can be transformed through a collaborative and interdisciplinary approach. She received her PhD from the University of Missouri–St. Louis.

Michelle Hoda Wilkerson is an assistant professor at the University of California, Berkeley. She studies how young people think and learn with computational representations—things like simulations and data visualizations. As part of this work, she designs and studies tools that leverage familiar expressive activities like storytelling or sketching as building blocks for scientific computing. Michelle employs design-based research approaches including participatory design, semi-clinical interviews, and curriculum enactments in partnership with classrooms and after-school programs. Her work has been funded by the National Science Foundation, including through a 2014 Early CAREER Award, and she has served as chair of the American Educational Research Association's Special Interest Group in Advanced Technologies for Learning (SIG-ATL). Before working at UC Berkeley, Michelle was faculty in the Department of Education at Tufts University, earned her PhD in Learning Sciences from Northwestern University, and was a member of the Center for Connected Learning and Computer-Based Modeling.

Jason Yip is an assistant professor at the Information School of the University of Washington. His research examines how technologies can support parents and children learning together. He is a co-principal investigator on a National Science Foundation Cyberlearning project on designing social media technologies to support neighborhoods learning science together. He is the director of KidsTeam UW, an intergenerational group of children (ages 7–11) and researchers co-designing new technologies and learning activities for children, with children. Dr. Yip is the principal investigator of a Google Faculty Research Award project that examines how Latino children search and broker online information for their English-language learning parents. He is a senior research fellow at the Joan Ganz Cooney Center at Sesame Workshop. He holds a BA (2001) in chemistry and M.S.Ed (2002) in science and math education from the University of Pennsylvania, and a PhD (2014) in curriculum and instruction from the University of Maryland.

INDEX

CPSIA information can be obtained
at www.ICGtesting.com
Printed in the USA
BVHW072133131218
535498BV00009B/55/P